T0221533

DISTRIBUTED DATA MANAGEMENT FOR GRID COMPUTING

DISTRIBUTED DATA MANAGEMENT FOR GRID COMPUTING

MICHAEL DI STEFANO

WILEY-INTERSCIENCE

A JOHN WILEY & SONS, INC. PUBLICATION

Library of Congress Cataloging-in-Publication Data:

Di Stefano, Michael, 1963–
    Distributed data management for grid computing / by Michael Di Stefano.
        p. cm.
    Includes bibliographical references.
    ISBN 0-471-68719-7 (cloth)
        1. Computational grids (Computer systems)   2. Database management. I. Title.

    QA76.9.C58D57 2005
    004.3′6--dc22   2004031017

This book is dedicated to my parents, who instilled in their children the importance of hard work, honesty, education, and dedication to family and friends, for making any sacrifice, no matter how great, to ensure that all of their children succeed to their fullest potential.

CONTENTS

FOREWORD   **xv**

PREFACE   **xvii**

ACKNOWLEDGMENTS   **xxi**

PART I   AN OVERVIEW OF GRID COMPUTING

1   What is Grid Computing?   **3**

The Basics of Grid Computing, 3
   Leveling the Playing Field of Buzzword Mania, 4
Paradigm Shift, 7
   Beyond the Client/Server, 7
New Topology, 10

2   Why are Businesses Looking at Grid Computing?   **13**

History Repeats Itself, 13
   Early Needs, 14
   Artists and Engineers, 14
The Whys and Wherefores of Grid Computing, 17
   Financial Factors, 17
   Business Drivers, 19
   Technology's Role, 19

3   Service-Oriented Architecture   **21**

What is Service-Oriented Architecture (SOA)?, 21
Driving Forces Behind SOA, 23
    Maturing Technology, 24
        Networking, 24
        Distributed Computing (Grid), 25
        Resource Provisioning, 25
        Web Services, 25
    Business, 25
    World Events, 26
Enter Basic Supply–Demand Economics, 27
Fundamental Shift in Computing, 29

4   Parallel Grid Planes   **31**

Using Art to Describe Life: Grid is the Borg, 31
Grid Planes, 32
    Compute Grids, 33
    Data Grids, 34
Compute and Data Grids—Parallel Planes, 35
True Grid Must Include Data Management, 36
    Basic Data Management Requirements, 36
        Coordinating the Compute and Data Grid Planes, 36
        Data Surfaces in a Data Grid Plane, 37
    Evolving the Data Grid, 38

PART II   DATA MANAGEMENT IN GRID COMPUTING

5   Scaling in the Grid Topology   **43**

Evolution in Data Management, 43
    Client/Server Evolution, 44
    Grid Evolution, 44
Different Implementations of a Data Grid, 45
    Level 0 Data Grids, 45
        FTP in Grid, 46
        Distributed Filing Systems, 47
        Faster Servers, 47
        Metadata Hubs and Distributed Data Integration, 48
    Level 1 Data Grids, 48
        Foundations, 49
        Case Study: Integrasoft Grid Fabric (IGF), 51
    Application Characteristics for Grid, 53

6 Traditional Data Management   **59**

Data Management, 59
   History, 59
   Features, 60
      Mechanics, 60
      Data Structure, 61
      Access, 62
      Integrity, 63
      Transaction, 63
      Events, 64
      Backup/Recovery/Availability, 64
      Security, 64
Key for Usability, 65

**7 Relational Data Management as a Baseline for
Understanding the Data Grid**   **67**

Evolution of the Relational Model, 67
Parallels to Data Management in Grid Environments, 68
   Analysis of the Functional Tiers, 69
      Language Interface, 69
      Data Management Engines, 69
      Resource Management Engines, 69
   Engines Determine the Type of Data Grid, 70
   Data Management Features, 70

8 Foundation for Comparing Data Grids   **73**

Core Engine Determines Performance and Flexibility, 73
   Replicated versus Distributed, 74
   Centralized versus Peer-to-Peer Synchronization, 75
Access to the Data Grid, 75
   User-Level APIs, 75
   Spring-Based Interfaces, 76
Support for Traditional Data Management Features, 76
Support for Data Management Features Specific to
Grid Computing, 76

9 Data Regionalization   **79**

What are Data Regions?, 80
Data Regions in Traditional Terms, 80
Data Management in a Data Grid, 84
   Data Distribution Policy, 85
      Data Distribution Policy Expression, 87

Data Replication Policy, 88
    Data Replication Policy Expression, 89
Synchronization Policy, 90
Load-and-Store Policy, 90
    Data Load Policy Expression, 93
    Data Store Policy Expression, 94
Event Notification Policy, 95
    Event Notification Policy Expression, 96
Quality-of-Service (QoS) Levels, 96

10 Data Synchronization   **99**

Intraregion Synchronization, 100
Interregion Synchronization, 101
Synchronization Architectures, 102
    Centralized Synchronization Manager, 102
    Peer-to-Peer Synchronization, 103
Synchronization Patterns, 104
    Synchronization Granularity, 105
    Synchronization Policy Expression, 106
    Synchronization Pattern Simulations, 108
Synchronization Policy as a Standard Interface, 109

11 Data Integration   **111**

Enterprise Application/Information Integration
(EAI/EII) in Grid, 111
    Straight-Through Processing (STP), EAI, and EII, 111
EII in Grid, 116
    Natural Separation of Process and Data, 118
    Data Load Policy, 120
    Data Store Policy, 124
    Load, Store, and Synchronization, 126
    Enterprise Data Grid Integration, 129

12 Data Affinity   **133**

A Measurable Quantity, 134
    What to Expect from Data Affinity, 135
How to Achieve Data Affinity, 135
    Regionalization, Synchronization, Distribution, and
    Data Affinity, 135
    Data Distribution is Key to Data Affinity, 137
    Data Affinity and Task Routing, 139
Integration of Compute and Data Grids, 139
Examples, 141

PART III PRACTICAL APPLICATIONS OF GRID COMPUTING

13 Which Applications are Good Candidates for the Grid 145

Grid Enabling Application Characteristics, 145
  Atomic Tasks, 145
  Complex Data Sets, 146
  Data Collection, 146
  Operations, 146
Gridable Applications, 147
  Compute-Intensive Applications, 147
  OLAP Data Analysis, 148
  Data Center Operations, 148
  Compute Utility Service, 149
Use Case Presentations, 149

14 Calculation-Intensive Applications 153

Description, 153
Use Cases, 154
General Architecture, 156
Data Grid Analysis, 160

15 Data Mining and Data Warehouses 165

Description, 165
Use Cases, 166
General Architecture, 168
  First Use Case, 168
  Second Use Case, 170
  Enter the Compute Grid, 172
Data Grid Analysis, 172
Benefits and Data Grid Specifics, 174

16 Spanning Geographic Boundary 177

Description, 177
Business Use Cases, 178
  Financial Services, 178
  Operations, 180
  Following the Sun, 183
General Architecture, 184
Data Grid Analysis, 185
Benefits and Data Grid Specifics, 188

17   Command and Control   **191**

Problem Description, 191
Solution Architecture, 192
   Command and Control Without a Data Grid, 193
   Command and Control with a Data Grid, 194
   Observations and Comparisons, 195
Data Grid Analysis, 196
Application Spinoffs, 202

18   Web Service's Role in the SOA/SONA Evolution   **203**

Definition of Web Services, 203
Description, 205
Data Management: The Keystone to Web Services, 206
Web Services, Grid Infrastructures, and SONA, 208
   The Undiscovered Past, 208
   The SONA Model, 210
      Connecting the Dots of the Past into the Continuum
      of the Present, 211
      Service-Oriented Network Architecture (SONA), 212
      Network Computing Power Explosion, 214
      Consequences of Moore's and Metcalfe's Laws, 215
      Isomorphism to Evolution of Previous Systems, 215
      Grid and Web Services as Manifestation of State Transition, 215
      Conclusion, 215

19   The Compute Utility   **217**

Overview, 218
Architecture, 220
   Geographic Boundary, 221
   Command-and-Control Systems, 221
   Macro/Microscheduling, 223

PART IV   REFERENCE MATERIAL

20   Language Interface   **229**

Programmatic, 230
Query-Based, 232
XML-Based, 234

21   Basic Programming Examples   **235**

HelloWorld Example, 236
   Coarse Granularity, 236

Coarse Data Atom, 236
Writer Program, 237
Reader Program, 239
Fine Granularity, 240
Writer Program, 240
Reader Program, 243
Random-Number Surface Example, 245

22 Additional Reading   **251**

Useful Information Sources, 251
White Papers, 252
Grid Computing, 252
GridFTP, 252
Distributed File Systems, 252
Standards Bodies, 253
Globus—Data Grid, 253
Global Grid Forum, 253
W3C, 253
Public and University Grid Efforts, 253
Scientific Research Use of Grid Computing, 254
Web Services, 254
Distributed Computing, 255
Compute Utility, 255
Service-Oriented Architectures, 256
Data Affinity, 256

**23 White Paper: Natural Attraction Forces of Data Bodies
within a Data Grid to Describe Efficient Data
Distribution Patterns**   **257**

Introduction, 257
Observation, 258
Hypothesis, 259
Laws of Attraction, 259
How Does This Fit in with Data Distribution Patterns of
Single Data Bodies within a Data Grid Fabric?, 260
Collision of Single Data Bodies, 261
Effects of the Data Grid on a Single Data Body, 265
Conclusions, 265

24 Glossary of Terms   **267**

REFERENCES   **273**

INDEX   **277**

FOREWORD

Commercial grid computing is inevitable. As certain as the sunrise or sunset, grid computing, or the ability to abstract the business logic (application) layer from the infrastructure layer, will be a reality. As firms' technology architecture continues to become more complex and technology budgets continue to come under increasing scrutiny, firms need to rethink the way they manage and utilize technology.

The current ways of tying applications to very specific hardware just will not scale. Firms are buying new technology when other servers are sitting underutilized. Firms are acquiring more hardware when they have thousands of desktops (after work hours) and even whole data centers (across the globe) sitting dormant. And even if we continue to throw hardware at our computational challenges, sooner or later the overhead of managing this infrastructure will become overwhelming.

Besides not being able to function without grid technology to help manage our increasingly complicated technology infrastructures, our 30 years of modern computing history all point toward a need for a better way to manage a widely distributed computing architecture. Whether it is called *grid computing* or *utility computing*, the shift toward hardware and software componentization cries out for a better technology management model.

Over the entire history of computing we have consistently experienced a pronounced increase in computational power and a continual decrease in both CPU size and cost (Moore's law). In the mid-1980s, there was the mainframe; in 1990 it was the Unix server, and today there is the virtually disposable Linux or Windows-based rack-mounted cluster. Concurrently we have witnessed a continual decomposition of traditional software applications from mainline COBOL programs, with embedded program calls, to client/server, the Web, and today service-oriented architecture (SOA)–based applications. While the COBOL and client/server-based applications ran on dedicated hardware, today's SOA-based applications can be run virtually anywhere.

But what happens when firms begin to roll out these new hardware and software architectures? How will firms be able to manage every single blade server running all of these Web services? Will they know what is running on the second partition of the third blade of the twenty-fifth cluster? Will corporate data centers be able to track the utilization rate of the eighteenth blade of the fourth cluster? Will they know when the blade was underutilized, and what could have been provisioned on that platform? What if the blade is down? How will they know, who will fix it, and what will happen to its workload?

None of these issues will be resolved without a more efficient, more fully automated technology management infrastructure. This is the challenge that grid computing is tackling.

Grid computing was initially targeted at decomposing computationally challenging problems into many pieces and parceling them out to a wide array of computational resources. Today grid computing is much more than high-performance computing; it is about virtualizing and abstracting the complete technology footprint from both users and software developers. It is about having technology manage technology.

This is not an easy problem to solve. It is more than lashing together a dozen computers. It is more than breaking a large problem into smaller pieces. It is more than provisioning on the fly. Grid computing is a comprehensive technology management infrastructure that decomposes, monitors, provisions, distributes, manages, and meters virtually all technologies within the organization and sometimes outside the organization.

That is why you are reading this book. Michael's book will help you get a much better understanding of grid computing—how it works, the theory, practice, and the challenges of pulling it all together. While I firmly believe that this technology is inevitable, the real question is "When will it be practical?" With this book, and Michael's help, the answer to that question will certainly be sooner rather than later.

LARRY TABB

Founder & CEO
TABB Group

PREFACE

Grid computing technology is breaking out of its birthplace in universities and research facilities and is quickly gaining acceptance in the commercial industry. In fact, the financial industry is where my company and I were first introduced to grid computing technology. I am very active in financial firms on Wall Street as they explore the potential use of grid technology for various business applications, restructuring data centers, and operations of data centers. With more years than I care to count or even mention, I have been an integral part of architecting and building distributed computing environments (client/server topology) for the financial industry and in the past few years (at the time of writing) have been working in the grid computing topology as it extends to financial institutions. This is not to say that this is the only industry to which this technology applies. As a result, it quickly became apparent that running business applications and services in the grid computing topology was not the same as the traditional client/server and new data management techniques were needed to leverage this new topology.

The first step is the buildout of the hardware infrastructure for grid computing (compute nodes, networks, etc.). Once in place, "Bob's your Uncle"; the rest should be as simple as migrating applications over to, or better yet, converting business line applications into, "services" for their "customers" to "purchase." However, the reality is that the hardware and the operating system of a grid at the end of the day is just another computer consisting of CPUs, memory, disks, and a communication bus. Granted, the internal components appear radically different from those of the big servers that we are accustomed to seeing in data centers. The *compute grid* is a logical computer that physically consists of many networked computers (or compute nodes) that spans one data center, multiple data centers, floors of a building, and even cities. When moving even the simplest of applications onto the new computer, there is at least one critical tool that the developers must have, a database, specifically, a data grid. The initial reaction is: "Our applications already have a database, we will use those" or "Why don't we use the relational databases that we have already paid licenses for?" However, given the difference in physical topology between the client/server and grid computing, the architects and developers will immediately realize that managing data in a grid computing environment is very different. Without the proper data management tools, developers are back to writing down to the bare metal of the grid to get data in and out of the grid, distributing the data among all the nodes where work needs to be performed, and must manage some sort of data synchronization (e.g., distribution of data across the nodes of the grid, and with external data sources that include not only databases but also all the various middleware tools, file systems, etc.). The information technology staff in many organizations have already received the green light to start to deliver applications on the compute grid without the required tools for providing data management. As a result, these projects will require more time and thus cannot achieve fast time to market, low costs, and so on since large amounts of time must be spent on creating pure infrastructure code customized for each application. The reusability of such code is small or nonexistent, resulting in additional resources and time to deal with the nuts and bolts of the grid. Without the proper data management tools, the migration will be slow and expensive at the cost of total acceptance of the technology into the commercial industry. This would jeopardize the whole "grid thing" altogether.

Working with our clients and the grid computing technology vendors, it became apparent that the management of data was not sufficiently addressed through the use of traditional data management techniques. The physical topology of the grid is as different from the client/server as the client/server was from the mainframe. Data management systems that were architected for the client/server are optimized and perform best in that topology, but not necessarily perform as needed by the grid topology. To gain optimal performance from of the grid topology, various levels of analysis are required, including the analysis of data types and their behaviors. The analysis drives different data management techniques that are required as part of the core for the data management system or the "engine" that needs to be redefined. The engine's (as an integral part of data management system) responsibility is to manage the mechanics required by the data storage devices and the movement of data into and out of the physical realm of the grid.

The first set of applications to run within the grid has operated over static data sets, and large files whose contents rarely, if ever, change. Naturally, the data management techniques for these types of data and the applications associated with them within the grid are geared toward the management and distribution of large static data sets across the nodes of the grid. Examples are GridFTP (Grid File Transfer Protocol) for distributed filing systems and various research projects such as Ocean-Store. However, these techniques do not translate to the management of dynamic data used by many applications within the financial services sectors (as well as other vertical sectors).

Throughout the evolution of the computer from mainframe/minicomputer to client/server to middleware to distributed computing, the early adopters piloted the transitions of each, followed by books and reference materials made readily available to the armies of architects and developers involved in the mass adoption of these respective technologies. As we are now working with the early adopters of grid computing in the financial community, most, if not all, of the reference materials on grid computing are white papers and research reports. There is an obvious vacuum of printed material specifically as it relates to how to manage data in the highly distributed topology of the grid. We, at Integrasoft, began to fill this void by creating user groups where the early adopters of grid technology regularly meet to discuss their activities and present some of the latest developments in grid computing and data management within this technology: a forum of open idea exchange and discussion. This is a small attempt since there are not enough user groups globally to reach the masses needed to acquire the technology knowledge required for this next evolutionary step in computing. I started this project of authoring a book on distributed data management in grid computing to assist in the adoption of grid computing within the commercial industry, to provide an introduction to grid computing for people who are just starting to hear about it for the first time; for those who have been studying or considering and started to use grid computing, by introducing the concepts for the management of data within grid computing; and for the early adopters of this technology who are familiar with the complexities of data management in grid computing, to hopefully spark research and development of practical product in these areas in order to establish this technology as a standard.

The audience for this book is not limited to the technical purist; the topic of grid computing is presented with the main drivers for its adoption, the economic and sociological impacts on an organization. Thus, this is an introduction for people who are along the managerial paths, who are aware of and familiar with the general terms of data management, as with relational databases, and is intended to introduce grid computing in business terms so that these individuals can see the benefits of using grid technology and become advocates for the use of this technology in their projects. It is hoped that they will be armed with the tools necessary to discuss grid computing with their technical staff with a sufficient level of understanding of this technology and to explain to the upper management and corporate leaders the benefits of using grid technology. Finally, to complete the lifecycle, project managers must be able to present their rationale for using grid computing in their projects to their corporate leaders such as the CIO and CFO (chief investment and financial officers). They, too, should, having read this book, possess an understanding of the business drivers behind grid computing and the benefits it brings to an organization as a whole.

To draw in such a wide range of audience, I leverage three techniques: drawing on a common baseline of knowledge, visitation through analogy, and finally practical applications of grid computing. For the first technique, a common baseline of knowledge, the relational database and relational data management systems are used to explain and introduce data management within the grid. Readers should be able to walk away with the tools to help them promote grid technology into their respective organizations and into the community as a whole. My intention is not to provide a deep level of detail on the relational data management concepts since technical people are typically familiar with them. Project managers should already have the level of understanding of relational data management technology on a par with what is discussed within, and drilling down into the bowels of the underlying technology would not be of practical use.

The second technique, visitation through analogy, coupled with the common baseline of relational data management, completes the conceptual bridge between what is familiar to what is not. Finally, by presenting the practical business and technical use cases that people and corporations are looking for the grid technology to solve, we will see the immediate benefits and widespread impact that the grid will have on our everyday business and information technology lives.

The field of data management in the grid is a broad one; individually the topics introduced warrant more in-depth discussion than the pages of this book can provide. In fact, each aspect or topic of distributed data management merits its own book or series of books. So, for the technical readers who are intimately familiar with the details of grid computing, this book should spark further thought and work within the topics presented and contribute in the advancement of distributed data management. The technical person becoming acquainted to grid computing will acquire a firm understand of the field and the concepts of distributed data management in grid computing. I encourage them to read the white papers and reference materials listed at the end of this book. The technologist will be able to take distributed data management products (such as the one that we have developed, from the ground up for data management within grid computing), and quickly get projects up and running by assessing the various strengths and weaknesses of each product and correlating that to their project needs.

A handful of people have been generous enough to read the manuscript of this book, some being the early adapters and some are the newcomers to the field. One person described my goals for this book as being the "rosetta stone" for grid computing. As generous as he was in that description, I tend to look at is as "beauty is in the eye of the beholder," as individuals can look at a piece of work and draw from it value particular to their respective backgrounds, experience, and job responsibilities with the ultimate goal of helping them perform their jobs better and contributing to the adoption of grid computing. Achievement of this objective will also mean that I have achieved my goal.

ACKNOWLEDGMENTS

I would like to thank my loving family for their understanding, support, and further sacrificing the already few precious moments we spent together while I took on the additional responsibility of authoring this book.

Special thanks to Dave Cohen of Merrill Lynch and my partner in business, Steve Yalovitser, for their contributions on Service Oriented Network Architecture (SONA), to Andrew Delaney of A-Team Consulting for transforming my "techese" into the English language, to Larry Tabb for his contributions in the Foreword of this book, and to my editor, Val Moliere of John Wiley & Sons for her insight into the importance of data management in grid computing and guidance during the authoring process.

PART I

AN OVERVIEW OF GRID COMPUTING

1

WHAT IS GRID COMPUTING?

Grid computing has emerged as a framework for supporting complex compilations over large data sets. In general, grids enable the efficient sharing and management of computing resources for the purpose of performing large complex tasks. In particular, grids have been defined as anything from batch schedulers to peer-to-peer (P2P) platforms.

Grid computing has evolved in the scientific and defense communities since the early 1990s. As with most maturing technologies, there is debate as to exactly what grid computing is. Some make a very clear distinction between cluster computing and grid computing. *Compute clusters* are defined as a dedicated group of machines (whether they are individual machines or racks of blades) that are dedicated for a specific purpose. Grid computing uses a process known as "cycle stealing": grabbing spare compute cycles on machines across a network, when available, to get a task done.

Since both compute clusters and grids coordinate their respective resources to perform tasks, when does a compute cluster start to become a grid? Specifically, does a compute cluster become a grid when it is leveraged to perform operations other than those for which it was originally intended?

THE BASICS OF GRID COMPUTING

Grid computing is an overloaded term. Depending on whom you talk to, it takes on different meanings. Some terms may better fit your practical usage of the

Distributed Data Management for Grid Computing, by Michael Di Stefano
Copyright © 2005 John Wiley & Sons, Inc.

technology, such as clusters. For the purposes of this discussion, however, we shall define grid computing as follows:

> Grid computing is any distributed cluster of compute resources that provides an environment for the sharing and managing of the resource for the distribution of tasks based on configurable service-level policies.

A grid fundamentally consists of two distinct parts, compute and data:

- *Compute grid*—provides the core resource and task management services for grid computing: sharing, management, and distribution of tasks based on configurable service-level policies
- *Data grid*—provides the data management features to enable data access, synchronization, and distribution of a grid

If the proliferation of jargon is a measure of a technology's viability and its promise to answer key issues that businesses are facing, then transformation of jargon to standards is a measure of the longevity of the technology in its ability to answer concretely those key business issues. The evolution of *grid computing* from jargon to standard can be measured by a number of converging influences: history, business dynamics, technology evolution, and external environmental pressures.

The drivers behind grid technology are remarkably similar to those that corporations are facing today: a starving business need for powerful, inexpensive, and flexible compute power, and limited funds to supply it. In the early 1990s, research facilities and universities used increasingly complex computational programs requiring the processing power of a supercomputer without the budget to supply it. Their answer was to create a compute environment that could leverage any spare compute cycles on campus to perform the required calculations.

Today, grid technology has evolved to the point where it is no longer a theory but a proven practice. It represents a viable direction for corporations to explore grid computing as an answer to their business needs within tight financial constraints.

There are additional forces in play that will present a fundamental paradigm shift in how computing is done. As it migrates from the hands of artistry to the realm of engineering—via the application of tried-and-true engineering principles—computing becomes a fundamental utility in the same way that gas and electricity generation and delivery is a utility. The quality of the service will be measured by its ability to meet the supply-and-demand curves of the producers and consumers.

Leveling the Playing Field of Buzzword Mania

There are many analogies in the development and adoption of grid computing to those of client/server technology. Both are fundamental paradigm shifts in the way computing is performed. As client/server technology ushered in the broad acceptance of relational database technology, grid technology will usher in new data management paradigms to address the specific topology of the physical compute grid.

To see how this is happening, it is best to untangle the concepts of data management in grid form by drawing on a fundamental baseline that we are all familiar with. The people who are going to use grid technology—developers, architects, and lines of businesses—are accustomed to thinking in terms of client/server technology and the relational data management features within a client/server paradigm. Irrespective of the compute topology—client/server, computer clusters, or a computer grid—from the user perspective, these data management service levels need to be consistently maintained.

In the early days of client/server technology one would attend a seminar sponsored by a relational database vendor, promoting relational technology in general, and the supplier's product in particular. The message was that the new compute paradigm of the client/server topology required new, more flexible data management techniques than do those currently in use. As a result, relational databases became synonymous with client/server technology and the standard for data management.

People attending those seminars were used to writing their own disk controllers for data storage, so popular questions centered on disk management. How fast does your product write to and/or read from disk? How efficient are your indices? How well does your product manage physical data positioning on the disk? The bulk of the seminar was spent on addressing these questions, and the only discussion of data management centered on the use of a new language called *Structured Query Language* (SQL) for storage and querying of the data. If you were interested, there were SQL training classes to attend, where only the basics of how to form a query were taught.

Figure 1.1 illustrates the parallels of the vocabulary and fundamentals between data management within relational databases and that within grid computing. This comparison is useful in two aspects: (1) it relates to terms that most are already very familiar with and (2) more importantly, it suggests that any data management system in grid computing must provide the same levels of service quality as within relational databases.

Figure 1.1 links a baseline of data grid vocabulary to well-known relational database terms. Relational database implementations have two fundamental components: (1) the underlying engine that manages physical resources, in this case a disk and (2) a layer on top of that to provide all the data management features and functionality that architects and developers would rely on for data management, querying, arrangement of data in highly ordered structures such as tables, the ability to transact on data, leveraging stored procedures, event triggerings, and transacting in and out of the database with external systems. These are the management features and functions that today are where our true interest lies. How do I manage tables/row locking? How do I structure indices for maximum performance? Very little attention today is given to the underlying engine.

In the same way that *relational database* is a generic term, so is *data grid*. Companies will offer implementations, products of their vision of what a data grid is. To analyze the differences between the products offered, it is possible to apply a

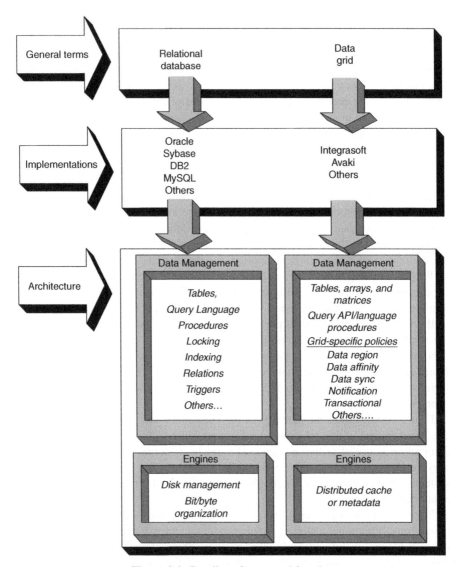

Figure 1.1. Baseline of terms and function.

baseline consisting of generic term, implementation, data management, and engine. Each implementation of a data grid will have an engine. That engine may be a meta-data dictionary or a distributed cache. It will also handle the data management aspects of this data grid, defining how to structure data in tables, arrays, or matrices; how to query data; and how to transact on the data.

Depending on the exact implementation of this engine—whether it is a metadata dictionary that routes requests to the true long-term persistent stores, or a distributed cache that spans all computers in the grid to form one virtual space—there are specific data management issues for this new topology. How to synchronize, how to transact on the data, how to address data affinity? These are all data management issues; issues that, no matter who the architect or application developer is, will need to be addressed within their applications. These are the quality-of-service (QoS) levels that are required of the data grid. If a data grid does not provide such service, then developers will have to write down to the lowest, most fundamental level of bit and byte management.

Data grid support for true data management extends to facilitation of the adoption and widescale acceptance of grid technology. Developers can easily transit from client/server-based applications to a grid topology by leveraging a product that provides the same levels of service quality that have become the standard with relational databases.

PARADIGM SHIFT

The technology concepts behind grids had their origins in distributed computing networks based on Distributed Computing Environment (DCE) and Common Object Reguest Broker Architecture (CORBA). The approach and value proposition, however, are radically different.

DCE- and CORBA-based distributed computing applications sought to separate client and server, and to move processing off to a server or set of servers, thereby reducing the requirement for large clients. Grids seek to harness large blocks of processors into a virtual pool. Once virtualized, these pools are managed by the grid, which provides a standard set of services that address

- Security
- Data management
- Discovery
- Reliability

Heterogeneity is key, and these pools range from desktop PCs for the purpose of AIDS and cancer research, to large servers for problems in computational physics and biology.

Beyond the Client/Server

Traditional client/server applications are typically configured as a client process connecting to a utility server such as a database. The client/server architecture can be further refined as to what a server is and what a client is. Clients that process the business logic ("fat" clients) can become "thin" clients by moving business logic processing to a separate server process, sometimes called an *application server*. The application servers would then in turn connect to the utility server (i.e., a database), thus forming a chain: clients connecting to an application server connecting to databases (see Figure 1.2).

Thus, client/server topology fundamentally is a piping of clients and applications. Operationally, for each line of business application, this implies a strict discipline of dedicated machines running the respective application and database servers. When planning the capacity of a data center, the rule of thumb is that the server capacity is twice that required at peak load. However, the peak load may occur only a few times a day for short intervals. Thus, for most of the time the machines are running far below their capacity (typically less than 30%). This leaves vast amounts of wasted compute capacity.

The use of distributed middleware products—such as a messaging—transforms the client/server piping topology into a "message bus" topology. Servers can now handle "requests" via the middleware messaging bus. Clients issue requests to the middleware, which routes the message to the appropriate the service. This is the beginning of a distributed processing environment, the decoupling of the physical resource to logical service. However, the capacity planning of the data centers follows the same rules as does the client/server topology, thus doing little to harness the vast, untapped compute capacity of the servers.

Grid computing is a further evolution of distributed computing that attempts to better utilize unused compute capacity. It enables the freedom to choose the hardware that is best suited to run the service at a specific point in time. This offers a better utilization of the physical resource. For example, machine A in a client/server topology was dedicated to one service. That same machine in a grid

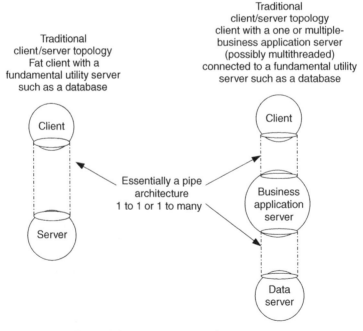

Figure 1.2. Traditional client/server topology.

topology can now support any service, with the limitation matching the machine's hardware/software provisioning to what is necessary to run a specific service.

Within a client/server environment, threading of servers allows for similar request processing—one thread for one request—thus allowing a single-server process to handle multiple clients at the same time. However, there is an upper limit to the practical number of threads that can efficiently run in that single process. Within grid technology, there is a similar concept. What would run in a thread can now be run on the best available machine in the grid. The end result is the elimination of any upper bound that exists in a single-machine, multithreaded process.

In a grid, a service can be further subdivided into tasks or worklets. The tasks can now be "sprayed" across the entire grid, thus transforming a sequential process into an *n*-way parallelizable event. What was a long-running process can now be completed in a fraction of the time.

As more capacity is needed to support the business, more hardware can be added to the grid. Once a service is grid-enabled, there are no programming changes necessary to take advantage of the additional capacity. This sets up the scenario of an infinitely wide grid, with "worklets" simultaneously accessing resources such as a database. What was a piping of client to server now resembles a funnel of clients trying to reach a single resource: orders of magnitude more "clients" trying to access data from a resource not designed for this wide-mouth funnel of requests (see Figure 1.3).

In attempting to handle large numbers of client requests efficiently, software companies have split up the servers by sharing or "striping" the workload across

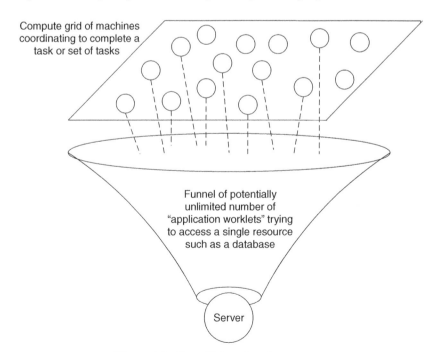

Compute grid of machines coordinating to complete a task or set of tasks

Funnel of potentially unlimited number of "application worklets" trying to access a single resource such as a database

Server

Figure 1.3. The grid funnel to data sources.

multiple server peers. This does increase the processing capacity of the servers behind the server wall but does not address the client request/response bottleneck. Attempting to use faster client/server technology in this way simply creates a processing hourglass (see Figure 1.4): wide client grid, and wide server process fanout with a bottleneck at client access to the server.

Data management in grid computing addresses the widening of the throat of the hourglass to the width of the grid to eliminate data access bottlenecks (see Figure 1.5).

NEW TOPOLOGY

Grid computing builds on established concepts of distributed computing to create a physical topology that is very different from that of the client/server. A computer becomes a network of smaller machines coordinating with one another to complete

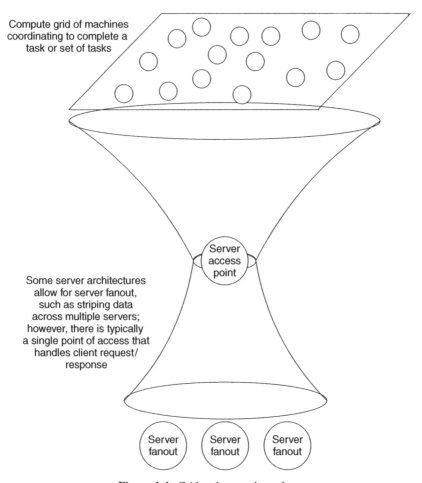

Figure 1.4. Grid and server hourglass.

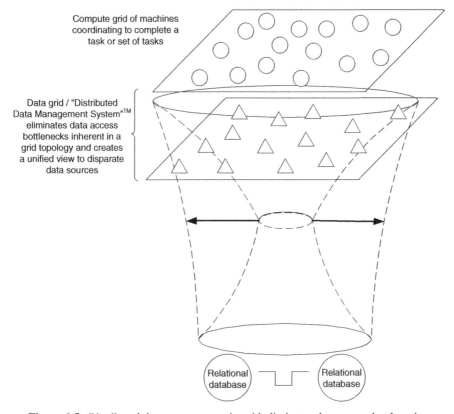

Compute grid of machines coordinating to complete a task or set of tasks

Data grid / "Distributed Data Management System"™ eliminates data access bottlenecks inherent in a grid topology and creates a unified view to disparate data sources

Relational database

Relational database

Figure 1.5. Distributed data management in grid eliminates data access bottlenecks.

a variety of tasks—a collection of reconfigurable nodes for performing a variety of different tasks without human intervention, in contrast to the siloed/specialized data centers of today:

- *Elasticity*—Information technology (IT) spending is being tied directly to business volume, forcing greater transparency and other benefits.
- *Pervasiveness*—There are a proliferation of uses of IT resources for basic needs much like a utility (electricity, telephone, etc.).
- *Defense spending*—IT spending is closely controlled by the upper management and corporate CIO/CFO.
- *Moore's law*—The cost of hardware is decreased.

Each of these forces has rippling effects throughout a grid architecture, thus forcing grid acceptance:

- *Elasticity*—increased emphasis on metering usage, and the utility concept within IT. For example, one utility must support multiple functions such as high-performance computing and Web Services.

- *Pervasiveness*—increased commoditization of basic functions [DNS (Domain Name System), Mail, Web, etc.].
- *Defense spending*—increased R&D in data integration, prediction, reliable infrastructures (à la ARPANET).
- *Moore's law*—increased emphasis on encoding more functions on chips themselves [i.e., Flash, PROM (programmable read-only memory), and RAM (random access memory) in everything, and nothing else].
- *Data management*—how to maintain the same "user experience" in data management and not hinder the realization of the full potential of the grid environment.

2

WHY ARE BUSINESSES LOOKING AT GRID COMPUTING?

Corporations today are looking at and investing in grid computing not because it is a "cool" technology but rather because it answers core business needs and stringent financial requirements. It also offers a high-performance compute infrastructure at low cost. The technology combines commodity, throwaway hardware with ever-increasing network bandwidths, and self-administration software, to promote

- Significantly lower operational costs compared to those of today's data centers
- Significant return on investment and return on asset

Grid computing is no accident, and its future is very predictable. History provides a clear view of its adoption today and its path in the future. It offers a practical solution to fundamental requirements ranging from operations to business development, to corporate fiscal pressures.

HISTORY REPEATS ITSELF

History repeats itself twice. Corporations are looking at grid computing today for the same reasons that originally prompted the evolution of this technology in the first place. The future of grid computing is predictable; the same engineering principle that has driven the evolution of the telecommunications industry will evolve computing into a utility service.

Distributed Data Management for Grid Computing, by Michael Di Stefano
Copyright © 2005 John Wiley & Sons, Inc.

Early Needs

The 1990s were an exciting time to be in the business of the computer technology and information technology fields. The excitement surrounding the Internet and the possibilities that opened up beyond it seemed endless. Some business ideas were well founded, some not; but the number of technologies that quickly sprang up to support the new business models was staggering. The euphoria within the investment community to fund the exploration of both business and technology seemed as endless as the ideas that it financed.

During that same time period, universities, typically strapped for cash, needed to support their own business of research, which relied on computers to perform increasingly complicated, highly computational tasks, but lacked the budget or the unlimited venture capital (VC) funding that was afforded to the private sector. Universities had to figure out a way to support their research business with modest budgets. Their solution was to leverage the brain trusts of professors and students alike to create a method of networking inexpensive machines, so they acted as one large supercomputer: grid computing.

With few exceptions, commercial industry—fueled by limitless money and hardware—paid little attention to the developments in grid technology. This is not the situation today; the burst of the Internet bubble brought an abrupt halt to the days of free spending and the universities; grid computing projects are today laying the foundation for the next round of technology spending in corporate America. Perhaps the people in business today once attended those universities and participated in the creation of a powerful computer platform from inexpensive machines. Perhaps they recognized the parallels of the business need and financial drivers of universities in the 1990s, with those IT organizations in corporate America's face today. The business/financial environment of the university in the 1990s was very similar to that of today's corporate America. One reason why corporate America is looking at grid computing today is that the students who were involved in grid research in universities in the 1990s are now in the workforce, seeing the similarities and thus serving as an influential voice in pushing grid technology into corporations.

The converging forces of business drivers, downward financial pressures, world events, and a mature technology are ushering in a disruptive force that will change the fundamental way computing is done and create new business opportunities that otherwise would not exist (see Figure 2.1). Had it not been for the burst of the technology bubble in 2000, it would be safe to say that the wide adoption of grid computing that we are experiencing today would not be occurring.

We are now going to look at the business drivers from the prospective of the financial controller, the business manager, and the IT department, and examine how grid computing is uniquely positioned to address their disparate needs.

Artists and Engineers

Grid computing is the beginning of the shift of computing control out of the hands of the artist and into the hands of the engineer. Today, compute environments and

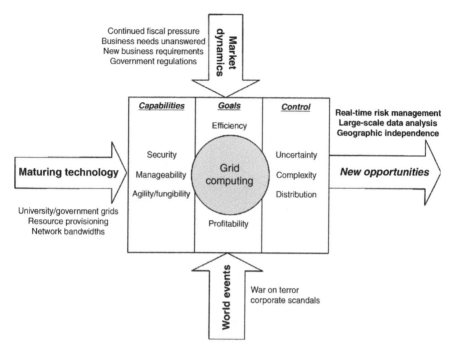

Figure 2.1. External forces, grid provisions, and new opportunities.

solutions are designed, integrated, developed, and operated by highly skilled indi-viduals, the "artists." Grid computing opens a path to leverage the tried-and-true engineering and economic principles of utility services, meeting supply and demand curves of the customer. Thus, into the hands of the engineer.

Service-oriented network architecture (SONA) will be mentioned more than once in our discussions. SONA applies a combination of virtualization and orchestration to planetary-scale, distributed middleware. It describes the fundamental paradigm shift away from the client/server computing that the grid provides.

The same laws and principles that have enabled the information age will apply to the paradigm shift of grid computing, the proliferation of the network (see Figure 2.2). We will stand on the shoulders of Claude Shannon, Norbert Weiner, John Holland, and others and apply the all-too-familiar laws of Moore, Metcalf, and Amdahl to usher in the age of customer-centric information, content, and trans-action standards of SONA.

It is the application of proven engineering techniques and methods that success-fully moved a direct-wired telephone system of the early 1900s to the communi-cation network utility that it is today. The same approach will change computing from a siloed data center to a grid utility that meets the economic principles of a free-market economy of supply and demand, and the reduction service of volatility.

The goal is to create a computer utility service that can be run and managed like a factory, with controlled costs, and the ability to increase output and change the

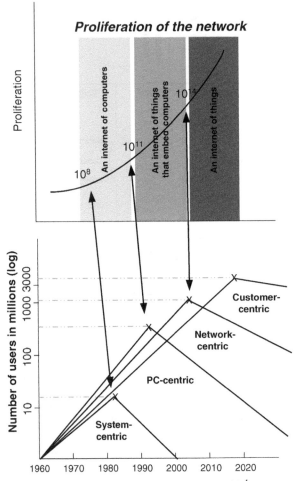

Figure 2.2. Proliferation of the network.[1]

production line as demand requires. This allows for better utilization of physical resources, which will drive down the operating costs.

The building blocks to achieve this start with the management of the physical resource for distribution of task—the compute grid—and must encompass:

- Data management techniques for the efficient movement of data
- Collection and use of metered data
- Application of feedback control logic, with metered data in, commands out
- The ability to provision your hardware quickly and efficiently
- Efficient administration without the need of an army of administrators.

The good news is that all these technologies are converging. They are not bleeding-edge; they demonstrate immediate return on investment (ROI) and, within a reasonably short amount of time (3–5 years), will yield significant cost savings for the organization.

THE WHYS AND WHEREFORES OF GRID COMPUTING

Recent events provide a logical path culminating in the emergence of grid computing. Starting at the burst of the technology bubble, there are financial pressures to control costs and unanswered business demands to cope with the changing economy, causing stress on IT personnel to manage both. At the same time, various technologies have been quietly maturing, each springing from different needs; for example, grid technology for low-cost, high-performance computing, self-provisioning software for operational management, and infiniband and other high-performance networking technology. These forces are converging, like the "perfect storm," to create a fundamental change in how computing and compute services are developed, managed, delivered, and paid for.

Financial Factors

Corporate CFOs have, in the years since the technology bubble burst, endured the burden of keeping their companies financially viable in the most difficult of business environments. Like the blade of a double-edged sword, changing business models demand new support from information technology; the other side of the blade is represented by changes in revenue streams that continue to squeeze profit margins, thus requiring tight cost controls and reductions.

This has led to a fundamental shift in how IT projects are developed and maintained. The use of IT outsourcing for project development and operations—barely existent prior to the burst of the technology bubble—has become the rule of the day. Companies that survived have done well, restructuring their respective organizations in both IT and long-term operational cost reduction. Unfortunately, there is continued pressure to further reduce costs.

How does grid technology assist the CFO? Let us look at how projects are developed and maintained within organizations. There is development, QA (quality assurance), production, and sometimes a step between QA and production for preproduction staging. Each of the steps requires dedicated hardware and support personnel to keep the centers running. (True, the developers can maintain their own machines.) However, environments outside the development environment (QA, preproduction, production; see Figure 2.3) will each reside in a proper data center, requiring trained staff to administer the hardware, network, core services (databases, middleware, etc.) as well as the business applications that run on them. Each environment is not a shared facility but rather separate, siloed copies of each other, each forming a closed and controlled environment to ensure that the production systems behave in a well-known manner resulting from the rigorous

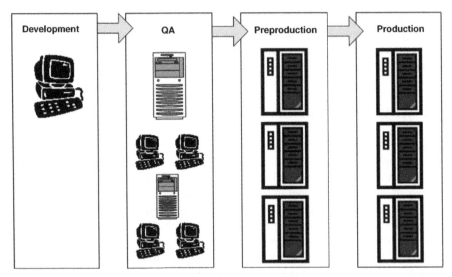

Figure 2.3. Dedicated and replicated environments.

testing done in both the QA and preproduction environments before being released to final production. This QA process and redundant physical setup is an expensive proposition in both physical resources (i.e. space, machines, and network) as well as in human resources.

The CFO looks to grid computing to reduce the long-term operational costs in a number of ways. First, each of these dedicated machines is not completely utilized. The rule of thumb is that the capacity for a machine should be twice what is required to handle the peak load, which may occur only at predictable, brief intervals throughout the day. In financial markets, these peaks occur at the market open and market close. Therefore, for most of the day, the dedicated and often expensive hardware is not completely utilized. When new projects come along, the purchase of additional machinery is necessary.

Grid technology allows us to run hardware closer to its full potential, typically at 70%, 80%, or even 90% utilization. This offers an organization a compute hardware environment that can support multiple business units according to their respective utilization requirements. No longer do their requirements need dedicated hardware for development, QA, and production. With grid technology there can exist a computer platform that is flexible and fungible to support the entire product development–production spectrum (see Figure 2.4).

Grid technology allows CFOs to buy inexpensive machines, and establishes a path to long-term operational cost reductions of an order of magnitude of today's data centers. The goal is to establish a compute utility service that obeys free-market economics, meets supply-and-demand (supply/demand) curves, and automates resource provisioning and commoditized hardware to the point where the value of a machine powered up and running in a data center is equivalent to its replacement sitting on a shelf in storage.

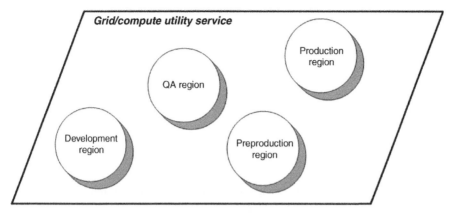

Figure 2.4. Grid: flexible and fungible compute environment.

Business Drivers

Business models have changed drastically since the technology bubble burst. The business units have had to be flexible and adaptive to quickly respond to external changes to continue to bring revenue into the organization. However, there is a lack of financial resources to spend on the technology needed to adapt to the new business models. As a result, the business's technology staff and the corporate IT organization supporting these business units have had to do more with less.

How does grid technology help? For the business manager, grid computing is a win–win scenario.

- *First Win*. As with their university counterparts, there are two opposing forces: business need and limited funds. Grid computing is a technology that offers computer power, flexibility, and high utilization at a low cost. A technological and financial model that supports the business and allows it to live within their respective budgets is available to the organization.
- *Second Win*. The use of grid technology creates new business opportunities. Grid technology enables new approaches to solving problems. This forces business heads, managers, and developers to start looking at things differently, thus creating new applications that would not exist without this technology. In Part III we will discuss practical business cases of grid technology and see how it ushers in a birth of new business and applications that otherwise would not be possible.

Technology's Role

We have discussed the business and financial pressures on the CFOs office to contain and reduce the ongoing operational costs, and the business's need to adapt quickly to changing business landscapes with limited technological resources. Now we will look at the people in the middle: the corporate IT organization.

IT finds itself caught between the pressures of demand from the business and supply in terms of limited resources from the CFO. IT is also under pressure to provide new services because simply maintaining existing services to the business is not an option. Grid technology is ideal for meeting both of these requirements and provides an inexpensive platform for the development and deployment of new applications, reduces operational costs, and offers higher resource utilization.

Grid computing represents a fundamental shift in how IT can support the business users when compared with a client/server environment. In a client/server data center, the business unit is financially responsible for the purchase of servers that are completely dedicated to that unit. The business is secure in its ability to support itself in peak environments but must live with additional hardware costs if demand increases and overpaying for resources should peak demand diminish. From the larger corporate perspective, the budget is used to purchase and operationally maintain hardware with low utilization levels.

The grid topology is a flexible infrastructure in which hardware can be used or shared by multiple groups depending on their usage demands. This implies cost structures different from that of a client/server data center. Grid technology is a decentralized flexible service that is owned and operated by IT, where business units' costs are shifted from a purchase/own/maintain-dedicated model to a "pay per use" model similar to that of a gas/electric utility service provider. Compute cycle usage must be metered and billed accordingly. The IT department must ensure that the resource is available when needed on a cost-effective basis, just like a gas/electric utility service provider.

3

SERVICE-ORIENTED ARCHITECTURE

In this chapter, we will discuss Service-Oriented Architecture (SOA) at a high level. Referenced within are various papers and articles that can go much deeper into the subject for interested readers. The objective is to explain what SOA is and how— along with business drivers and readily available technologies—it will lead to a paradigm shift in computing and compute service delivery. The technical reader can expect to be reacquainted with SOA and the technology behind it, while the business reader will learn about the economic forces driving SOA and how business (in terms of both current and future opportunities) will generate revenue streams sooner rather than later.

The importance to this shift of grid technologies and data grid in particular will be in supporting and enabling SOA. Data grid's role is less in how to implement SOA, but more in enabling SOA to deliver services to the customer when and where they are needed in a timely and cost-effective manner.

WHAT IS SERVICE-ORIENTED ARCHITECTURE (SOA)?

Service-Oriented Architecture is not a new concept in engineering and computer science; it touches our everyday lives in ways that we do not realize. Examples include television sets, DVD and CD players, the telephone, and electricity. In each case, the devices are interchangeable by make, model, and manufacturer, taking advantage of advancements in technology, but still offering the same respect- ive service. In the software industry, SOA delivery paths have evolved. Examples of

Distributed Data Management for Grid Computing, by Michael Di Stefano
Copyright © 2005 John Wiley & Sons, Inc.

early attempts to deliver SOA are based on the evolution of middleware architectures such as Common Object Request Broker (CORBA) and Distributed Component Object Model (DCOM). Those of us who have delivered systems based on CORBA are all too used to such terms such as "CORBA Services," "locating the service," and "registering the service" and having the services available to anyone who needs them. Any "CORBA client" can "connect to" a "CORBA service" if it "knows" the service's Interface Definition Language (IDL).

Listen to the vocabulary, and you will quickly see why these early attempts at delivering SOA failed. The clients and services must be CORBA-based. Therefore systems built using any other middleware paradigm (of which there are many) could not leverage the services simply because of the tight coupling of connectivity, definition, and message (data). We will see that SOA must have "loose couplings" in order to be of value to a broad customer base.[2]

The concepts of loose coupling of services and the customer are very important in SOA. Systems built by leveraging the services of other systems in an enterprise have a "real dependency" on those services. However, to access the services, a number of human-made obstacles must be overcome. These are "artificial dependencies."[3] The CORBA example above is an example of an artificial dependency. While real dependencies cannot be eliminated, artificial ones can be reduced to a minimum. "Loose coupling" refers to the minimizing of artificial dependencies. Basic criteria are applied to achieve loose coupling of services and customers:

- Simple interfaces must be widely accepted by the community.
- Messaging (consisting of a schema) is self-describing in structure, both limiting vocabulary and enabling change for service versioning.
- Messaging does not have system behavior.
- Services need to be dynamically located by the customer.
- Services must be self-contained.

These criteria are purely technical in nature. To deliver a SOA, there are some non-technical aspects of defining the service that need to be addressed Services must be "coarse on boundary." This implies that interfaces or boundaries of the service to the users of the service must describe the service from a business prospective, enough to describe what the service offers so that the consumer can make an educated decision. A service must provide a business function; it must make something happen. Services that simply move data are too fine-grained.[4]

Clients must be able to locate the service that best fits their requirements. There may be three billing services available, but the client must be able to reach all three and select the one that provides the best service to meet its needs. The latter is done via interface and messaging per the criteria listed above. Figure 3.1 shows how dynamic discovery can be achieved.[5]

There is a lot of buzz around Web Services and the tight correlation between Web Services and SOA. It is important to realize that Web Services is one way to

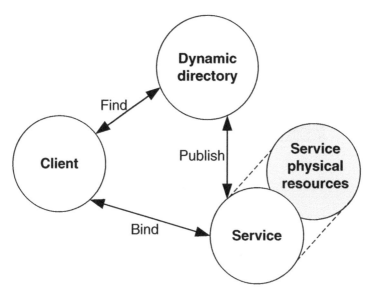

Figure 3.1. Dynamic location of services.

implement a SOA. Other technologies and methods can be used to implement SOA, provided they meet the criteria listed above. Web Services addresses many of the SOA criteria today. It is a technology that not only provides for loose coupling but also is in wide use by the industry. The correlation of the ability of Web Services to deliver SOA is

- *Interface*—HTTP, FTP, SMTP (Simple Mail Transfer Protocol)
- *Message*—XML (eXtensible Markup Language)

These enablers are in place and proven and give rebirth to SOA. It is the convergence of available technology in production and widespread acceptance that will quickly enable the delivery of services to a wide variety of customers.

DRIVING FORCES BEHIND SOA

As in the movie *Perfect Storm*, there are forces converging at the right time and place under the right conditions that are resulting in a fundamental paradigm shift in computing. As shown in Figure 3.2, these forces are market dynamics, maturing technology, and world events. Within each is its own miniature "perfect storm." It is interesting to see how these seemingly unrelated events and advances in technology are converging, opening the window for new opportunities for business and information technology.

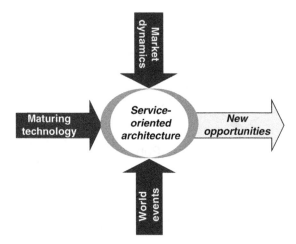

Figure 3.2. The SOA "perfect storm."

The opportunities emerging range from new business to improvements in information technology operations.

- New business
    - Real-time risk management
    - Large-scale data analysis
    - Utility services
- Operational improvements
    - Dramatic lower operational costs
    - Increase in compute utilization
    - Geographic independence

In-depth examples of these new opportunities are discussed in Part III of this book.

Maturing Technology

The advances in technology leading up to this point do not represent a single, revolutionary breakthrough. Rather, it is an evolution that is taking place in four areas of the IT world: Web Services, networking, distributed (grid) computing, and operational resource provisioning. Each has made advances in their respective areas that, on the surface, have no correlation to the others. However, advances in networking are the primary enabler for the rest.

Networking. Starting with the Ethernet, networking speeds have steadily increased since the late 1980s, 10 megabits per second (Mbits/s), giving way to 100 Mbits, giving way to 1 gigabit (Gbits). Enter Fiber Channel at 2 Gbits. Infiniband technology—first appearing as device interconnects for use in things such as storage area network (SAN) solutions—is now making its way into data center local-area networking with network speeds of ≥ 10 Gbits/s.

Distributed Computing (Grid). Grid technology takes two forms: computational or compute grid, and data grids. Each has its origins in academia and research, where complex analytical methods operating over large data sets were becoming the norm. However, the norm was also the limited budget to purchase supercomputers to do the work. The result was utilization of existing idle compute resources on a network, either private or public (the Internet), and distributing and coordinating work, thus yielding a seemingly limitless compute backbone for little to no financial cost.

As grid computing gains favor in commercial industry, further advances are being made to continue to evolve both the compute and data grids. Early problems involved large static data sets. As commercial applications have come online (via SOA), the data sets are becoming more dynamic in nature, thus requiring an evolution in data grid and distributed data management in grid.

Resource Provisioning. Resource provisioning, or data center automation, addresses issues for lowering the cost of administration of data centers by automating the mundane, manual-labor tasks found in most data centers. Tasks such as software installation and machine configuration can be automated, thus reducing cost of administration, improving the consistency of server profiles, and increasing data center uptime or reliability. Spinoff benefits include further cost savings from leveraging idle systems by reprovisioning them on the basis of usage demand.

Web Services. The evolution of SOA and Web Services has been discussed. The benefits of SOA via Web Services are

- Improved return on investment (ROI) via
  Lower infrastructure and operations costs
  Development focused on business problems, not service delivery
- Reliability due to
  Better quality assurance testing
  Improved service maintainability
  Improved service uptime
- Opening up business to a new and broader customer base

Business

Things always happen for a reason. But sometimes it can be difficult to see what those reasons are. For those who have lived through the technology and Internet boom of the late 1990s and seen the bubble burst, it was hard to understand the difficulties in the economic climate that occurred in the years that followed. Now that we have gotten past this, we can see that without the boom and bust of that bubble, the economic and business climate would not have existed to promote the elevated interest in grid computing and SOA that we are experiencing today.

If grid computing and SOA only provided a better and faster way to run applications, no one would be interested. The interest in grid computing and SOA is due to their collective financial benefits and their ability to address the climate that exists in business today, of tight fiscal spending and continued pursuit of ways to control costs and operational expenses. The added bonus of grid computing and SOA is that they both offer an improved way of running current business applications while offering an avenue for creating new business opportunities using a technology that is not bleeding-edge. None of these technologies is new. They have been explored and tested, and have been running in a production environment for many years. As such, the business—the CIOs, CTOs, and CFOs—do not view them as experimental. Rather, they see this as an application of an existing technology that can be quickly leveraged to put together IT infrastructures that not only support current business and promote new business but also reduce long-term operational costs.

It also becomes apparent to the business that widespread adoption of a SOA, implemented using Web Services and grid technology, fundamentally changes the way in which data centers are operated, moving them away from the dedicated silo-based structures that they are today to assume the appearance of a factory. As services are used by a growing number of customers—both internal or external—the price that can be charged for those services and the costs to the manufacturer begin to follow basic economic principles of supply and demand. It would not be economically feasible to deliver services given the current silo-based structure of the data center; it is not economically feasible to run a factory when your equipment is only 30% utilized. Grid technology addresses issues of delivery of service and economic costs by allowing data centers to run at efficiency/capacity rates of 50%, 60%, 70%, and higher using commoditized hardware components. Provisioning software allows the shift of physical resource to meet a service need when the demand now dictates. Below, we will discuss the business fundamentals of this paradigm shift in computing and tie them to the basic economic principles of supply and demand—in other words, market dynamics. In addition, we will see how this shift can leverage the same tried-and-true economic and engineering principles that govern utilities such as telephone companies to transform the silo-based data center into a compute utility service.

World Events

The third element in the *"perfect storm"* we described above is represented by the world events occurring during this same post-bubble-burst time period. We have seen a new war on terror, which is forcing an unprecedented level of communication and information sharing between the various law enforcement and intelligence agencies, and the judicial communities. It becoming apparent that the most important weapons we have in this war are information collected from a wide range of sources and the ability to analyze and correlate the data as quickly as possible. It is also part of the as-yet uneffected offense. How to foster this level of information sharing has become a driving factor in the advancement of grid computing, data grid, and SOA among the various government agencies fighting this war.

This same thirst for information sharing is being driven elsewhere by investigations relating to the seemingly endless series of corporate scandals afflicting American business. In this case, rather than tracking terrorists' movements or the diversion of illicit funds through money laundering schemes, law enforcement officials, and regulators are joining forces to share information on the timing of stockmarket trades, emails, and telephone calls.

In both cases, grid computing, data grid, and SOA have a role to play in achieving the level of interagency communications required to deal with the threat at hand.

ENTER BASIC SUPPLY–DEMAND ECONOMICS

In the movie *Trading Places*, an elaborate plot by Randolph and Mortimer Duke to corner the frozen orange juice market was foiled by Billy Ray Valentine and Louis Winthorpe III once they "acquired" the farm reports from Clarence Beeks. How did this happen?

1. The true farm reports stated a "good" or abundant supply of oranges.
2. Valentine and Winthorpe gave the Dukes a false report stating the opposite: a bad orange crop, thus a shortage of oranges.
3. The Dukes having the farm report in advance of the government announcing it to the public (just a few SEC rules were broken here alone), went on a buying spree to purchase as much of the available orange crop at a low price, knowing that once the shortage was announced, their orange crop holdings would be worth more that what they paid for them.
4. This caused a feeding frenzy that caused others to "follow" the Dukes' lead of buying the orange crop. The result of all this buying caused the price to rise.
5. Valentine and Winthorpe, knowing the content of the true farm report, sold orange crops at what was becoming an artificially high price due to all the Dukes (and others') buying. Technically, they were "selling short," selling something that they did not own, knowing that at some point in the future they would have to deliver the oranges they sold. They were not worried, for they knew that soon they would have all the orange crops they would need to meet these commitments.
6. Once the government announced an abundance of oranges, the value of the orange crops decreased; therefore the price started to go down as well.
7. As the price went down, Valentine and Winthorpe started buying back the same orange crops they had just sold but now at a much lower price. Buy low and sell high, and you make a profit.
8. The Dukes bought high and sold low, so they lost a lot of money (not to mention all the legal trouble they were in for insider trading).

Service-oriented economies follow the basic economic principles of supply and demand. Service-oriented architectures produce "business services" or product for anyone who desires them (consumers). The ability to supply a quality service to the customer will determine customer demand for the service.

In the example presented above, a supply of a product or service that falls short of demand forces the price up. This is what the Dukes were led to believe by the false report. So, no matter what price they bought the orange crops at, once the public knew of a supply shortage, the prices would rise even further, thus allowing them to sell at the higher price. But Valentine and Winthorpe knew that the opposite was true: an excess supply of oranges. In this case, oranges in excess of demand will force the fair market or equilibrium price down. The end result was that the Dukes lost money by buying high and selling low, while Valentine and Winthorpe made a profit by buying low and selling high.

Supply–Demand 101: Vocabulary

- *Desire* refers to people's willingness to own a good.
- *Demand* is the amount of a good that consumers are willing and able to buy at a given price.
- *Utility* is the satisfaction people get from *consuming* (using) a good or a service.
- *Supply* is the amount of a good that producers are willing and able to sell at a given price.

Figure 3.3 shows that "excess supply" forces the equilibrium price (P^*) down while "excess demand" forces the equilibrium price up. In a market economy, whether the product is oranges or billing systems, the ability of the producer to meet the market demand will determine the value of the product.

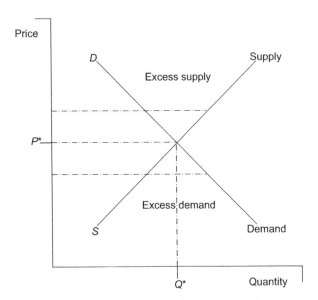

Figure 3.3. Basic supply–demand economics.

Service-oriented architectures, when successful, will package a product in such a fashion that renders it palatable or of a sufficiently high "utility" to encourage consumers to purchase the product rather that produce it themselves. As service offerings to customers increase, a true market economy will emerge that will be driven by the basic economic principles that guide a free-market economy.

As evidenced by Randolph and Mortimer Duke, the price of a product or service is determined in part by the ability to supply the product to the market. If the cost is too high, the size of the market is limited only to those who can afford to pay the higher price. There is little difference between a late winter frost destroying the orange crops, causing a supply shortage and a silo-based data center incapable of producing a quality service at a sufficient quantity and reasonable cost. Data centers need to run more efficiently to produce a quality product/service at a market cost indicated by the convergence of the supply/demand curves.

Distributed computing technology (compute grid, data grid, networking, provisioning, etc.) is an enabler that offers service-oriented architectures and shifts the operations of a data center from a custom "silo per product" offering to a factory producing quality product at affordable prices. The methods to do this are not new, for the telephone and electricity companies produce their respective products and distribute them across vast networks of devices to a broad consumer base. The quality of service is judged on ease of access, availability on demand, cost, and responsiveness to correct supply outages. Information technology can, via the evolutionary state of distributed computing, apply the tried and true principles of Shannon, Weiner, and others to transform the data center into a "compute utility service."

FUNDAMENTAL SHIFT IN COMPUTING

Technical communications in the latter half of the twentieth century were a function of computing innovation. Historically, communications relied on improvements in switching and resource allocation technologies. Switching technologies, in turn, have depended on the evolution of computing capabilities. This symbiotic equation, linking communications and computing, has become particularly important in the present environment of service-oriented architectures.

Today, a significant increase in computing power is driving a fundamental paradigm shift in technical communication.[6] The evolution of technical communication and its present-day drivers all point to a convergence point, a paradigm shift. This shift stands on the shoulders of history but also satisfies the elasticity, fungibility, granularity, and dependability needs of SOA. The shift is toward *Service-Oriented Network Architecture* (SONA). SONA is characterized as an overlay network, of Internet scale. It is architected to take advantage of virtualized hardware and policy-based dynamic resource allocation. It is multipurpose, and can be thought of as a learning system through its use of a continuous feedback loop for service improvements. The implementation of SONA is a nexus of grid computing and Web Services. We will discuss SONA and its relationship to grid computing and Web Services in Chapter 20 of this book.

4

PARALLEL GRID PLANES

USING ART TO DESCRIBE LIFE: GRID IS THE BORG

For anyone who has seen *Star Trek—the Next Generation*, grid computing can be described using a very simple analogy: Grid is the Borg. For anyone who has not, the Borg is an evil race of half-men, half-machines who terrorize the stars of the television/movie series, and are now an attraction at a Las Vegas casino.

The Borg displays all the characteristics of grid computing: the roles of its two most fundamental components, and how these components must exist in harmony in order for any grid environment to succeed.

I do not want to give the impression that grid computing is going to evolve into a consciousness that will take over and dominate humankind. System administrators are not going to be assimilated into the grid "Collective" and become part human/part machine drones that recharge while standing up in "regeneration chambers." Grid computing is a positive development for information technology and the businesses that will embrace to create flexible compute backbones and eventually utility services.

The Borg is a race of humanoids that are enhanced with machine (cybernetic) implants that are melded together so that flesh and machine form a single being. This melding did not stop at the physical but also extended to the consciousness. The person's uniqueness was blended into a collective mind—"the Collective" or "hive"—so that the Collective's consciousness comprised all the experiences and knowledge of the entire species that was assimilated.

Distributed Data Management for Grid Computing, by Michael Di Stefano
Copyright © 2005 John Wiley & Sons, Inc.

The Borg's social environment is very similar to a bee's or an ant's, where there are many drones, these biomechanical organisms. In the Borg society, the drones are

- Large in number.
- Replicable; when a drone is wounded or killed, there is always another right behind it to take its place.
- Capable of performing any task given to them by the Collective.

The Collective, meanwhile, knows implicitly:

- Where all the drones are.
- What the drones are doing.
- What tasks the drones are capable of performing.
- What tasks need to be performed (something to fix, defense against an intruder, etc.).

The Collective, given this information, would assign the best available drone to perform the required task. The most obvious example of this is when one Borg drone is recharging in a regeneration chamber when it would suddenly wake up and go do something. In this analogy, the Collective's role is played by the compute grid plane: management of resources and the distribution of tasks to the best possible resource to do the work.

The Borg, as a race, assimilates other races to proliferate itself. Borg assimilation is the absorption of the experiences and knowledge of the individual and the race. When a human was captured by Borgs, probes were plunged into the neck of the victim, who would be transformed into a Borg drone, and the victim's knowledge and experiences would be transferred into the Collective. Once the victim's knowledge is assimilated, then every Borg drone, no matter where they were in the universe, would immediately become aware of the new data now held by the Collective. This process of taking data and sharing and distributing them across all the nodes, no matter where they were, is paralleled by the data grid plane.

Any environment where many machines coordinate and synchronize tasks needs to organize the computer and the data resources. The Borg example offers an insightful way to visualize these two halves of the grid equation and how they must interact to become an effective, unified unit. If the Borg were merely the compute grid plane, it would simply be a mindless machine that fell far short of its potential. And so, any grid environment without the inclusion of smart and efficient data management will not be effective and will never reach its full potential.

GRID PLANES

Physically, grid computing involves using large numbers of computers, arranged as clusters and connected via a network, that are controlled using efficient task management techniques. Typically, this results in an infrastructure capable of tasks ranging from the small to computational problems too large for a single server or even supercomputer to handle. But it is also important to broaden our view of grid computing beyond the physical compute resource, compute cycles and network, and the coordination of tasks, as represented by the compute grid. The compute grid is merely half of any grid environment. To view grid in its entirety, it is essential to consider data management within the grid: the so-called data grid.

In any grid computing environment (see Figure 4.1), how to address data management is essential to realizing the grid's full potential. Grid topology is a fundamentally different from the topology of the current standard computing model, client/server. It is this difference that will force new thinking on how best to manage data within the grid. Traditional data management techniques were not designed for the highly distributed physical grid topology and therefore are not best suited to realizing its full potential.

Grid represents a paradigm shift in how we view computing, leading to the birth of new compute utility services and applications that are possible only within a complete grid computing paradigm consisting of both compute and data grids.

Compute Grids

Compute grids form a high-performance computer in a topology very different from that of today's typical compute backbone, with communities of hundreds or thousands of computers that

- Tap underutilized computers in an enterprise
- Create "compute farms"
- Share enterprise resources
- Perform tasks orchestrated across the grid as if it were one virtual machine

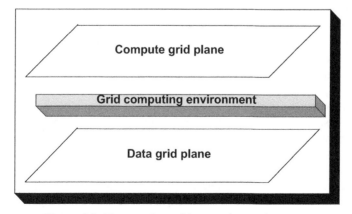

Figure 4.1. The complete grid computing environment.

The standards body Globus has evolved as the center of the grid computing community and the driver of a "reference platform." The Globus toolkit provides a reference platform for the implementation of Grid networks. It includes standard protocols, as well as libraries for resource discovery, management, and distribution.

Most grid implantations have their own toolkit and protocol, which follow the Globus standard, and enhance it to support, in most cases proprietary resource allocation, data distribution, and quality-of-service (QoS) models.

Currently, the Globus community is developing a standard Open Grid Services Architecture (OGSA), based on Web Services, allowing for the introduction of a variety of vertical services for the support of financial, commercial, and life science grid applications. Grid is now in its third generation:

- First-generation implementations of grids were highly oriented around jobs and job scheduling across clusters of distributed Unix platforms.
- Second-generation implementations tended to be based on the P2P computing model for managing jobs across both Unix and Intel platforms. P2P models were driven into the limelight by Internet-based efforts to solve complex life sciences as well as extraterrestrial signal processing problems.
- Third-generation implementations, in their infancy now, have evolved beyond the P2P platform to enable true, guaranteed distributed computing, are more similar to distributed computing environments, and as such include basic services such as directory, reliability, and security.

Globus is establishing specifications for third-generation grid. This organization's members include universities and major grid vendors.

For a more in-depth discussion of computational grids, please see the white paper by Foster et al.[7]

Data Grids

Grids evolved to address highly parallelizable problems in the scientific community. These problems typically involved computational processing of large data sets (static in nature, stored as files) to derive result sets. The data sets are made available to the grid nodes via an FTP-like process. The current Globus reference architecture includes a service called GridFTP that addresses the distribution of static data throughout a grid.

As grid computing is adopted in the commercial community, the problem sets that it must support broaden beyond the traditional-use case. Most commercial applications rely on a combination of static, derived, and real-time data to perform their business functions. For example, a typical portfolio pricing applications are state machines tying together dynamic and static data sets that originate from various sources, each with its own access and performance characteristics.

Current grid technology provides the capability to create a compute grid plane for the distribution of tasks. It does not, however, address data distribution and management. Rudimentary implantations of data grids attempt to address the issues of real-time distribution and caching of nonstatic data. However, they do not take into consideration data management. Examples such as data passing through a variety of ad hoc mechanisms, including arguments, databases, and flat files, limit grid implementations in two ways:

- Data available only centrally to a grid become a performance bottleneck.
- Grid nodes cannot efficiently cooperate and thus can address only problems that do not require coordination.

To address the requirements of the new grid topology, more sophisticated methods of data distribution—and, more importantly, data management—are needed for a reliable, transactional, and real-time data grid plane. This need is evident when taking a closer look into what is meant by a *data grid* and its requirement to easily manage disparate, large, and complex data sets.

COMPUTE AND DATA GRIDS—PARALLEL PLANES

The compute grid can be viewed as a two-dimensional plane—like the surface of a table—that encompasses the physical machines that can reside within a data center, or across a local network or a WAN (wide-area network) that spans multiple data centers. This two-dimensional plane is called the "compute grid plane," with an individual machine in the compute grid termed a "compute node" or simply a "node." The logical grouping of the physical compute nodes in the compute grid plane is flexible, according to the architect's preference. Possible logical groupings are by data center (e.g., New York, London, and Tokyo), by physical provisioning of machines, independent of location, or by any other view that best meets the needs of the architect, developer, or operations manager. The compute grid plane manages its compute nodes and the coordination of tasks to the best available compute node.

The data grid is also viewed as a two-dimensional plane called the *data grid plane*. Physically, the data grid plane spans all the nodes within the compute grid plane. The data grid plane provides a completely separate function for the compute grid plane by addressing the distribution and management of data between the nodes. A piece of data can physically reside on any one or on multiple nodes in the data grid plane.

Individually, the compute grid plane the data grid plane respectively provide unique service and function. Only when these two planes work together does the whole equal more than the sum of the two parts. One way to visualize these planes and how they functioned together is to view them as parallel to each other. Placing the compute and data grid planes in parallel, as if to stack one on top of the other, reinforces the view of one physical world split into two functionally separate and parallel planes. The interconnections between the two parallel planes are like

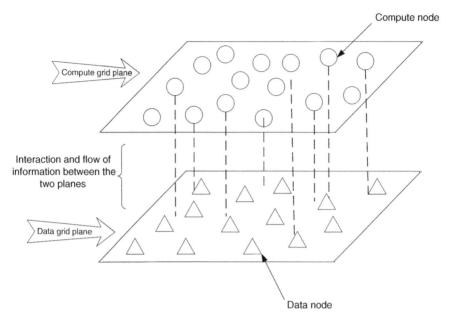

Figure 4.2. Parallel compute and data grid planes.

electrons flowing between the two plates of the capacitor. The compute grid plane draws on the information in the data grid plane, while the data grid plane draws on the physical resources of the machines that constitute the compute grid plane.

Figure 4.2 depicts these two planes and the interconnections conducting the flow of information and resources between them.

TRUE GRID MUST INCLUDE DATA MANAGEMENT

At the most fundamental level, the data grid plane is a set of functionality that has become expected in today's client/server environments. It also addresses the new data management issues in a grid topology so as to facilitate transparent access of shared data across a grid. The plane provides both a localized and a distributed caching function to support intranode and internode collaboration. The compute grid plane utilizes the APIs provided by the data grid plane to enable this collaboration.

Basic Data Management Requirements

Coordinating the Compute and Data Grid Planes. The grid, as a whole, functions well with the simplest flow of application data from the data grid plane to the compute grid plane. However, there are additional areas of coordination between these two planes that can greatly enhance the performance as well as function of the grid. This is accomplished by allowing the task and resource management functions of the compute grid plane to have access to some of the underlying and most fundamental workings of the data grid plane.

Sharing data distribution and location information of the data grid plane with the resource and task management logic of the compute grid plane enables the grid environment as a whole to function at a much higher level than it would otherwise. This leveraging of sharing data locality with the task and distribution functions is a concept known as *data affinity*, which will be discussed later in this book.

Data Surfaces in a Data Grid Plane. The data grid plane is viewed as a two-dimensional plane with the individual data elements as nodes that can logically reside at any point in the plane. If the location of the data is defined using X and Y coordinates, you can quickly view the data contained within the data plane. A third coordinate, Z, gives us a three-dimensional surface, where the X and Y axes indicate the location of the data node and the Z axis indicates the data point residing on each node. Figure 4.3 shows the data grid plane in the $X-Y$ axis as a two-dimensional surface R and the data contained in the nodes of the data grid plane as a surface that extends into the third dimension or Z axis. This three-dimensional view of a data surfaces is very helpful because for the first time we can see data transition through its processing lifecycle. You can see these data surfaces build as the compute processes create, access, and change the data points.

Once a three-dimensional view is established, it is easy to extend it to an N-dimensional data space. The three-dimensional space is created as a single point by each data point within this data grid plane. To go beyond a three-dimensional view, each data point can vector off into another set of data points or collection of data points.

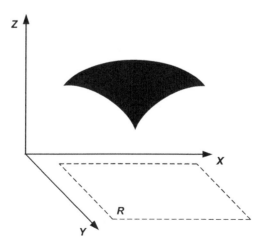

Figure 4.3. Data surface in a data grid plane.

Evolving the Data Grid

The rudimentary implantations of a data grid plane attempt to address data distribution. But they fall short of some the grid-specific data management requirements. Examples of this are

- *Data Passing with Task.* This is similar to a programmatic function call, where data are passed in as arguments and data are returned as the function return argument. This implies such mechanics as marshaling and unmarshaling for both in and return data passing.
- *Localized Caching of Parameters.* This is the next step beyond data passing with task, aimed at reducing data transport/marshaling overhead. Once a piece of data is moved with the task, a copy of it is kept locally on the node that performs the task. Thus, for future tasks requiring the same data sets, it is already there. This method does nothing for data consistency across nodes and the data source.
- *Data Pulling by a Task.* When a task is distributed to a node and the data are not locally cached, then the data sets are requested by some central data manager. This method does nothing for data consistency across nodes and the data source.
- *Traditional Data Management Techniques.* These are not designed for grid environments and thus have inherent data access bottlenecks as the physical size and complexity of task increase on the grid.

Therefore, new architectures for the data grid plane are required to support data management with a perspective on a fully distributed compute environment that is the grid. Some features and functions to be supported by data grid plane architecture are

- Support traditional data management features
    - Queries
    - Transactionality
    - Support high-ordered data structures, such as tables, arrays, and matrices
- Support grid-related data management issues
    - Data regionalization
    - Data synchronization both within and between data regions
    - Data distribution with data regions
    - Data transactionality for within a data region and with external data grid data sources
    - Fault tolerance and high availability
    - Others
- Match a compute grid's functionality
    - *Dependability* on a massive scale
    - *Consistency* across heterogeneous data sources
    - *Pervasiveness* on a massive scale

Security on a massive scale

Inexpensive

Offer *varying levels of service*

- Enhance a compute grid's functionality

Influence scheduling based on data locality

Enable *task/grid migration*

Enable *legacy integration*

Enable *vertical extensions* for common industry problems

Enable *interactivity*

PART II

DATA MANAGEMENT IN GRID COMPUTING

5

SCALING IN THE GRID TOPOLOGY

In this chapter we will discuss the various levels of data management within the grid and its enabling role in allowing the grid topology to scale to its full potential. We will start with the evolution of data management within the grid and investigate the various implementations of the data grids that are in place today as well as those currently emerging.

EVOLUTION IN DATA MANAGEMENT

It is important to acknowledge the long and rich history of data management and give credit to those who have applied the science of mathematics to computers, catapulting their use into our everyday lives. I have a personal appreciation of APL and its application of mathematic expressions applied to data. APL's mathematic programming language reveals its beauty to the mathematicians and its complexity to the nonmathematicians.

The evolution of computer science can be charted by the growth of data management techniques and products. Initially, the mainframe and mini-computers utilized APL, network databases and hierarchical architecture. Today, client/servers are heavily in use and rely on both relational and object databases. The emerging technology for distributed computing relies on in-memory as well as relational databases.

For our discussions, I am choosing the client/server architecture as a baseline for establishing an understanding to distributed computing because of its widespread use in industry. This allows us to draw on the common knowledge among managers, architects, and developers, and to leverage that knowledge so as to describe the data management needs within the grid topology.

Data management in a grid topology must provide the same QoS levels that are provided within a relational database. Only by maintaining the same QoS levels that are commonplace in today's environment can the widespread adoption of the grid succeed.

Client/Server Evolution

In the late 1980s and early 1990s, client/server technology began to gain wide acceptance. This change in compute topology, a change from mainframes and mini-computers to a more distributed environment—where the separation of a program functions was made between "service" as a separate execution program, a "server," and the business "client"—started to usher in the need for relational data management systems. Relational database technology matured during the 1970s and 1980s, with the emergence of such companies as Oracle, Sybase, and IBM introducing the concept of relational database technology with it's DB2 product. These companies positioned themselves to take advantage of the paradigm shift toward client/server topology. They offered training and educational seminars, at which attendees explored client/server computing as a possible architecture for new projects. The seminars would introduce relational database and data management systems. Some of the most common questions centered by the attendees' frame of reference were efficient file and disk management, with substantially less focus on accessing data via something well known today as Structured Query Language (SQL).

Typically, the follow-up to a seminar consisted of training classes in relational database technology and SQL, perhaps 2, 3, or 5 days in length, with "hands on" labs that emphasized the database structures that included tables, rows, indices, and the like, as well as how to structure a query and how to utilize a stored procedure.

As more projects began to migrate to client/server topology, the importance of data management rose to the surface, which was well deserved. Issues such as how to structure the database both to support the business data and gain maximum performance began to receive more attention, while file and disk management lost focus. Specialists in relational data management quickly focused on system performance optimization, and how to provide the proper tools and methods to operate the system. Today, when we talk to the same groups of people who are now developing in the client/server architecture, their main focus and/or concerns are less on the engine of the relational database and more on the data management features as well as levels of service that these data management systems provide.

Grid Evolution

Data management within grid computing has evolved with the applications of grid technology. The earliest applications were complex analysis, often traversing large data sets. Examples of this include protein folding, semiconductor manufacturing, energy exploration research, seismic data analysis, and analysis of DNA sequences (which is covered in more detail in a later chapter). The data sets for these applications are normally static in nature; DNA sequences and seismic data, once recorded, seldom change.

Data management of the static data sets is adequately handled via common data storage techniques such as file systems. The problem to resolve is how to take the data stored in files, typically large in size, and move that data to the nodes in the grid that require the data in order to perform their designated tasks. Most common methods used today are File Transfer Protocol (FTP) and distributed file systems.

Since these are the first generation of data management tools for the grid—and as such address the movement of a subset of data type, primarily data sets that are static in nature—they are considered a level 0 data grid. As the use of grid computing expands to support increasing fields of work and businesses, dynamic data sets become a more common problem that needs to be solved. Therefore, the level 0 data grids, which work well for static data, will not work and scale for data sets that exhibit dynamic behavioral properties.

New data management techniques and infrastructures are required to address the dynamic data sets within the grid environment. These level 1 data grids, unlike the level 0 data grid, take into account both static and dynamic data sets and address the unique data management issues posed when data are to be managed in the highly distributed compute environments of the grid.

DIFFERENT IMPLEMENTATIONS OF A DATA GRID

Level 0 Data Grids

Level 0 data grids were the earliest to address data requirements in a grid topology. Their main function is the distribution of large, static data sets to the nodes in the grid. They do not address data management issues such as updates, transactions, or integration with external systems, as illustrated by the following academic examples. The first example is found in the white paper by Chervenak et al.[8] as quoted below:

> In an increasing number of scientic disciplines, large data collections are emerging as important community resources. In this paper, we introduce design principles for a data management architecture called the Data Grid. We describe two basic services that we believe are fundamental to the design of a data grid, namely, storage systems and metadata management. Next, we explain how these services can be used to develop higher-level services for replica management and replica selection. We conclude by describing our initial implementation of data grid functionality.

Another similar argument is presented in the white paper called by Moore et al.:[9]

> Data grids link distributed, heterogeneous storage resources into a coherent data management system. From a user perspective, the data grid provides a uniform

name space across the underlying storage systems, while supporting retrieval and storage of files. In the high energy physics community, at least six data grids have been implemented for the storage and distribution of experimental data. Data grids are also being used to support projects as diverse as digital libraries (National Library of Medicine Visible Embryo project), federation of multiple astronomy sky surveys (NSF National Virtual Observatory project), and integration of distributed data sets (Long Term Ecological Reserve). Data grids also form the core interoperability mechanisms for creating persistent archives, in which data collections are migrated to new technologies over time. The ability to provide a uniform name space across multiple administration domains is becoming a critical component of national-scale, collaborative projects.

FTP in Grid. The File Transfer Protocol (FTP) is one of the most widely used protocols for the movement of files across a network. It is amazing that it remains in heavy use even in today's technology advanced society. Therefore, it is an obvious choice for data movement within a grid environment. The standards body Globus is investigating the use of FTP as the data transfer protocol for a data grid implementation, termed *GridFTP*.

In Chapter 1, in the section entitled "Leveling the Playing Field of Buzzword Mania," an allusion was made between the relational database and the data grids to establish a common vocabulary. Each contains an engine that establishes a data transfer protocol to manage the process of how the bits and bytes of data are moved at the physical level. A close look at GridFTP shows it as a data transfer protocol; therefore, applying our definition, GridFTP is an engine in the larger picture of data management within the grid. It does not address the data management techniques of transactions, distribution, synchronization, or querying of data.

GridFTP, as a protocol engine, is a good choice for static data sets. It allows data to be transferred between nodes but does not address data management beyond data movement. Since it is based on the common used FTP, it is a common protocol that is well proven and works well. There is no need to reinvent something for managing the distribution of files across many machines in the network. The Globus effort describes how to take FTP as the file transfer protocol and extend it to support issues such as security, stripping of data in parallel with data transfers, and automatic negotiation of TCP/IP (Transmission Control Protocol/Internet Protocol) buffers and window sizes. These are all part of the protocol for moving the data reliably across the grid. For additional reading on GridFTP, please refer to the papers by Allcock et al.[10] and the Globus Project.[11]

The physical architecture of the FTP protocol requires a central server to manage the FTP requests and the movement of data. Therefore, if a machine is to make public its files through the FTP protocol, that machine must be running a FTP server; thus, any machine requesting data must be a FTP client. The respective FTP libraries and processes must be running on both the client and server machines in order for the FTP process to work properly. This is a client/server paradigm with both FTP servers and clients. One key feature of FTP is that each source of data is its own server, and the client must know where that data reside on the network in order to access them.

Distributed Filing Systems. Similar to GridFTP, a distributed file system is a way to manage the distribution of files across a network. From the user's perspective, a distributed file system is a common filing system with a directory tree structure. However, although the branches of the trees appear to be sourced from one filing system, in reality, the files can physically reside on different machines on the network making it virtually one file system to the end user. For example, the files in branch A may physically reside in one machine while files in branch B physically reside on another machine, and so on. The user who is changing directories from branch A to branch B will not realize that the data are actually been served from different machines on the network.

The architecture of a distributed file system is server-based; a server manages the mapping of the disparate physical file systems into a logical, unified file system. As the user of the distributed file system, the client in this case, traverses the tree structure, client requests are made to the server, which in turn negotiates with the true sources of data and pulls the data back to the client in the common directory tree view.

Similar to the GridFTP, a distributed file system has the following characteristics:

- An effective method to distribute data across the grid for data sets that are static
- A protocol for data movement
- An engine for the mechanics of distributing bits and bytes across many machines
- Inability to resolve the data management issues of transactions, synchronization, integration, and querying of data

Distributed filing systems differ from GridFTP in that the server in distributed filing systems provides a common and logical view of the data. Therefore, a client requesting data does not need to know where the data physically reside. A distributed file system is not like the GridFTP, where the FTP client must know the physical location of data across the network.

An example of a distributed filing system is CODA, "a file system for a large-scale distributed computing environment composed of Unix workstations. It provides resiliency to server and network failures through the use of two distinct but complementary mechanisms. One mechanism, *server replication*, involves storing copies of a file at multiple servers. The other mechanism, *disconnected operation*, is a mode of execution in which a caching site temporarily assumes the role of a replication site."[12]

Faster Servers. One of the fastest paths to maintaining quality of service for true data management within the grid is to leverage the traditional data management techniques of client/server by leveraging existing relational databases and interfacing them into the grid. This works well for smaller grid implementations, where the numbers of CPUs are relatively low. However, scaling becomes an issue as the size of the grid increases, thus increasing in the number of CPUs. It is important to note that the grid nodes are required to know that they must connect to the database in order to query and transact on the data.

The traditional relational database companies, in an effort to support larger grid environments, will take steps to increase the performance of their engines. However, as described in an earlier chapter, the physical differences between client/server and grid topologies will not allow the efficient application of data management architecture for one topology to be applied to another topology. Technology that was designed, implemented, and tuned for client/server applications will not scale well within the highly distributed computing environment of the grid.

Metadata Hubs and Distributed Data Integration. Metadata hubs facilitate the integration of data from various sources and formats the data into a structure that is consistent with the format of the receiving application that is requesting or querying the data. This is a layer of abstraction required between the business application and the data source so as to encapsulate the complexities of the mechanical process of connecting, retrieving, and transforming data, making it possible to access and correlate data that otherwise would not be available.

Efforts to bring this concept to the data grid are described in a white paper by Foster et al.[13] The paper discusses the mechanisms for delivering such a distributed data integration platform and introduces an example of such a prototype system, known as *Chimera*, in which some of the virtual data grid concepts are implemented.[13] Commercial implementations of a metadata hub are available from Avaki. Their version 5.0 product claims to deliver data from multiple data sources through a single service.[14]

Level 1 Data Grids

Level 1 data grids support data sets that are dynamic in nature: data sets that change daily, hourly, minute-to-minute, second-to-second, or at any other intervals. Level 1 data grids address the distribution of and the ready access to data across the many nodes of the compute grid. They supply, among other things

- Access methods
- Management methods
- Transactional methods
- Synchronization methods

In this book, I will discuss the various data management policies that are compatible with level 1 data grids. The engines that support level 1 data grids are readily available today. These engines and the data management products built with them supply some of the data management features required for grid computing. Some examples include JavaSpaces and projects such as OpenStore and OpenMP. OpenMP has existed in the industry for a number of years. However, it is not directed toward solving data management in the grid computing space. Rather, OpenMP addresses multithreaded applications across clusters and how to manage interactive data across the clusters. There is a similarity between OpenMP's distributed memory model of data access and that of a level 1 data grid. Finally, I will close with a use case of a level 1 data grid product from Integrasoft, called the *Integrasoft Grid Fabric* (IGF), designed from its inception as a level 1 data grid.

Foundations. I will look at three basic technologies for providing level 1 data grids: JavaSpaces, global replication of data across the grid, and distributed memory. I am not implying that these are the only ways of a providing a level 1 data grid. However, these are the technologies currently leveraged to supply level 1 data grids. I will asses each of the three solutions to determine how they meet the requirements imposed by a level 1 data grid.

JavaSpaces. JavaSpaces has its roots in the Linda project developed by Dr. David Gelernter,[15] in which persistent stores (tuples), combined with simple operations, can easily and effectively address distributed problems that, if using conventional middleware techniques (messaging and invoking methods over networks), would be significantly more complex. Where middleware techniques involve message or transactional passing of data and remote method/object invocation across networks, JavaSpaces creates a shared memory environment that not only exchanges information between distributed processes but is also a vehicle for distributed processes to coordinate operations and tasks with each other. I will illustrate that JavaSpaces exhibits some distributed data management features as well as attempt to address some of the requirements of a compute grid.

A process can "write" to and "read" from a JavaSpace, but it cannot modify an object while it is in a JavaSpace. For an object to be modified, it must first be removed from the space, changed, and then put back into the space. The read operation makes a "local copy" of the object to the reading process. This implies that not only can data be read from the space, but since the reading process has its own "local copy" of the object, the object's methods can be invoked by the process. This is where JavaSpaces begins to blend compute and data grid features. In addition to shared memory and computational invocation of objects, additional properties of JavaSpaces include

- *Persistence.* An object read into a JavaSpace is persistent in the space until it is removed. There are several ways to remove an object, either explicitly or through a "leasing" process.
- *Transactions.* Operations into and out of the space, as well as those where spaces interact with each other are transactional.
- *Query.* JavaSpaces supports a filtering or associative lookup mechanism where queries can be made to the space on the basis of a filter or template; the space will return objects that meet that filtered criteria.

JavaSpaces as a Data Grid. JavaSpaces exhibits some of the properties of a distributed data management system:

- Shared access of data across a network of machines
- Persistence
- Transactions

However, since JavaSpaces shares "objects," it shares the data attributes of the object and its executable methods, thus exhibiting the other properties of a compute grid as well. Finally, JavaSpaces is just that: Java. Distributed applications that do not support Java cannot participate without gyrations of interfaces and bridges into the space.

Global Replication. Global replication is a process of providing distributed and durable storage of data across a large grid of computers. One such system is the Ocean-Store project.[16] Data objects are distributed and stored locally on the nodes of the grid. OceanStore's storage and replication algorithms are such that they ensure strong consistency among the object replicas. However, realizing that not all applications will have the same requirement for strong consistency and fault tolerance, global replication also allows applications to move to a weaker consistency policy that will boost performance.

One of OceanStore's more interesting aspects is its ability to manage *data affinity*, the ability to move data to the nodes that most frequently use these data, keeping them cached locally to that node and thus reducing network traffic and increasing overall performance. OceanStore analyzes usage patterns of data and migrates the data to areas or nodes where they are frequently used. Data affinity of objects also reduces the time needed to find objects, caching objects either at or near—as defined by the number of local network hops—the local node that much more quickly, thus reducing the latency time of locating an object.

However, like JavaSpaces, the global replication method is currently being prototyped only in Java, thus introducing the issues of integrating non-Java applications.

Distributed Memory. Distributed and shared memory is an effective mechanism for building a data grid. OpenMP, although not designed for grid computing, is designed for the splitting of large processing loops into smaller bits of work in a multi-threaded, multiprocessor environment.[17] It also creates a distributed memory space to eliminate the use of traditional network communication methods and middleware to allow the threads to share data. Sounds a lot like grid computing, or does it? I will examine some of the properties of OpenMP and its parallels to grid computing, to determine the benefits of a distributed memory data grid engine.

Some of the features of OpenMP are as follows:

- It is compiler-based. Any program using the OpenMP API (Application Program Interface) set must compiled with these APIs in order to take advantage of the benefits it provides. Current OpenMP APIs supports only for C/C++ and FORTRAN programming languages.

- It is thread-based. A master thread forks (or splits) into "child" threads, each with its own environment that include process and memory space in the "shared multiprocessor" (SMP) environment.
- It creates a shared memory space among the threads so that data among threads can be shared at either a coarse or fine granular level, where *fine granularity* is defined as one set of instructions (thread) operating on multiple pieces of data and *coarse granularity*, where multiple code segments run concurrently across multiple processors.
- Its distributed memory for data sharing eliminates the overhead of traditional message passing (which, designed for client/server topologies, does not translate well to applications running on scalable systems with a globally addressable distributed memory space) between threads, thus yielding

    Dynamic threading, adding and removing threads dynamically as required

    Dynamic load balancing, where load distribution is performed during runtime automatically

    Application parallelization options and incremental levels of parallelization

- ANSI, which is an industry standard yielding single source portability for shared memory parallelism. Members of the OpenMP Architecture Review Board (ARB) include

    ASCI program of the U.S. Department of Energy

    Compaq

    Fujitsu

    HP

    IBM

    Intel

    KAI

    SGI

    Sun

Performance of thread execution, time spent processing within a thread, increases as the number of compute nodes or processors increases. Depending on the characteristics of the code parallelized, improvements of up to two times can be expected.[18]

Reading the OpenMP description on processing and distributed shared memory, it will sound very similar to descriptions of compute and data grid engines. In fact, replace terms such as "threads" with "worklets," which are almost indistinguishable.

Case Study: Integrasoft Grid Fabric (IGF). The Integrasoft Grid Fabric (IGF) by the company called Integrasoft (www. integrasoftware.com) has been designed from the ground up as a data management system for highly distributed computing environments such as clusters and the grids. The objective of IGF is to provide an effective way to manage data, from the user's perspective, in the grid environments—the management of fast-moving, transient data and the provision of the same levels of service that we have become used to with relational database management systems.

IGF's engine establishes a distributed memory space that spans the physical nodes of the grid. Within this space, various levels of data management are applied, including the ability to create the regions, to transact on the data, to query the data, to integrate the data from legacy systems, and to provide data affinity. All of these terms, and more, will be addressed subsequently in this book. IGF brings the data within its distributed memory space to coexist with the applications that have been enabled to run within the grid, offering immediate access to the data and transacting on the data as if the application were working in a client/server environment, dealing directly with the data sources themselves.

IGF, as a product, is differentiated from JavaSpaces in that

- IGF is not a Java-only solution.
- The long-term persistence of data is defined through policies that the application can set with the data grid.
- IGF provides additional distributed data management features not supported in JavaSpaces.

Like OceanStore, IGF supports data affinity. However, the data affinity support in IGF extends beyond what the data grid can achieve by itself, by integrating with the computer grid and feeding the compute grid's task scheduler with data-locality-type information.

Integrasoft has a track record for designing systems using distributed compute architectures and thus is very familiar with the data management requirements of applications to work effectively in the topology of grid. By working with the user community in the financial sector, many of the practical issues, such as ease of use, migration, reuse of existing code, and integration of legacy systems and data, are integrated into IGF, lowering the barrier of entry to the grid computing and thus yielding higher acceptance of this new technology.

IGF is one of the first commercially available distributed data management systems incorporating the data management issues demanded by the grid architecture, providing levels of service similar to that of its relational counterparts. User community research and feedback is incorporated into the product and presented in this book in the form of

- Introduction of data management within the grid
- Practical, user-driven interest for its application (see Part III of this book, on practical applications of grid computing)
- Code examples (see Part IV, "Reference Materials")

APPLICATION CHARACTERISTICS FOR GRID

The data grid plane, which originated as a mechanism for distributing files to compute servers, is undergoing a substantial evolution. The evolution is centered on the needs of next-generation grid applications, which include integrity and quality of service for both static and real-time or nonstatic data. Figure 5.1 shows the current evolution of the data grid plane in relation to the demands of an application.

One topic frequently discussed throughout this book is the policies for the management of data in the highly distributed compute environment of the grid. The various policies, their implementations and effects on data, and the resulting combinations of the interactions of the policies, will determine the data grid's effectiveness in supporting the business requirements. There are numerous factors describing how the interdependencies of application data requirements, data integrity, quality of service (QoS), data dynamics, and application events interact with

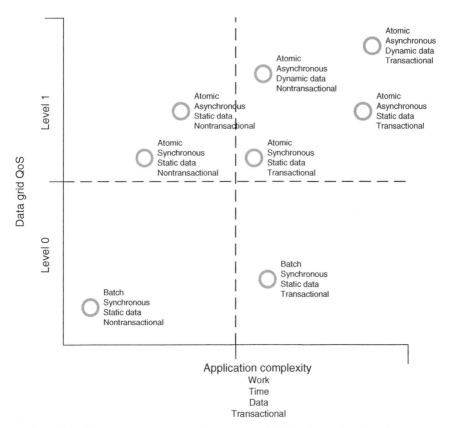

Figure 5.1. Data grid quality of service versus application demand and requirements.

each other at various levels depending on the complexity of the application.[19] I will define some of the characteristics of an application with respect to the selection of the various data management policies so as to best meet the application requirements.

The issue to resolve is how best to represent the parameters describing an application's properties and correlate them to the policies for data management in grid computing. The use of tables, matrices, and graphs is not sufficient to visualize the various interdependencies, due to the multidimensional relationships that quickly form between the various parameters of work, data, time, geographic boundaries, and complexity of data analysis. The expression of an application's properties in mathematical notation is presented below. This method provides a way for us to clearly and accurately define functional areas of an application and the parameterized arguments composing each part of the application. The definition for an application in a distributed environment can be defined as a function driven by of other functions as indicated below:

$$Application(Work(\ ), Data(\ ), Time(\ ), Geography(\ ), Query(\ ))$$

where the following are the driven parameters of the functions:

$$Work(batch/atomic, synchronous/nonsynchronous)$$
$$Data(overallsize, atomicsize, transactional, transient, queryable)$$
$$Time(Real\text{-}Time, NotReal\text{-}Time, NearReal\text{-}Time)$$
$$Geography(Topology, NetworkBandwidth)$$
$$Query(basic, complex)$$

The functions of this equation are described as follows:

- *Work(batch/atomic, synchronous/nonsynchronous)*. The *Work*( ) is the application processing mode addressing the type of work being performed from a communication perspective. This indicates whether the application is a single process (where threading is not relevant) or can be subdivided into atomic worklets. If it can be subdivided into worklets, is there any coordination between them? For example, is the execution of one worklet dependent on the output of other worklets? Is there any synchronization between the worklets?

- *Data(overallsize, atomicsize, transactional, transient, queryable)*. The *Data*( ) defines the application data requirements and characters addressing many questions that require answers from a data perspective. What is the overall size of the data set over which the application operates? If the application consists of atomic worklets, what is the data size over which each worklet operates? Are the data either within a data region or other systems external to the data region, or both? Are the data generated and then discarded during the operation of the application or worklet? Are there any transient data sets?

Are the data to be queried either for internal purposes or for generating user reports?

- *Time(Real-Time, NotReal-Time, NearReal-Time)*.   The *Time*( ) defines the application data requirements from a time perspective, addressing some questions regarding data availability. What are the timing interactions of the application with other external systems and events? Does the application consume or produce data in "real time," or is it purely event-driven? Does the application require all input data sets to be static before it can run and its output produced at the completion of its execution—is it "non-real-time"? Does the application operate on "snapshots" of data that are produced by external systems—is the application "near-real-time"?

- *Geography(Topology, NetworkBandwidth)*. The *Geography*( ) defines the application in relationship to the network capacity and design. What is the physical topology of the application's execution? Is this application targeted to support a local business unit, or is the business unit geographically distributed across the enterprise? This will imply how the application and data region are to be structured within the grid. Geography as it relates to the grid has less to do with physical distance than with network bandwidth as WANs imply lower bandwidth than do LAN (local-area networks). However, bandwidth can vary greatly within a LAN from 10baseT all the way up to infiniband. This, too, must be taken into consideration.

- *Query(basic, complex)*. The *Query*( ) defines the application need for data and the complexity of the type of query that will be associated with the request. If the data are to be queried, what is the level of complexity of the queries? Complex queries can be optimized by various data management policies of the data grid.

I will refer to these definitions associated with application characteristics, particularly when discussing policies for synchronization and distribution. If the application characteristics are taken into account when defining the policies for data management in the grid, the performance of the overall system will be maximized; not only for the applications in question but for the overall utilization of the grid in the larger scope of a compute utility service.

Some examples of how the grid can optimize performance as a compute utility service are

Monte Carlo Application. A Monte Carlo simulation within a data grid plane yields many interesting processing efficiencies that are otherwise not realizable. For example, there are a number of "interim" result surfaces that can be built atomically on an individual basis. However, some the building of interim results may be dependent on other interim surfaces being partially or completely built. Therefore, there is also an element of synchronization of "batch" processing with regard to when to start building interim surface *b* only when "*X%*" of surface *a* is complete, where the internal processing of both *a* and *b* are completely atomic and nonsynchronous. The following is a representation of the Monte Carlo simulation function:

$$MonteCarloSimulation \begin{pmatrix} Work(W\_T1(),W\_group1(W\_T2(),W\_T3())\ldots,W\_Tn()), \\ Data\_input(),Data\_output(),Data\_S1(),\ldots Data\_Sk(), \\ Time(), \\ Geography() \\ Query() \end{pmatrix}$$

where
For the work function, we obtain

$$W\_T1(atomic, nonsynchronous)$$

$$W\_T2(atomic, nonsynchronous)$$

$$W\_T3(atomic, nonsynchronous)$$

$$W\_Tn(atomic, nonsynchronous)$$

$$W\_group1(batch, synchronous)$$

For the data functions, we have

$$Data\_input(1\,kbit, 100\,bit, nontransactional, transient, nonqueryable)$$

$$Data\_output(1\,kbit, 100\,bits, transactional, transient, nonqueryable)$$

$$Data\_S1(3\,Gbits, 100\,bits, nontransactional, transient, queryable)$$

$$Data\_Sn(3\,Gbits, 100\,bits, nontransactional, nontransient, queryable)$$

For *Time( )*, *Geography( )*, and *Query( )*, we obtain

$$Time(NearReal\text{-}Time)$$

$$Geography(DataCenter, 1\,GbitEthernet)$$

$$Query(basic)$$

The QoS–Monte Carlo application demand graph is shown in Figure 5.2.

An OLAP Application. An online analytical processing (OLAP) application performs the functions of collecting, managing, processing, and presenting multidimensional data for analysis and management purposes. The data grid plane acts as an information integration plane for OLAP processing of data from a datamart or integration from various sources. In general, a data grid plane will increase the

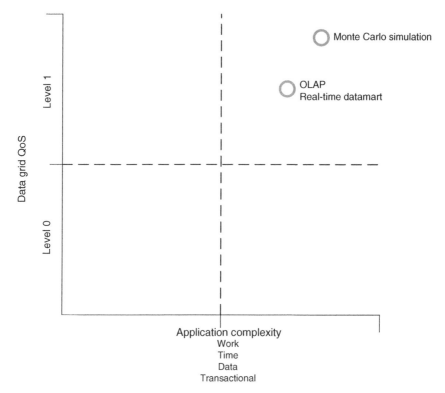

Figure 5.2. QoS versus application requirement.

performance of any OLAP process. Depending on the supported QoS levels, the OLAP process can also increase sophistication of the analysis and provide results in real time or near real time.

The example below assumes a simple OLAP process that can be broken into atomic worklets. However, as OLAP processing increases in sophistication, the *Work*( ) interactions can increase in degree and dependency as with the Monte Carlo analysis example.

$$OLAPProcess \begin{pmatrix} Work\_T, \\ Data\_output(\ ), Data\_S1(\ ), \dots Data\_Sk(\ ), \\ Time(\ ), \\ Geography(\ ), \\ Query(\ ) \end{pmatrix}$$

where, for the work function:

$$Work\_T(atomic, nonsynchronous)$$

and for data:

> *Data_output*("*x*" *kbits*,"*y*" *bits*, *transactional*, *nontransient*, *queryable*)
> *Data_S1*("*z*" *Tbits*,"*k*" *Mbits*, *nontransactional*, *transient*, *queryable*)
> *Data_Sn*("*z*" *Tbits*,"*k*" *Mbits*, *nontransactional*, *transient*, *queryable*)
> *Time*(*Near-Real-Time*)
> *Geography*(*DataCenter*, 1*GbitEthernet*)
> *Query*(*complex*)

The QoS–OLAP application demand graph is shown in Figure 5.2.

6

TRADITIONAL DATA MANAGEMENT

DATA MANAGEMENT

Electronic data management has a long and rich history dating back to the 1950s. Many data management systems have tried to make their way into the mainstream of information technology, some more successfully than others; hierarchical, network, object, and in-memory are only a few examples. The most successful data management system has been the relational data management technology. For our purposes, I will start at this point to look at its development and what has made it succeed. This is the "yardstick" used to measure how far forward it has moved in comparison to any other data management system.

History

Dr. E. F. Codd, a researcher at IBM, defined the relational model in a 1970 paper entitled "A Relational Model of Data for Large Shared Data Banks,"[20] which initiated a chain reaction of research into the concepts, both internally at IBM and everywhere else. The research timeline included

- 1974—the System/R project gave birth to the Structured English Query Language (SEQUEL).
- 1976–1977—SEQUEL is extended to support multiple users, tables, and so on and later eventually renamed Structured Query Language (SQL).

Distributed Data Management for Grid Computing, by Michael Di Stefano
Copyright © 2005 John Wiley & Sons, Inc.

- 1979—Oracle is launched.
- 1983—IBM introduces DB2.
- Other products are introduced to the marketplace during this same period, including Sybase.

Dr. Codd was also responsible for the mathematical foundation on which SQL is built, namely, relational algebra. SQL is the interface that allows most users to simply access and modify relational data. Through a series of publications in the 1970s and 1980s, Dr. Codd introduced such concepts as the separation of the physical and logical aspects of data management, a model that is understood by a wide user community. The ability to process multiple records simultaneously via an access method that enables ad hoc queries into the data management system has fostered the widespread adoption of the relational model more widely than perhaps any other data management system today.

Features

I will highlight some of the features of a data management system that are essential from the user perspective. I will not go into great detail as to how relational data management systems implement these features as these are complex topics in their own right. Rather, I will discuss these features at a high level including what they are, what they are designed to address, and in some cases, by way of example, highlight how a relational data management system addresses specific features. These topics include

- The mechanics or engine of the data management system
- How data are structured within the data management system
- Data integrity
- Transactional support
- Support for external events and event handling within the data management system
- Backup, recovery, and availability of the data management system
- Security

Each of these features is important, and in some instances one feature plays a supporting role for another feature, as is the case of data integrity. For a more in-depth analysis of these and other topics, the reader can refer to Richard T. Watson, *Data Management, Databases and Organizations*, 4th edition, Wiley, 2004.

Mechanics. The data engine is the part of the data management system that ties the logical representation of data to the physical media that stores the data. It is this engine that binds the data management system to the physical topology of the compute environment that supports it. A generic diagram of an engine consists of the media manager (i.e., the disk manager) and the data container manager (i.e., the file manager) as illustrated in Figure 6.1.

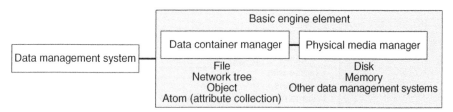

Figure 6.1. Data management system and its engine.

The characteristics of the engine determine the data management system's ability to support the user community for issues such as speed of access, storage of data, scalability, and data replication speed as well as efficiency. The separation of the physical and the logical representations of the data have allowed relational database technology to evolve in terms of increased speed performance and the ability to query and access data without adversely affecting the user community or forcing it to reprogram its data access logic.

I will illustrate that in a distributed compute topology the architecture and the implementation of the engine will have direct consequences for the data management system's ability to support the features and quality-of-service (QoS) levels expected by the users of the system.

Data Structure. In the relational model, the basic data structure is a table that is a two-dimensional structure of rows and columns. Physically, a table is mapped to a file on disk via the engine, which is an integral part of the relational data management system. The relational data management system provides the tools to organize tables so as to describe more complex data relationships. A breakdown of the data structure in the relational model, its extensibility to model complex relationships, and its ability to maintain ease of use is presented in the following text. This combination has lead it to its widespread acceptance as the de facto standard in data management and as a long-term data persistence store.

The relational model starts with a collection of one-dimensional structures made up of rows and columns that form the table. Columns are the fields (attributes) that define the structure of an entity (record) of the table. The fields of the table support basic data types such as numeric, string, date/time, graphic, and Boolean. Records are the rows of the table. Entity uniqueness can be established by creating and maintaining a primary key in the table. The primary key establishes uniqueness of entity identity within the table. Primary keys must not be an empty or have a null value. The primary keys must be unique for each record of the table, and cannot change during the life of the record.

Relationships are established between multiple tables on the basis of common data types or columns of the tables to be joined. The columns establishing the join are called "secondary" or "foreign keys." Matching foreign keys in two tables establishes the relationship and enforces "referential integrity" between the tables. Both primary and foreign keys are discussed in maintaining data integrity

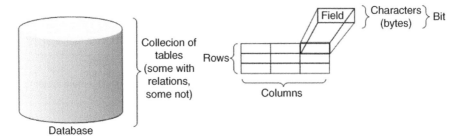

Figure 6.2. Data structure.

later in this chapter. Figure 6.2 illustrates the database made up of collections of tables and the composition of a table.

The logical structure of the relational model is quite simple, starting with the two-dimensional structure of the table (rows and columns) combined with the ability to be joined with other tables so as to extend the complexity of the data management system and enable it to model the more complex data structures as they actually exist in the real world. The basis of the relational model is simple to comprehend and is capable of modeling complex systems, thus enabling a wide range of users to build real-world systems very quickly.

Access. Access to the data in the data management system is primarily through the Structured Query Language (SQL). SQL is a powerful query language that is simple to understand. The learning curve for SQL is very reasonable for a programming-proficient individual to quickly access to the relational data model of tables within the data management system. SQL allows the users to process multiple rows of a table and related tables without requiring an intimate knowledge of the low-level mechanics required to do so.

SQL is a perfect example of the separation between the logical data model and the physical representation that enables developers, programmers, and architects to model data closer to the business without requiring an intimate knowledge of both the physical disk representation and access of the physical disk layer. Through the use of SQL it is simple for the user to

- Create a data scheme is through commands such as "create table"
- Query the data via the simple syntax of a selected statement
- Create relations between tables
- Query tables with multiple relations with simple extensions to the select statement such as the "where" clause
- Modify existing tables via the update and delete statements

Through the simple interface of SQL, the relational model can be accessed and manipulated by a vast number of users. The foundation of SQL is based on an in sound mathematical principle that allows for the extensibility of the system to represent complex structures.

Integrity. The data going (updated or inserted) into the database has to ensure that the data are correct and accurate; this cannot be done through the data management system—it must be done through the business applications. The applications need to ensure that the data they are inserting into the database are accurate. Once in the data management system, it is the responsibility of that to maintain the integrity of the data. Data integrity is essential for a data management system, since the users must be confident in the quality of the data on which their business is depending in making key business decisions. Otherwise, the data management system would be of little value. In the relational model, data integrity has two levels: entry-level integrity rules and referential integrity rules. The entry-level integrity rule is for primary keys that must be assigned to a valid value. The referential integrity rule, on the other hand, guarantees that the relationships between the tables are valid. So, integrity within the table as well as integrity between tables must be maintained by the data management system.

The end result of data integrity is data availability, data quality, and confidentiality. Each of these outcomes is required and achieved through other key features of the data management system, for example, events, transactions, and backup/recovery/availability of the system.

Additional levels of data integrity begin to enter into the realm of the architects and developers alike. The data management system must support event-driven mechanisms so that when data are inserted, changed, or deleted, these events will enforce the data integrity rules for entity and reference. External to the database, data integrity has to be maintained and manage by the user community, here the adage of "garbage in, garbage out" has special meaning.

Transaction. The data management system must be able to support data transactions internally within the database, with external systems to the database, and with "user programs." Support of transactions integrity is also important to many business applications, to ensure that any of the changes, updates, and deletes are guaranteed and delivered from start to finish (end to end). Typically, transactions are implemented via a technique called a "two-phase commit."

Transactions are used to support and ensure data integrity, which in turn guarantee the user that the data represented in the application are secured all the way down to the long-term physical storage, which in this case would be the database or disk. The transaction is processed so that there exists a recoverable state typically through the use and maintenance of transaction logs, managed by the data management system. A transaction log is a detailed record of all changes that have been applied to the data within a database including information on who made the change, when the change was made, and what the exact change was for audit trail purposes. With this information also being logged, the recovery of the database is both possible and simple. The recovery is merely the reenactment of the steps recorded in the transaction log starting from the "last known good state" of the system.

Events. The data management system must be able to support and manage events, both internal and external to the system. Events are real-time mechanisms, typically user-based, starting as an external event to the data management system that can also trigger subsequent events within the data management system. Events are a tool used to support data integrity as well. For example, referential integrity can be supported through event mechanisms; should a user (with the proper entitlements) delete a record in a table, this deletion will need to be reflected in other tables to maintain referential integrity between two joined tables.

Backup/Recovery/Availability. The data management system must be a reliable resource of information technology. It contains the knowledge required by the business units in order to perform their functions. The quality of the data and availability of the data must be ensured. If this were not the case, then the community would have little confidence in the data management system and would be little value to the business. Therefore, the goal is how to ensure that the data are protected from loss and are available when needed.

First, ability to back up the images of the database makes this possible. The data management system must support methods of backing up the data and the state of the data management system at regular intervals. The database must be recoverable; some methods used to achieve this are "backward recovery." Backward recovery unwinds the state of the database to a previous well-known, high-confidence-state level of the complete data management system. Another method is "forward recovery," which starts from the last well-known state and reapplies the changes and updates to bring in the more current states that existed after the last of the full backup of the system. Both methods require the ability to reprocess transactions.

The availability that the database must meet is driven by the demands of the business for the information contained within to be available and in a well-known reliable state. The system must support the ability for disaster recovery in a quick and efficient manner. Some of the more traditional implementations for data availability are the mirroring of data across multiple instances of the database. One instance is the primary database; the second instance is the fallback/recovery system. The primary and failover/recovery systems are maintained in transactional lock with each other through a mechanism that is implemented by the data management system provider. This technique is called "mirroring" databases. In conjunction with the database mirroring is the ability to determine when the primary system is no longer available to the user community and to take action to reestablish the "service" of the database to the users. Techniques such as high availability (HA) detect full or partial system failures and switching to the redundant systems automatically in a relatively short time so that the user community does not notice the system failure and recovery taking place.

Security. System security is an important aspect for assuring the user community that the system is protecting the data from unwanted eyes. Securing data starts with user entitlements, defining each user with the authority to read, change, insert, or delete specific data sets within the system. Security models must include the following capabilities at a minimum:

- Identify users and check their authorization levels through the use of user profiles.
- Ensure the security of the data stored on the physical medium. Implementations may include some level of encryption of the data to prevent unwanted interception or "listening" to the data. It may even carry the encryption all the way to the storage medium or disk in an effort to secure the data from programs other than the data management system itself and bypassing the security and access channels of the system by directly accessing the data that reside on the disk.

KEY FOR USABILITY

The usability of any system or product is driven by two factors; simplicity and consistency. The saying "keep it simple" are words to live by and is never more evident than when designing a system intended for a broad consumer audience and to last beyond the moment. Ergonomics needs to be applied to system design so that a broad range of people can understand and effectively use the product. Simple examples of this are in the automotive industry; examples can be found in companies such as General Motors, Ford, Toyota, Mercedes, Ferrari, BMW, and Kia. Yet, just about anyone in the world can get behind the wheel of these products; of complex, intertwined mechanical, hydraulic, and electronic systems; and be able to drive them with very little or no car-manufacturer-specific training. The interface to the automobile is simple and standardized; each automobile must provide the same basic features and functions for it to be usable. The steering wheel, brake and gas pedals, the braking system, the headlights and turn signals, the engine and transmission (automatic or manual, which will then include a clutch pedal and stick shift), seatbelts and airbags, and the position of lease instruments are all in the usual place and function in the usual way.

Other industries are starting to follow the example that has been set by the automotive industry. One such example is in air travel, namely, the small-aircraft industry.[21] In an effort to make the small-aircraft industry safer, cheaper, ubiquitous, and routine, aircraft vendors (and their supporting industry groups) are starting to standardize on instrumentation and controls of the aircraft. So, when moving from one make of aircraft to another, a pilot will not require special training for each of these individual machines. Aircraft companies, taking the lead of the auto industry, can standardize on interfaces. The end result is a consistent operation of the plane from one vendor to another. It also instills a sense of comfort and security for passengers.

Just as with these industries, distributed data management systems must follow the same usability and levels of interface previously established as the de facto standard by the relational data management systems. The majority of data management systems in use today are relational, and generally have the same basic interface and support the same feature sets. Yet, each vendor may deviate slightly from the other as a way to "differentiate themselves" from the pack. Oracle differs from Sybase, which may differ from DB2; however, they are pretty much the same. The learning curve to go from one to the other is not steep, especially with regard to the basic data management and access features.

Any new data management system such as in the area of distributed computing that is specifically designed to fit a distributed compute topology such as the grid must maintain the same level of ease of user interface and must support, at a minimum, the same feature sets described in this chapter and throughout this book. The basic data structures that the majority of the developers, application architects, and managers understand revolve around the ability to support transactions, data integrity, and security, and most of the system as a whole must be equally usable by the development team and other types of staff currently in place within corporations. Failure to meet this de facto standard that has been set will hinder the adoption of not only the data management system itself but the spread of distributed computing, and grid computing, as a whole.

7

RELATIONAL DATA MANAGEMENT AS A BASELINE FOR UNDERSTANDING THE DATA GRID

This book uses analogies that are completely unrelated to computer science in order to drive home a concept. In this chapter, we will use relational data management as a baseline for introducing distributed data management. We will see that this analogy is more than just a visualization tool; it is a practical necessity.

Relational data management systems are the prevalent data management systems in use throughout information technology. They provide levels of service that not only have we become accustomed to but also have become a necessity for supporting the needs and requirements of the business. Therefore, a comparison at both the physical and functional levels of the two is not only helpful but also required.

We will break down the main components of the comparisons with the objective of using the parallels between the two data management systems to better understand the data management issues that are particular to the data grid and necessary in order to maintain the quality of service levels for the business applications dependent on the data grid.

EVOLUTION OF THE RELATIONAL MODEL

The late 1980s and early 1990s saw a shift away from a centralized compute topology of mainframes and minicomputers and toward a more distributed topology of client/server technology. As a result, the need for a data management system to meet the requirements of that topology emerged. This shift could not have taken place if it were not for the relational data management systems that matured

Distributed Data Management for Grid Computing, by Michael Di Stefano
Copyright © 2005 John Wiley & Sons, Inc.

during the 1970s and 1980s as the data management technology evolved to meet the new computer client/server topology.

As client/server technology was being adopted by the industry, relational database companies were educating the general population of managers, architects, and developers on the characteristics client/server and relational database technologies, how they are used, and how the business as a whole can benefit from this new and better way of building systems. At these educational seminars (typically a full-day event followed by a 3–5-day training course), the most common questions asked would have less to do with data management for relational databases than with how these relational databases managed the physical resource available to them. These questions were to be expected; with relational databases, the physical resources are files, disks, and spindles, and prior to this point, this is how developers kept data viable; they wrote the file and disk management systems. They understood the lower-function input/output (I/O) of file and disk management, the importance and difficulty of achieving efficient disk and spindle management. Less attention was given to the relational data management and even how to access the data through something called SQL. As time progressed, relational database technology became mainstream, and attention shifted away from the engine and how fast it wrote to and read from disk and maintained indices. More concern was directed toward the relational model, with management, access, and administration of these systems as the key to performance and reliability. Issues such as table-level locking, row-level locking, event-driven triggers, and the ability for complex indexing and relating tables, were the domain of the specialist.

Today, with the emergence of a highly distributed compute environments such as the grid, most developers are focusing on the engine. What is the engine, and how does it manage the fiscal resource, whether that resource is routing queries to a heterogeneous variety of data sources (databases, file systems, queuing systems, etc.) or is a distributed cache. Absent are the questions related to data management or the effort required simply to manage and maintain the same levels of service quality offered by traditional relational data systems.

We will highlight the two main components of a distributed data management system: the engine and the data management functions.

PARALLELS TO DATA MANAGEMENT IN GRID ENVIRONMENTS

Relational models provide a good foundation for understanding the development and evolution of data management in grid environments. However, the grid requires a fundamentally new paradigm, and so the foundation becomes to some extent less interesting as one scales the problem out.

Anatomy of the comparison is as follows. There are three functional tiers: language interface, data management engine, and resource management engine.

- *Language Interface.* This consists of a set of tools that enable application developers to control, transact, and manage data organized and managed by the technology. This typically includes language-specific APIs as well as entire language sets that address the domain (ANSI-SQL).

- *Data Management Engine.* This provides an organizational methodology for handling data within the store. Each type of data management engine can have unique traits, concepts, or objects (relational, time-series, hybrid, etc.).
- *Resource Management Engine.* This engine manages the mapping between logical organization and data sets, and the physical location (storage) onto which those data sets map. Resource management engines can include raw partition managers, shared memory managers, and flat file managers.

Analysis of the Functional Tiers

Language Interface. As with relational technologies, data management in grid computing requires a language interface component. The language interface can be specific to a type of language or can be a generic input spec similar to XML. Application developers use the language interface to specify particular objects as data-grid-aware, and also manipulate them within the data grid context. The data grid needs to know particular aspects of the object structure in order to properly distribute objects within a data grid. This knowledge is a key difference between relational and grid-based language interfaces.

Data Management Engines. Data management engines within a grid provide a set of functionalities similar to those provided by relational management engines in relational data management systems. Key functionality of engines includes

- Data regionalization
- Data synchronization policy
- Data transactional policy
- Coordination of task scheduling to data locality
- Event notification policy
- Data load policy

Resource Management Engines. Resource management engines—within data grid environments—provide the core transport and caching facilities. As such, each type of engine provides a specifically different set of functionalities, which directly reflects on the overall functionality of a data grid. There are two distinct types of resource management engines: distributed and replicated. Within these categories, certain engines also support shared memory, memory-mapped files, and relational-database-based backing storage.

- *Distributed Resource Managers.* Distributed resource managers enable the spanning of multiple memory domains via either a peer-to-peer or a replicate-as-needed mechanism. These managers scale better toward problems of large memory requirements with reasonable latency and/or access time requirements. These managers also enable segments of the data grid to be completely autonomous of one another, thereby facilitating greater robustness.

- *Replicated Resource Managers.* Replicated resource managers support a "replicate everywhere" policy for all data. These managers maintain a "virtual synchrony" of sorts among all the nodes and guarantee that every update is provided to every peer. This mechanism typically uses a multicast transport, and as such has some limitation in scaling. Additionally, the smallest memory machine participating in the grid typically limits total data grid storage.

Engines Determine the Type of Data Grid

The engine of a relational database manages the physical resource: how the files are organized, how they are managed, how they are stored or organized on the physical disk, how disk fragmentation is minimized, and what is the optimal data placement on the physical disk to minimize a spindle movement. These are all important features, and as the technologies at the physical level have advanced, relational databases have been able to take advantage of improvements due to the separation of the engine and the higher-level data management.

With data grid, there is a similar separation of engine and data management. Within data grids, however, the engine is not a single form as with relational databases. Data grids can take any number of forms, each requiring a different engine to support it. For example, in today's enterprise, data exist in various heterogeneous systems, and as a matter of practicality, disrupting those systems is not an option. If the customer transaction database resides in a relational engine and the customer information databases reside in a mainframe, it is reasonable to expect that the data will remain in those respective permanent data stores. Some view data grids as a virtualization of data to where they actually reside in the physical data stores. The engine for this type of a data grid would be a metadictionary that formulates and parses out specific query syntax to each target system and conversely receives data from the data sources and unifies them back into a cohesive form.

Other types of data grids bring the physical data as close to the compute nodes of the compute grid as possible for speed of access. This type of a data grid engine can take the form of a distributed cache.

Data Management Features

With the introduction of relational database and client/server technologies, the main focus was on how the engine works and less on data management. Today, it is the reverse. The focus now is on data management and the data management supported by relational database technology that we have become accustomed to and expect in a data management system. Moving toward a new topology, these levels of data management must be maintained. We need to look at some of the data management features that are supported within relational databases, such as support for transactions, the ability to organize data in logical groupings like databases and tables, the ability to bring data into the database from external sources and extract data out to those sources, and to query data in an effective and efficient manner. Data management in data grids must support much the same features of transact, load, and query with the same level of confidence, from the user perspective, as with a relational database. We will see that there are additional data management issues particular to data grid in addition to these baseline features.

8

FOUNDATION FOR COMPARING DATA GRIDS

In this chapter we will itemize the key points of comparison of various data grid implementations so as to provide the reader with a methodology for selecting the best "tool for the job." Recalling Figure 1.1, the two major areas of comparison are in the "engine" of the data grid itself and the support for the necessary data management features required by the business application. The latter includes support for traditional data management techniques, data management features specific to the data grid, as well as accessibility to the data grid. It is expected that the reader understands the traditional data management features such as those supported by a relational database. The chapters subsequent to this will focus on data management features that are unique to a data grid.

CORE ENGINE DETERMINES PERFORMANCE AND FLEXIBILITY

Data grid architecture and the associated characteristics can vary widely. With many different options in architecting the data grid, there are two that are most prevalent: (1) "data replication" versus "data distribution" and (2) "centralized" versus "peer-to-peer"-based synchronization management. Each of these architectures provides support for a global or common feature sets as well as unique feature sets. We will also see that there are "policy"-based data management features for the data grid's data distribution/replication and for data synchronization. The policy-based

Distributed Data Management for Grid Computing, by Michael Di Stefano
Copyright © 2005 John Wiley & Sons, Inc.

data management features can be supported only if the underlying engines support the mechanics of those features. For example, if the underlying engine only supports data replication, then data management policies involving a distributed data scheme cannot be implemented with that engine. Similarly, the engine must also support the mechanics for all the data grid management policies, for example, "event notification" and not just the management policies for data synchronization and distribution.

The sections that follow highlight the most common data grid architecture and the associated feature sets.

Replicated versus Distributed

Replication-based architectures rely on a duplicating cache across engines that guarantees that any data modified in one cache are shared across all members. This allows for total cache synchronization regardless of where the data modifications occurred. The common features of replication-based architecture are a high degree of reliability and data integrity since the data resides on many nodes but at the cost of scaling and performance due to data concurrency across the nodes of the data grid. The replication schema is typically achieved through levels of reliability built on top of the multicast or broadcast protocols.

The *distribution-based architecture* of the data grid, on the other hand, tends to share data on a peer-to-peer (P2P)-oriented nature. The advantage of such architecture over the replicated architecture is greater scalability since all the data are not replicated across all nodes of the data grid. One way to visualize this is to compare data distribution to how a RAID (redundant array of inexpensive disks) device "stripes" data across the disk array. Data distribution involves striping a piece of data across a number of the physical nodes of the data grid. These nodes are a subset of the total nodes in the data grid and will be considered as peers to each other for data update, distribution, and access. As does a RAID device, this method of data distribution yields an upper bound of available data grid storage capacity solely as a limit of the number of physical nodes to the data grid. (Conversely, in a replicated engine, the upper bound of data grid storage capacity is limited to the physical node in the data grid with the least physical capacity.)

The disadvantage of such architecture is data reliability and data integrity. Even though the distribution-based architectures does not replicate the data completely, some degree of replication is achieved, thus yielding a level of resilience to failure. If a piece of data is distributed or "stripped" across 10 of the 100 nodes of the data grid, for example, then that data are resilient if at least one of those nodes remains operational. Should all 10 of those nodes fail while the other 90 remain operational, then that piece of data is lost. The ratio of nodes to stripe a piece of data across is managed by the data management policies described below. Adjusting this ratio of nodes to stripe or "replicate" a piece of data across to the total number of nodes in the data grid will determine the level of resilience of the data grid for that piece of data.

Centralized versus Peer-to-Peer Synchronization

The implementation of an engine of a data grid will follow one of two general architectures (distributed or replicated) as it relates to how it physically manages data integrity across the nodes. There is a centralized manager for data integrity among the nodes of a data grid as well as for synchronizing data in and out of the data grid with external data sources. The second method employs a decentralized manager for data integrity. In this approach, only those nodes of a data grid that have a piece of data stored locally in it will be involved in managing the integrity of that data among themselves. Drawing from the example in distribution engines, if a distributed data engine also supports a P2P synchronization implementation, then only those 10 nodes on which a piece of data resides will be involved in any transactional operation for that piece of data. The other 90 nodes are free to go about supporting other usage requests made on the data grid.

ACCESS TO THE DATA GRID

Access to the data grid must support methods similar to those found in traditional data management tools. There needs to be a programmatic API set as well as some method to query the data grid through a string-based query, and finally there needs to be a management interface for the data grid as a system. These topics are addressed in more detail in Chapter 20. However, when comparing which data grid is best suited for your purposes, you must consider the following:

- The support of a programmatic API in the languages (Java, C++, C#, etc.) in which the business applications are implemented. The quality and flexibility of those APIs are important points of comparison.
- For a string-based access method, one must consider how the data grid will be integrated into the environment and which class of applications are required to leverage it. For example, if the business application is Web-oriented, then support for an XML-based query is more useful than a standard SQL-type access method.

User-Level APIs

The data grids offer a variety of application-level APIs depending on the vendor and the type of architecture. All vendors and architectures support a concept of a data-grid-aware structure; for example, if the data grid engine supports an "object-oriented" API set, then it will have the concept of a collectable object and a collection object such as a bag or list. In addition, the APIs support rudimentary querying, updating, and retrieval of data in and out of the collections of the data grid. For operational functions, the APIs support a set of both traditional (startup, shutdown, user and user entitlements, etc.) and data-grid-specific data management features such as synchronization, distribution, replication, and event notification.

String-Based Interfaces

As straightforward as a programmatic API interfaces are, string-based queries of a data grid are less clearly defined. In Chapter 20, an argument is posed regarding which is the best method to use for string-based queries as there currently is no standard similar to SQL in the relational data models. Is a SQL or SQL-like interface best since the majority of developers are familiar with it as a tool, as well as its properties and syntax? Or is a more Web Services–like interfaces best, such as an XML-based interface? The answers to these questions have yet to find a consensus among technology specialists and the marketplace in general.

SUPPORT FOR TRADITIONAL DATA MANAGEMENT FEATURES

In order for the APIs to support the traditional data management features, they need to provide capabilities that include querying, indexing, administration, and replication. These features typically need to be "loosely" available within data grid products.

The *querying* feature is typically supported through a proprietary XML interface that has some of the features available in ANSI-SQL. Since a data query is typically unstructured or hierarchical data in nature, traditional ANSI-SQL specifications are not commonly used.

Indexing and reorganization is typically loosely supported in data grids through both garbage collection and graph transformations. The garbage collection and graphic transformation allow unstructured data to be formatted, reorganized, and structured to the requirements of the receiving application.

Data grid administration is currently supported through command-line interfaces. Most administration is achieved via modifications to configuration files.

Replication is supported through processes that allow data replication across engines, database servers, and nodes.

SUPPORT FOR DATA MANAGEMENT FEATURES SPECIFIC TO GRID COMPUTING

With new technology come new features that are required and the associated data management specific to that technology. This, too, is also true for the many unique aspects of data management in a grid environment. Services specific to data management in grid environments include data regionalization, data synchronization policy, transactional data policy, coordination of task scheduling to data locality, event notification policy, and data load policy, which are discussed in the sections that follow.

- *Data Regionalization.* Regionalization of data within a grid is a key performance and management feature that is seldom available within other infrastructures. A data region within a grid is an organization of data that spans machines and potentially geographies and caters to the needs of the users of that region. "Region" is the highest level of constructing the data in the data grid. Region drives the aggregation of the data and the policy instructions regarding the data. For example, a data region is analogous to the "database" in the relational model. It contains other structures of data or data schema specific to a line of business. The management policies of the region will describe the behavior of the region in order for it to best meet the requirements of the line of business or "business services" that it supports. The data-grid-specific management policies are listed below.

- *Data Synchronization.* Dynamic data synchronization is performed per the defined management policy. The "data region" definition encompasses the data synchronization features and enables the control of different types of consistency policies across the data grid. Data synchronization typically falls into two spectra: strong synchronization and weak synchronization. Strong synchronization policies enforce a tight replication of "like" patterns of data among the nodes of the data region as well as strictly enforcing the replication policies among the nodes of the data region. The strong synchronization mechanism is used when low latency and high consistency are required from the data grid at the cost of scalability and flexibility. Weak synchronization policies, on the other hand, enable data to be synchronized on an "as needed" basis and sometimes not at all. The weak synchronization mechanism allows for less data consistency but for higher scalability and flexibility.

- *Transactional Data Synchronization.* Transactional data synchronization is very important even in the data grid since the ability to recover, commit, roll back, and the like are important to data integrity. Transactional data policies fall into basic categories within a data grid: *optimistic* and *pessimistic*. One of the main drivers of the transactionality with external data sources is the transactional features and semantics supported by that external source. The data grid must support a level of transactionality equivalent to that external source in order to maintain a quality of service as required by the line of business that the data region (data grid) supports. *Optimistic* transactions are typically implemented with little or no locking and coordination; they are transactions only in the sense that in a possible conflict situation, an exception is thrown and the user is notified. *Pessimistic* transactions are typically multiphase with the proper locking, unlocking, commit, and rollback that are typical for transactional integrity. The mechanism used is that of XA, which is associated with the destination, and all transactional management (e.g., all locking) is done through that destination.

- *Data Locality (Data Distribution).* The ability to locate and group data depending on data usage is essential to the data grid from a performance perspective. Data locality thus can be defined as the clustering of data depending on usage. This feature, which is specific to the data grid, enables the architectures to scale significantly better than did previous technologies architectures. The data grid implements data locality through two sets of synergistic architectures: (1) data within a data grid are associated with a locality that pinpoints the exact resource that owns a primary copy of the data and its neighboring topology (this information is provided through the APIs to the architecture using the data grid in order to propagate and distribute work to the particular resource) and (2) metrics of data usage improve the availability of the data in the data grid. Data are monitored through a set of metrics, and individual data blocks can migrate from resource to resource depending on the usage patterns and history of use.

- *Event Notification.* The data grid supports a variety of push-based and pull-based event notification policies, depending on the product and its associated architecture. In general, event notification is supported around a particular data type, which can be by region, collection, or individual data object, as well as a particular transaction type. APIs for event notification involve either callback handlers or queues, and typically require the handler to be in the same data region as the event source.

- *Data Load/Save.* Data loading and data saving is an essential part of the data grid. Without capability of loading and saving data, any import and export of data would be haphazard and require custom code development. The data grid supports the "load and save" feature through a variety of mechanisms, some coupled with pessimistic transactional support and some without. Transactional load/save mechanisms work by allowing users to specify a block of code (or in the vocabulary of enterprise information integration, a data adapter) that would map inbound data to the transaction source and query (load) or commit (save) within the context of a data transaction. Transactional mechanisms are activated at demand time and will complete before any access or update to data within the grid is allowed. Nontransactional load/save allows users to specify individual procedures (adapters) to map data into and out of the data grid. These procedures are executed on data demand but are not required to complete successfully before any access or updates are permitted.

9

DATA REGIONALIZATION

A scene as serene and innocuous as clouds rolling across a clear, crisp blue sky offers a useful analogy for regarding the concept of data regionalization. Like the clouds crossing the sky, data regions float across the data grid plane (DGP). Like the droplets of water held within the clouds, the data within a data region can be gathered from a variety of sources and are now united to form this region of ever-changing size and shape as it traverses across the data grid plane. And, as with the effect of atmospheric conditions on our vision of a clear blue sky, the data region continually adjusts to changing external factors, such as business need, usage demand, overall data size, and performance requirements, so as not to allow its data to fall to Earth.

Data region management policies for distribution, synchronization, and other functions affect the region's size, shape, and traversal in the data grid plane (see Figure 9.1).

Other external forces play a hand. They include hardware, mean time between failures, scheduling and routing of tasks (in the compute grid plane), time of day, and cycling of available resources in the data region's size, shape, and traversal across the data grid plane. This complex interaction of forces is counterbalanced by the data management policies of the data region, continually adjusting its characteristics to keep itself in an optimal state to meet the supply–demand curves imposed on it.

Leveraging this concept of the data region as condensation and the data grid plane as the sky allows us to bridge to the physical implementation with the right tools of analysis and mathematical modeling. All these affect data distribution

Distributed Data Management for Grid Computing, by Michael Di Stefano
Copyright © 2005 John Wiley & Sons, Inc.

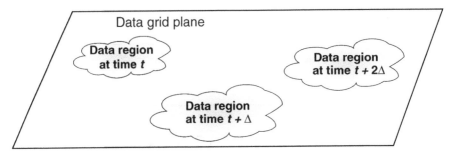

Figure 9.1. Data regions in the data grid plane.

and data synchronization policies, as well as other concrete data management policies involved in the proper access and management of a data region in the highly distributed environment of grid computing.

WHAT ARE DATA REGIONS?

Traditional client/server data architectures defined a concept of multiply siloed databases, or a data warehouse that contained the entire set of information required to run a particular business. Applications built around this concept promulgated this notion and themselves became associated with a set of information and a particular business. As businesses grew, many different, and sometimes competing silos were created to deal with different aspects of the business. In finance, the back office and the front office tended to have similar information, but could rarely share. Data grid architectures are designed to specifically decouple the location of particular data from the resources that use them. In order to accomplish this, the concept of a data region needs to be defined. Once defined, the data region can be managed through data management policies.

Data regions are defined as a logical organization of virtual resources that provide the storage necessary to house data. That storage and the virtual resource that provides it are typically unspecified in terms of service level and locale. In addition to virtual resources, regions have a set of management policies associated with them. The data contained within a data region represent a logical grouping independent of source.

DATA REGIONS IN TRADITIONAL TERMS

Data regions are similar to databases in traditional terms. Figure 9.2 illustrates this relationship.

It is always best to establish a baseline that is grounded in concepts that most of us are familiar with, a common knowledge that we can use to visualize and build on when learning new concepts. In introducing data regions within a data grid, we

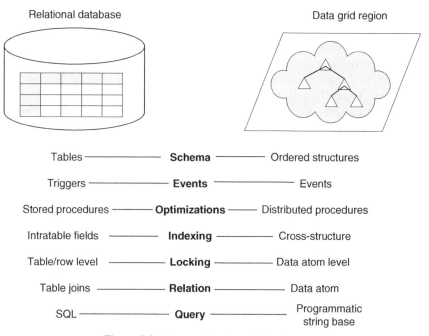

Relational database   Data grid region

Tables	—	**Schema**	—	Ordered structures
Triggers	—	**Events**	—	Events
Stored procedures	—	**Optimizations**	—	Distributed procedures
Intratable fields	—	**Indexing**	—	Cross-structure
Table/row level	—	**Locking**	—	Data atom level
Table joins	—	**Relation**	—	Data atom
SQL	—	**Query**	—	Programmatic string base

Figure 9.2. Data regions in traditional terms.

will use relational data management as the baseline. This analogy is as functional as it is visual; the traditional elements of data management need to be maintained and expanded on when entering into a data grid environment:

- *Logical Data Groupings.* Data are logically grouped, typically aligned with a business vertical. In the relational data management realm, this grouping is by a database. In the case of the data grid, this grouping is a data region.
- *Schema.* The schema relates to the way data are organized within the database: a definite structure organized in a logical grouping and aligned with the business and data applications where data storage, retrieval, and updates are applied to the database. In a relational database, the fundamental organization for the schema is a table, a two-dimensional matrix of rows and columns. Typically, databases contain many tables. [*Note*: Within a data region the choice of data structure goes beyond the two-dimensional rows and columns that constitute a table.] The fundamental structural elements for data schema within a data region are dependent on the implementation of the data grid. It is important to make clear that the data grid implementation is independent of the underlying engine (i.e., file system or distributed cache; see Figure 1.1). The engine defines the data grid's ability to fulfill other QoS levels, but imposes no limit on the kinds of data schema structures that can be defined. Again referring back to Figure 1.1, this is purely a function of

the data management layer and its implementation. Structures are dependent only on the implementation of the data management layer and its support for *N*-dimensional structures, including arrays, tables, matrices, and trees.

- *Events.* An event is an occurrence or happening at a single point in time and space. In computer science, events trigger a change of state for an object or system. Typically, a system's state is defined by its data attributes. Programmatic paradigms are based on the concept of events and form the basis for event-based processing that drive straight-through processing (STP). In relation to data management, an event triggers a change in state of an array, table, database, or data region. Programmatic "event handlers" or "triggers" are registered for a specific event and are invoked when that event occurs. A common use of triggers in a relational database is to maintain referential data integrity among the tables of the database. Triggers tie together or are set to a specific event, such as the insertion or deletion of data to a table. When these events occur, the triggers are programmed to make the required changes, such as insertions, deletes, or updates to the other structures in the database or data region to ensure data integrity. Events caused by triggers can in turn set other triggers into motion; thus a chaining effect can take place. Data regions can extend event handling by allowing systems external to the region to "register" interest in data region events. The external systems can either be notified directly by the data region or invoke an event handler registered by the external system when an event, with its associated triggers, occurs.

- *Optimizations.* Data management systems support various optimization tools for data access and update. One of the more common methods is the precompiling of queries. In the case of the relational databases, SQL statements are precompiled into procedures that are given well-known handles so that user programs can invoke them directly. For example, when an application queries the database, a certain amount of processing must be done by the database to transform the SQL into executable code. If the query is frequently used by one or more applications, it can be optimized within the database to eliminate many of the preprocessing steps. This optimization improves the performance of the database queries. In some implementations of relational databases, these are called "stored procedures." Similarly, procedures can be maintained within the data grids and their associated data regions. However, given the nature of the implementation of a data grid, the exact meaning of a stored procedure can vary. For example, a data grid that is based on a distributed cache can distribute the precompiled procedures across all the nodes of the data region. When invoked, the data grid can execute the "distributed stored procedure" in parallel, each node processing it against its own set of data within that region.

- *Indexing.* Indexing is a way to gain faster access to atoms of data within the database or data region. In the relational model, a column, or groups of columns, within a table can be indexed in ascending or descending order. The cost of creating and maintaining indexes is extra overhead for the data management system. The amount of overhead is dependent on the design and implementation of the data management system. In the case of a relational database, an index is an extra data structure that needs to be maintained each time an indexed table is updated or changed. Indexing within a data region is conceptually the same as that within the relational model; however, data grids can support additional data structures, including arrays, tables, matrices, and trees. Therefore, the exact implementation and benefit of indexing within the data grids can vary greatly depending on specific data grid designs and implementations.

- *Locking.* For a multiuser system, maintaining data integrity is essential, and therefore locking is required. Locking data atoms assists in maintaining data integrity when multiple users have permission to update and change data within a database or data region. When updates, inserts, or deletions are performed on a data set, it may be necessary to block others from accessing that data until the data modifications are complete and committed. This process of blocking access to data from other users when they are being changed is called "locking." Typically, the updating application "acquires" the lock from the database before starting and then "releases" it when the operation is completed. In a relational database, the level of data atom locking can be at table level within the database or at a much finer level of granularity: the row within a table. When row-level locking is employed, other users can acquire locks on different rows of the same table without being blocked. Thus users are not interfering with each other. On the other hand, locking within a data region will take place at the data atom level. Therefore, the finest atom of locking of a data structure is dependent on the type of data structures supported by the data grid. When structures in a relational database are mirrored in a data grid, the data grid must support the same locking features and same level of granularity as those in a relational database. However, for more complex structures, the granularity of data atom locking is dependent on the data grid implementation.

- *Relation.* How are the various data structures and data atoms related to each other? In the world of relational databases, where the fundamental schema is a table—a two-dimensional structure of rows and columns—additional dimensions can be created by joining tables based on common fields, allowing relationships to be established between two or more tables. Within the data region, relations between data structures can be as fine as the most basic data atom joining a heterogeneous set of data structures offering more granular flexibility. For example, trees can be joined to arrays that can be joined to matrices. Depending on the implementations of the data grid, a single data atom may be a member of multiple structures, thus providing the relation between the structures.

- *Query.* Relational databases have standardized on structured query language (SQL), a text-based query language. Within the data grids and data regions there are fundamentally two ways to query data: (1) a string-based query language similar to SQL and (2) a programmatic querying or filtering.

Programmatic querying is a higher-level language such as C++ or Java, where the query is done via a set of programmatic APIs. Early implementations of data grids will support the programmatic query interface first. String-based query languages for data grids are an area that today requires industry standardization on exactly what the language syntax needs to be. This is primarily because data grids can support a wide range of data structures and the most optimal query language may not be SQL. Rather, it may be more of an XML-like language, or a hybrid of SQL, Object SQL, and based on other theories. Such standards are necessary, especially if the data grid is to succeed in the commercial arena.

Data grid queries must support two types of functions: queries into user-defined data structures and queries into the operational structures resulting from data management. For data grids, the operational data include most of the same administrative data sets for users, entitlements, and logging. However, additional information is needed for data-grid-specific data management features. The most obvious is the support for data affinity, which is discussed later in this book. Statistical information on each data atom is required to support data affinity, including

- The physical data location of each data atom and all its replicas
- Access patterns
- Movement patterns

Therefore, just as with relational database engines, administrative query support is an integral part of the data grid system.

DATA MANAGEMENT IN A DATA GRID

As with many other solutions, data management is very important in the data grid; the ability to define data management policies specific to each data grid region is very powerful at implementation:

- *Data Grid Resources*. Many components or resources are required for the data grid. A data grid resource includes the processors and storage associated with a data grid (the nodes constituting the grid), and the data grid "daemon" that monitors and manages the physical nodes of the data grid. The data grid daemon tracks and records "metered information" describing the state of each node of the data grid. Metered information includes details about the memory layout, processor, and size of the CPUs of the grid's nodes, local node transaction/storage, and load sources. Together this information provides the data grid normalized information that it uses to determine the proper amount of resources required to efficiently and effectively service usage demand.

- *Management Policies*. Flexible data management policies are required. The management policies are applied at region level, enabling a region to behave similarly to a relational database instance. Management policies for the regions include data distribution/data replication, synchronization, and load/store. Each of these policies addresses a particular behavior of the region. Data management policies include (1) data distribution, (2) data replication, (3) synchronization, (4) data load and store, and (5) event notification. The interrelationships between these policies are discussed in the sections that follow.

For each of the data management policies listed above, we will express the key parameters that define them. These expressions are not intended as a complete expression of the respective policies, but simply as a basis on which to build insight into their roles and interactions with each other and affect on the system as a whole. As in Chapter 5, section entitled "Application Characteristics for Grid," the expression for an application is in equation form. For similar reasons—namely, for the purpose of quickly developing multidimensional relationships among the parameters and policies themselves—we will follow that notation here.

Data Distribution Policy

Regions contain collections of resources that manage data. Data associated with a particular region can be distributed or replicated through a number of methods. Distribution of data takes individual data "atoms," associating them with a particular resource and resource ownership of that data atom. Distributions of data "atoms" include simple techniques such as round-robin, mathematical models (e.g., Gaussian and Poisson distribution), and dynamic schemes based on real-time system behaviors. Each of these distributions results in a specific data topology:

- *Round-Robin Distribution*. Round-robin distribution is a simplistic distribution scheme that distributes data "atoms" in a sequential mechanism. It does not guarantee a particular distribution except if all the resources have exactly the same capacity.
- *Gaussian Distribution*. Gaussian or normal distribution takes as its parameters a central machine or machines, a standard deviation, and a set of distances, and attempts to distribute most of the data in close proximity to the central machine.
- *Random (White Noise) Distribution*. Data atoms are randomly distributed across the data region.
- *Poisson Distribution*. Poisson or jump distribution uses parameters similar to those of Gaussian distribution and in addition takes into account the probability of jumps. It attempts to distribute the data within the proximity of a central machine, but also adds the possibility of data "jumping" away from the central machine on the basis of some probability algorithm.

1. *Dynamic-Data Movement Pattern Analysis.* For efficiency reasons, a large part of data distribution policy is aimed at minimizing data movement within a data grid. Replication of a data atom across a data region to the physical nodes where the data are accessed most often minimizes network traffic. There are numerous methods for achieving this goal, one of which is to monitor data movement within a data region and continually evaluate and redistribute the data according to data access and usage patterns. This implies a continual feedback control loop that evaluates the following:

- *Input*—data location, data request points, data movement, distance that data travel on the network, frequency of data requests, and other parameters
- *Logic*—an algorithm that best estimates the placement of physical data locality to minimize or eliminate future data movement within the data region
- *Control Commands*—the ability to manage data movement in the data grid to manually tune system performance

The "control commands" can be manual, involving people analyzing "macroscale" data patterns and manually redistributing data over long periods of time. Alternatively, the process can be automated via a programmatic analytical process causing "microscale" data distributions and redistributions over short periods of time. Finally, a combination of both automated (microscale) and manual (macroscale) data distributions may be used.

2. *Implied Properties of Data Distribution.* A number of implied properties of data distribution are important to system behavior, including the distribution policy and its interactions with other policies, data management features, and the external systems. The implied properties that affect the abovementioned system behaviors are

- *Locality*—the position of the data atom.
- *Manipulation* of the data atom position.
- *Query* of the data atom position.
- *Distribution policy* that includes all data atoms and their replicas.

3. *Locality.* The data distribution policy implies an intimate knowledge of the exact location of each data atom (including its replicas) in the data region. This is key to the successful implementation of any data distribution policy. The data distribution policy determines where each of the data atoms is to be physically located in the data region. Knowledge of exactly where a data atom resides will result in an efficient use of the network resource, since data atom movement will be minimized during the operation of or access to data in the region by the applications or services it supports. This concept is known as *data affinity*, which will be addressed in the chapters that follow.

4. *Inclusion of Replicas.* The distribution of data in a data region must also include all the data atoms and the replicas as determined by the data replication

policy. Only in this way can maximum data affinity and data grid resilience (data grid high availability) be achieved.

5. *Location Manipulation.* Data distribution policy inherently implies that implementation will provide the ability to manipulate the exact physical location of each data atom in the data region.

6. *Query of Locality.* To implement the data management policies of a data grid and support a full range of data management features, data affinity, for example, all the administrative attributes of a data atom must be known and can be managed. These attributes include physical location in the data region as well as history of data movement (location and time of access).

Data Distribution Policy Expression. The data distribution expression defines the key parameters for the distribution of data atoms within a data region identified in the formula

$$DataDistributionPolicy = DDP \begin{bmatrix} PolicyName, \\ Region, \\ Scope(\,), \\ Pattern(\,) \end{bmatrix}$$

where

- *PolicyName* = logical name for this policy. This is the logical name for this instance of a data distribution policy. Since there may be many distribution policies, this name provides a unique identification. Depending on the implementation of the data grid, this name may or may not be unique.
- *Region* = primary region name. This is the primary data region to which this data distribution is applied. A data distribution of identical characteristics [as determined by the *Scope(\,)* and *Pattern(\,)* attributes] can be applied to other regions in the data grid.
  - *Scope(\,)* = *F(All, List(DataAtoms)* = *NULL)*. The scope of the data distribution can span the entire data region as indicated by the "all" attribute or apply only to a specific range of data atoms identified in the supplied list. Note that these parameters are mutually exclusive.
  - *Pattern(\,)* = *Function(Automatic/Specified, DP(\,))*, where

$$DistributionPolicy = F \begin{bmatrix} PatternName, \\ DeployPattern(\,), \\ DataAtom, \\ Currentlocation, \\ NewLocation, \\ Move/Add/Delete \end{bmatrix}$$

This distribution pattern is used to apply to the data atoms identified in the Policy's *Scope(\,)*. The pattern can be automatic in nature, one that follows a predetermined mathematical principle such as randomness or Gaussian distribution. In this case, the pattern expression is the *DeployPattern*( ) parameter and the parameters of data atom, including its current and new locations, and operation (*Move/Add/Delete*) are not required. The second option is to manipulate the exact physical location of a specific data atom manually. In this case, the *DeployPattern*( ) parameter is not required. However, the parameters of the data atom, including its location (current and new), and operation (*Move/Add/Delete*) are essential.

Data Replication Policy

Within a data region, data atoms are distributed on the basis of policies. The distribution policies can be grounded in mathematical formula or heuristic usage patterns of data movements within the data region through time. The distribution policy determines the physical location where each data atom will be cached within the data region. The data replication policy goes hand in hand with the data distribution policy. Data replication addresses the number of "copies" of a data atom that exist within a data region.

Both the data distribution and the replication policies should be statistically tied to the physical size of the data grid; or, more specifically, to the physical size of the data region within the data grid. The physical size of the data region—for example, in a peer-to-peer topology—is the number of compute nodes assigned to a data region. The number of nodes that can execute the tasks of a service or services supported by the data region determines the physical size of a data region. (*Note*: More sophisticated data regions can be constructed and maintained to span nodes where there is no intersection of task execution capability. However, for this discussion we will consider only the simple case of the intersection of nodes to execute tasks for a single or multiple services.) Therefore, the maximum size of a data region is the entire grid of T nodes. Typically, as the grid grows to support more services, the data region size will be R number of nodes less than or equal to those of T. As R increases in number, a sophisticated model (e.g., statistical, heuristic) for data distribution policy becomes possible and preferable. Also, the data replication policy can not only reflect the size R of the region but also take into account the geographic/network topology that the data region spans. As the data region size R shrinks to a minimum of one or two nodes, the data distribution policy begins to look like the data replication policy.

The combination of data distribution and replication policies characterizes the data region's ability to support a task or service with minimal data movement and thus minimum network traffic with a region; adding in the data synchronization policy, the robustness of the data region to any failures is then defined.

Figure 9.3 shows an example of a modified data atom synchronized with its peers and replicas. This is not to suggest that all data synchronization relationships represent a single master/replica orientation. Various data atom synchronization relationships can be supported as part of the data synchronization policy.

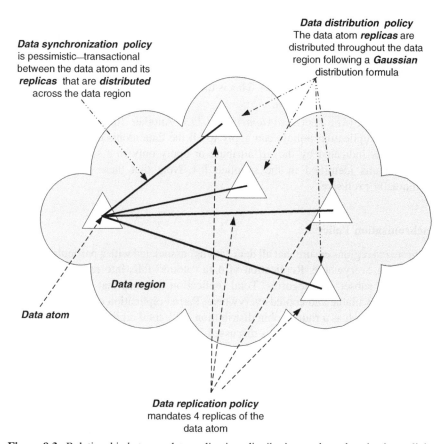

Data distribution policy
The data atom **replicas** are distributed throughout the data region following a **Gaussian** distribution formula

Data synchronization policy
is pessimistic—transactional between the data atom and its **replicas** that are **distributed** across the data region

Data region

Data atom

Data replication policy
mandates 4 replicas of the data atom

Figure 9.3. Relationship between data replication, distribution, and synchronization policies.

Data Replication Policy Expression. The data replication policy expression defines the key parameters for the replication of data atoms within a data region. The expression can be expressed as

$$DataReplicationPolicy = DRP \begin{bmatrix} PolicyName, \\ Region, \\ Quantity, \\ Scope() \end{bmatrix}$$

where *DRP* is the data replication policy. The following parameters influence the policy:

- *PolicyName* = logical name for this policy. This is the logical name for this instance of a data replication policy. Depending on the implementation of the data grid, this name may or may not be unique.

- *Region* = primary region name. This is the primary data region to which this data replication policy is applied. A data replication policy of identical characteristics [as determined by the *Scope*( ) and *Quantity*( ) attributes] can be applied to other regions in the data grid.
- *Quantity* = number of replicas. This is the number of replicas that a data atom will have in the data region.
- *Scope*( ) = *F(All, List(DataAtoms)* = *NULL)*. Another function, *Scope*( ) of the data replication policy, can apply to all the data atoms of the entire data region as indicated by the *All* attribute or apply only to a specific range of data atoms identified in the supplied list. Note that these parameters are mutually exclusive.

Synchronization Policy

Synchronized regions ensure that all data "atoms" associated with a particular region are available everywhere. Replication of data "atoms" falls into replicating all or replicating a subset of categories. Total replication assumes that all the data for the region is available and copied everywhere. Partial replication combines a distribution policy, such as a round-robin distribution, with total replication of some data "atoms." Synchronization policy is discussed in more detail in a later chapter.

Load-and-Store Policy

A load-and-store (load/store) policy is needed when data are integrated from data sources external to the application data region. These external sources can include other data regions, legacy systems, databases, middleware (i.e., messaging), and files. The data load policies will define how and when data are to be obtained for the data region, for example, whether the data are to be "preloaded" or "loaded on demand." The data store policies will determine when and how data are to be pushed out of the data region to the appropriate external data destinations, for example, persisting to an external database. Data store policies can be transactional as well as nontransactional. Both load and store policies can also follow a data distribution policy.

One way to think of the data load/store policies is as an interregion synchronization policy. Virtualization of the external data sources and the interaction properties of those data sources allows the application that is running in synchronization to behave similarly to the synchronization policies of the data region. One must take into account whether the external data sources support such policies. A load/store policy is needed when data are integrated from data sources external to the application and its associated data regions. Those external sources that require load and/or store could include

- Other data regions
- Legacy systems

- Databases
- Middleware (i.e., messaging)
- Files
- Custom APIs

The data load policies will define how and when data are to be brought into the data region. Examples of data load policies are:

- *Preloaded*—load the data region with the external data before the application needs it.
- *Load on demand*—data from the external source are to be loaded to the data region on request from the application.

The data store policies will determine how and when data are to be pushed out of the data region to the appropriate external data source or sources. For example

- *Store all*—all or portions of the data in the data region is predefined for storage to the external systems with the data remaining in the data region after the store operation is executed.
- *Store on demand*—specific data atoms in the data region are stored or copied to the external systems as the application requires. The data remain in the data region after the operation completes. In this situation, the application controls the storage.
- *Purge*—data atoms are removed from the data region.

There are a number of implied properties to data load/store policies, including

- Granularity
- Grouping/frequency
- Invocation

Granularity. One property of the data load/store policies is granularity. Note that there are policy attributes that define just how many atoms are to be loaded into and stored out of the data region. The "xxx on demand" policy attribute implies a varying level of granularity from the smallest data atom to a grouping of any size as defined by the application. The "xxx-all" policy attribute implies that the data pertaining to a specific external system are to be loaded into or out of the data region in a complete block.

Grouping/Frequency. The mechanics of data load and store into and out of the data region involve, either as directed by the application or transparent to the application, when the operation physically is to take place. Each invocation of a load or store (typically for the "on demand" operations) can be done one at a time, or the policy can define a store-and-execute strategy that will group loads and updates for execution at a later time. This strategy is particularly useful for performance optimizations when

Data atoms are fine-grained

The frequency of the load/store operations are greater than the time period of the external system's ability to transact the operation

Invocation. A third implied property of the data load and store policies is the invocation of the required enterprise information integration (EII) or enterprise application integration (EAI) adapters. The policies must tie the data atom grouping and manage the invocation of the physical data movement into and out of the region via the respective adapters.

Just as there is a relationship between data distribution and replication policies, there is a relationship between data synchronization and data load/store policies. Figure 9.4 illustrates this relationship.

The data management policies of the data grid are interconnected. The data synchronization policy determines the transactional level of the system, and the data

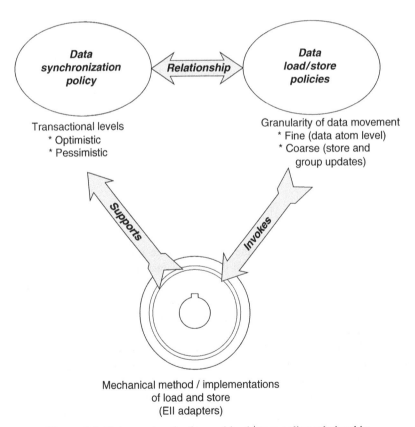

Figure 9.4. Data synchronization and load/store policy relationship.

load/store policies define the granularity and frequency of the process. There is, however, a third part of the equation: the EAI/EII adapter. The adaptor must be able to support the synchronization policy set in the region. For example, if the synchronization policy is optimistic but the EII adapter is a XA transactional, then there is a policy/implementation impedance mismatch. The end result is a system behavior that will not meet the application requirements for data management, performance, and throughput. The physical implementations must support the data management policy set in order for the data grid to operate properly in accordance with the set policies.

Data load/store policies are integral parts of enterprise information integration and are discussed in more depth in a later chapter.

Data Load Policy Expression. The data load policy expression defines the key parameters for loading data into a data region from external sources:

$$DataLoadPolicy = DLP \begin{bmatrix} PolicyName, \\ Region, \\ Granularity(\ ), \\ Adapter(\ ) \end{bmatrix}$$

where

- *DPL* is the data load policy function.
- *PolicyName* = logical name of this policy. This is the logical name for this instance of a data load policy. Depending on the implementation of the data grid, this name may or may not be unique.
- *Region* = primary region name. This identifies the primary data region to which this data load policy is applied. A data load policy of identical characteristics—as determined by the *Granularity(\ )*, *Scope(\ )*, and *Operation(\ )* attributes—can be applied to other regions in the data grid.
- *Granularity* = *F(Grouping(\ ), Frequency(\ ))*. The granularity of a data load is defined by the parameters of grouping and frequency. The *Grouping(\ )* parameter defines the number of updates that are to be grouped in the data region as a result of queries before the queued updates are applied to the data region. The *Frequency(\ )* parameter indicates the minimum frequency or time interval for data load into the data region. Both the grouping and frequency parameters can be static numbers and user-defined functions based on application/service requirements for data load. A *Frequency(\ )* of zero identifies a one-time data load into the data region, thereby preloading the data region. Frequency of any other value (negative values do not apply) indicates a load on demand operation (e.g., a frequency of 2 means updating every 2 s).
- *Adapter(\ )* = *EIIAdapter(...)*. The *Adapter* refers to the physical enterprise integration information (EII) or enterprise application integration (EAI)

adapters that will physically perform the loading of data into the data region. Included in these adapters can be the data atom schema and translation logic from the external source into the data atom of the region being loaded. The parameters of the *EIIAdapter( )* attribute can vary from adapter to adapter implementation as required to perform the required function.

Data Store Policy Expression. The data store policy expression defines the key parameters for loading data into an external data store:

$$DataStorePolicy = DSP \begin{pmatrix} PolicyName, \\ Region, \\ Granularity( ), \\ Operation( ), \\ Adapter( ) \end{pmatrix}$$

where

- *DSP* is the data store policy function.
- *PolicyName* = logical name of this policy. This is the logical name for this instance of a data load policy. Depending on the implementation of the data grid, this name may or may not be unique.
- *Region* = primary region name. This is the primary data region to which this data store policy is applied. A data store policy of identical characteristics [as determined by the *Granularity( )*, *Scope( )*, and *Operation( )* attributes] can be applied to other regions in the data grid.
- *Granularity* = *F(Grouping( ), Frequency( ))*. The granularity of a data store is defined by the parameters of grouping and frequency. The *Grouping( )* parameter defines the number of updates to be exported out of the data region that are to be queued before the queued exports are applied. The *Frequency( )* parameter indicates the minimum frequency or time (maximum time interval) with or during which any data export out of the data region must occur. Both the *Grouping( )* and *Frequency( )* parameters can be static numbers and user-defined functions based on application/service requirements for data store. A *Frequency( )* of zero identifies a one-time data export out of the data region. A frequency of any other value (negative values do not apply) indicates a store on demand at a defined interval.
- *Operation* = *F(Store/Purge)*. This defines the resulting state of the data region after a data atom has been exported. *Store( )* leaves the data region populated with the data atom in the last known state at the time of the store. The *Purge( )* attribute deletes the data atom from the region after it has been stored.
- *Adapter( )* = *EIIAdapter(...)*. The *Adapter( )* refers to the physical EII, or EAI adapters that will physically perform the export of data out of the data region. Included in the adapter can be the data atom schema and translation logic from the data atom to the external source to which the data are being exported.

The parameters of the *EIIAdapter*( ) attribute can vary among implementations as required, thus meeting the required functions.

Event Notification Policy

Event notification policy is a common paradigm—a tool common to real-time event processing or straight-through processing (STP). Most databases and middleware products support event notification in some way. Databases support event notification through "triggers." The triggering mechanism monitors the state of a database at varying degrees of granularity: a table within a database, a row within a table, or a field within a row. When a monitored entity changes state (due to an event that modifies its state, via an insert, update, or delete action), the database will toggle all "registered triggers" for this event, which will execute the respective registered triggered operations. These operations are typically user-defined. The trigger passes into the user-defined operation (or function) that describes, in detail, what event invoked the trigger. Typical examples of triggers and corresponding user-defined functions are:

- Internal database operations when a row in table A is deleted. The first thing that happens is to find the rows in related tables for which this action effects and then take the appropriate action to other tables maintain referential.
- External operations to database: user-defined programs that will cause a cascade of events or state changes to systems external to the database.

In straight-through processing, or more specifically with message-based middleware, which is a concept of publish and subscribe, an external program will "subscribe" to a published event in the middleware. Any single published event can have many subscribing programs. The published event may trigger cascading events by the invocation of all subscribed programs.

Similarly, within the data grid, event notification plays an integral role. When a data region's state has changed, the following could occur:

- A data atom is added to or deleted from a data region.
- A data management policy is changed.
- A data atom is changed.

Other data regions within the data grid, applications/services, or legacy systems, can register interest in order to be notified should an event take place. The event notification policy is a standard interface that describes how events are to be handled within the data region. Some of the key parameters described via the event notification policy are the events themselves. Programs can register interest in events, and exactly how the invocations are to be managed.

As with the data load and data store policies, event notification policy is an integral part of information integration into and out of the data grid. This will be discussed in more detail in a later chapter.

Event Notification Policy Expression. The event notification policy expression defines the key parameters for the management of events within a data region:

$$EventNotificationPolicy = ENP \begin{pmatrix} PolicyName, \\ Region(\,), \\ Scope(\,), \\ Operation(\,) \end{pmatrix}$$

where

- *ENP* is the event notification policy.
- *PolicyName* = logical name for this policy. The *PolicyName* is the logical name for this instance of an event notification policy. Depending on the implementation of the data grid, this name may or may not be unique.
- *Region* = primary region name. This is the primary data region to which this policy is applied. An event notification policy of identical characteristics [as determined by the *Scope*(\,) and *Operation*(\,) attributes] can be applied to other regions in the data grid.
- *Scope*(\,) = *F(All, List(DataAtoms)* = *NULL)*. The *Scope*(\,) of the event notification policy can be applied to the data atoms of the entire data region as indicated by the *All* attribute or apply only to a specific range of data atoms identified in the supplied list. Note that these parameters are mutually exclusive.
- *Operation* = *F*(\,). This is the user-defined function to be invoked on the occurrence of an event.

QUALITY-OF-SERVICE (QoS) LEVELS

Throughout the our discussions on data grid—and its management policies of synchronization, distribution, replication, and load and store—we will be using the terms *quality of service* (QoS) and *QoS levels*. The objective of a distributed data management system, through its data management policies, is to provide a level of end-user support found with traditional data management systems. It is necessary to identify QoS levels on the basis of application requirements when both the business applications and services are running in a distributed grid computing environment. Various categories of QoS levels must be accounted for, including

- Service availability
- Service performance
- Geographic boundary (desktop, data center, cross data center, etc.)
- Data management
- Others

Our discussions will focus on the QoS levels for data management. Some of the QoS features for data management in grid are computing

- Traditional data management service levels, such as support for transactions, query, and embedded logic (i.e., stored procedures).
- Data grid management service levels—for example, regionalization and synchronization.

There are numerous ways to implement the data grid, depending on the user application's requirements as well as the level of service that it demands from a data management system in order for it function properly; this will determine the type of data grid and the QoS level that the data grid must provide.

In Chapter 5 we discussed ways in which to express an application in an equation format via the definition of its parameters and to quantify its data management needs (QoS levels) for the data grid.

The definition for an application in a distributed environment is

$$Application(Work(\ ), Data(\ ), Time(\ ), Geography(\ ), Query(\ ))$$

where the various functions can have the following parameters:

Work(batch/atomic, synchronous/nonsynchronous)

Data(overallsize, atomicsize, transactional, transient, queryable)

Time(Real-Time, NotReal-Time, NearReal-Time)

Geography(Topology, NetworkBandwidth)

Query(basic, complex)

This equation is broken up into functions: *Work(\ ), Data(\ ), Time(\ ), Geography(\ ),* and *Query(\ )*. Each of these parameters quantifies a level of service that a data grid must provide to support the service or application. The QoS level that a data grid provides is determined by its management policies within the data region. These policies are mentioned in this chapter, but will be discussed in more detail in the chapters to follow.

As with most service-oriented architectures, the service is judged by the customer's satisfaction level as a result of using the service. The most fundamental aspect to customer satisfaction is the service's ability to meet the business need. However, there are additional key factors necessary to measure customer satisfaction, such as

- Availability when needed during peak as well as off-peak times
- Cost of the service
- Performance time to run the service

Therefore, the responsibility of the data grid is to meet the QoS demands on all levels in order to accommodate and manage the overall customer experience.

10

DATA SYNCHRONIZATION

The vocabulary of data synchronization is similar to that of a motivational speaker. Is the application optimistic or pessimistic? Or is it somewhere in between these two extremes? Does the application trust the data grid to deliver data? Does it even care whether the data are delivered at all?

Optimistic synchronization policies relate to instances where the application has a great deal of trust in the data grid to deliver data of its own accord. This synchronization policy lends itself to high performance. The opposite end of the spectrum is a pessimistic synchronization policy. Here, the application needs to ensure the delivery of data before continuing to process. These applications need to "see it for themselves" in order to "believe" that the data reach their intended destination. These applications tend to be transactional in nature.

One of the data management policies within the data grid is synchronization, as discussed in earlier chapters. There are two types of synchronization: intraregion and interregion. These respective synchronization types identify data synchronization within a data region with other data sources either external or internal to the region. These are distinctly separate synchronizations, each with its own definition, scope, impact, and effect on the application and others around it.

The data synchronization policy, like other data management policies of the data grid, is heavily dependent on the requirements of the applications. Intraregion synchronization supports the application's behavior and its characteristics for inbound and outbound data, the generation of interim data sets, and other applications interacting within that region. For example, are the data characteristics of the application transient or transactional in nature?

Distributed Data Management for Grid Computing, by Michael Di Stefano
Copyright © 2005 John Wiley & Sons, Inc.

Interregion synchronization manages the dependencies of the data region's inter-actions with external data sources, whether those sources are external systems, such as legacy systems, or other data regions in the data grid. Typical behavioral charac-teristics are read-only, and read and update where transactional constraints apply.

A proper analysis of the application will determine the synchronization policies required to best meet the application's goals. The data grid must support a wide range of synchronization policies in order for the data grid to be of maximum use, efficiency, and scalability for application within the data region.

INTRAREGION SYNCHRONIZATION

Intraregion synchronization (see Figure 10.1) policies support the transient and transactional behavioral data requirements of applications whose scope is internal to the data region itself and involve other applications and systems that participate in the contribution or consumption of data managed by that data region.

The data management requirements of contributors (or producers) and consumers of data within the data region have a direct impact on the selection of data grid implementation and its ability to fully or partially support those requirements. One choice, for example, could be GridFTP, where the data producers and consu-mers are the FTP clients and the data stores are FTP servers. Synchronization between FTP clients and servers implies a transaction manager that resides within the data region managing updates between the FTP clients and servers involved in the transaction. The transaction manager is responsible for implementing the syn-chronization policy for the data region. This implies that GridFTP is best suited for pessimistic (transactional) synchronization policies and not well suited for optimis-tic synchronization policies where speed of processing is paramount.

The FTP transaction manager itself can have a centralized architecture so that all transactions are managed via this one manager. Alternatives include having trans-action managers logically reside in each data region producer and consumer process. The transaction managers are peers to each other and coordinate between them-selves on the transaction. Each approach has its own pros and cons for giving the

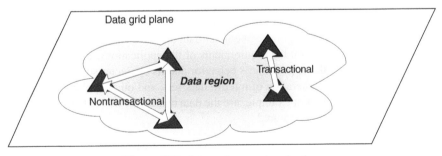

Figure 10.1. Intraregion synchronization.

synchronization policy support for the data region and its own unique intraregion synchronization QoS level.

The two architectures of centralized and peer-to-peer synchronization are common, and will be an important consideration when choosing the data grid implementation in terms of its ability to deliver the best intraregion data synchronization QoS levels for the application requirements.

Another example of data grid implementation is a metadata dictionary, which gives an abstraction layer between data producers, consumers, and the physical data sources. Intraregion synchronization policies are managed by the metadata dictionary, thus assuming the characteristics of a centralized synchronization architecture. The metadata dictionary provides the abstraction layer and is the transaction manager for synchronization between the various sources.

Data grids that are based on distributed caching; thus intraregion synchronization is internode synchronization per atom of data. The applications themselves become the producers and consumers of data.

Intraregion data synchronization policies govern transient and transactional data behaviors in support of the specific requirements of the application using the data within the data region. However, the intraregion synchronization QoS levels available to support those policies depend greatly on implementation of the underlying data grid.

INTERREGION SYNCHRONIZATION

Interregion synchronization (see Figure 10.2) policies—synchronization between a data region and data sources that are external to that region—follow the same general guidelines as do intraregion synchronization policies. With interregion

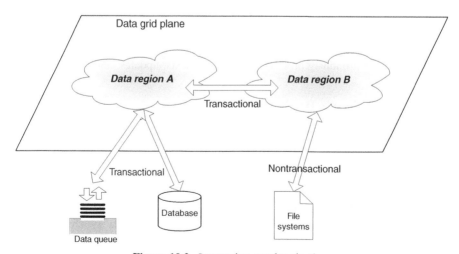

Figure 10.2. Interregion synchronization.

synchronization, the participants involved could be other data regions as well as external systems, applications, databases, or middleware. The external partners can be other data regions within the data grid or a legacy system. The legacy system is any other data source outside the data region. Examples include a relational database; a middleware bus, such as a queuing system; a publish-and-subscribe bus; a filing system; a mail server; and even other data grids. The synchronization policy defines the interaction with another system that is external to the data region.

Even more in evidence here than with intraregion synchronization is the dependency on the implementation of a data partner. These partners can be a wide range of systems each with their own characteristics and ability to support purely transient or transactional behavior. Some standards do exist to define a transaction such as XA; however, not all transactional systems support an XA interface. For nontransactional behavior, too, there is a dearth of standard interfaces, if indeed any exists. Therefore, extra attention must be paid to the available levels of QoS needed to be considered when architecting an application in a distributed environment.

SYNCHRONIZATION ARCHITECTURES

There are various ways to implement synchronization between n numbers of partners. We will look at two methods: (1) a centralized controller and (2) a decentralized, peer-to-peer mechanism. It is important to realize that these architectures are implementation-based and not policy-based.

Synchronization architectures control the interaction between two or more partners interested in maintaining a constant view of the data. This interaction can be regarded as a transaction between these partners. In a centralized architecture, the controller or "synchronization manager" coordinates the transactional update between the partners. In a peer-to-peer architecture, that has to be a quorum established between the partners as to which partner "owns" the master version of the data. The synchronization of the data among the transaction partners of the quorum involves only those partners, thus allowing the other nodes in the data grid free to asynchronously process their data requests, updates, and transactions.

Centralized Synchronization Manager

The centralized synchronization manager architecture implies one central process, the synchronization manager, with which all the nodes coordinate when receiving updates. It is the responsibility of the synchronization manager to know the identities of the other partners interested in maintaining the latest view of the data atom. The synchronization manager will, in a coordinated fashion, update all the interested partners with the latest data. From the user's perspective, all the requests or notifications go to the synchronization manager, at which point the synchronization manager operates on the data. The synchronization manager can operate in several modes, one of which is the transactional mode. In this mode the user will wait for a successful acknowledgment before processing with the other tasks. This ensures that all parties have received and acknowledged the receipt of the information. Another mode of operation is nontransactional. Here the synchronization manager returns to the user a successful receipt of the data even though further synchronization with other parties needs to be performed. Therefore the user can continue with its tasks while the synchronization manager processes to update all required endpoints (data regions, systems, databases, etc.). The synchronization manager will then continue to update the rest of the parties involved in the synchronization. However, these users will not be waiting for all parties to be synchronized; the user trusts the synchronization manager to perform this function. The user in this case also has the understanding that should something catastrophic happen—either with this synchronization manager or if one of the transaction partners is not available to receive the update—data will be lost and updates to all interested parties cannot be guaranteed. This mode of behavior for the synchronization manager is policy-driven.

The advantage of the centralized synchronization manager is that there is one manager to administer, monitor, and ensure that all parties involved receive the update. However, this simplicity of design cuts both ways. The disadvantage is that it is one manager yielding scaling limits to performance. Various engineering methods can be used to circumvent this, including an architecture hybrid between the centralized and peer-to-peer architectures, a federation of synchronization managers, where each manager is responsible for its own group of transaction partners. When a group becomes too large for one manager to service, new managers are added to the federation and the grouping will be subdivided among them. However, now the federation of managers must coordinate among themselves. This yields a tiered approach, a quorum of synchronization managers, each responsible for a grouping of nodes interested in receiving data updates. The federation begins to resemble a peer-to-peer architecture. However, on the upside, few synchronization managers are needed relative to the total number of nodes to be administered. The downside is that should a synchronization manager fail, then an entire group of nodes will stop receiving updates.

Peer-to-Peer Synchronization

In the peer-to-peer (P2P) architecture, each data source is responsible for identifying all the potential partners interested in being updated when a piece of data is changed and for coordinating directly with those partners without the middleperson, a centralized manager. For an update and only for the duration of that update, will the nodes coordinate with each other. This implies that there is a primary owner for a piece of information, and it is the responsibility of the owner to notify all interested parties and coordinate the propagation of the update among them.

Administration of a P2P architecture is different from that of a centralized architecture. There is no central administration manager to monitor in order to view the transaction process, performance statistics, and the various status logs maintained. Thus, a different administration approach must be taken in P2P architectures. One possibility is to view the chain of events across the data grid from the data's perspective. Performance and transaction statistics can be identified and monitored by the owners of a data atom.

The advantage of the P2P architecture is scalability. Without having to worry about the number of nodes in the data grid, the amount of data under management or synchronization scaling and latency, the system will intuitively scale without having to add layers of managers for the increased load.

SYNCHRONIZATION PATTERNS

There are various synchronization patterns from which one can choose when defining and selecting policies for synchronization. These patterns can be transactional or nontransactional; they can define frequency and granularity of synchronization. There is also an intertwining between synchronization policy and distribution policy when it comes to a replicated distribution policy. For example, the replicated distribution policy employs the transactional mode of synchronization. A distributed distribution policy makes no such vocation.

The synchronization must take into account the distribution policy, the granularity of the data sets involved, and the geography of the region: specifically, the geography of the transaction partners involved in the synchronization. If it is inter-region, the bandwidth and geography constraints need to be considered, as do the constraints of the other system characteristics—their ability to support a transactional and nontransactional synchronization. For intraregion synchronization, the external transaction partners' characteristics and behavior are not a primary concern. However, the geography and network bandwidth characteristics of the region need to be considered.

In the case of the replicated distribution policy, issues such as data granularity in frequency and network bandwidth are less of an issue because the distribution policy itself dictates that for every update, whenever a piece of information is changed, all parties involved must receive an update in transactional mode. Therefore, the speed of the system is not of primary concern; rather, it is the security of the data. However, for other distribution policies, data granularity and frequency of synchronization become important. For example, if the data set is very fine (i.e., the data atoms are small in size) and is typically updated frequently, then the load on the synchronization manager in keeping up with all the updates can be high. If the physical surroundings, such as geography and network constraints, can support high-speed interconnections (e.g., high network bandwidth), then fine granularity and high frequency of update become less of a gating factor to performance. Otherwise, low network bandwidth, either local-area network (LAN) or wide-area network (WAN), and synchronization patterns of frequency and per atom update rates need to be adjusted. In these cases, it will be efficient or scalable to synchronize small pieces of information frequently across a network. The synchronization pattern may have a group of updates and synchronize groups of updates with less frequency. This works well for nontransactional policies; in a transactional policy, all updates must be synchronized regardless of the data atom size, network bandwidth, or geography.

Synchronization Granularity

We have yet to address the granularity of a synchronization policy. For intraregion synchronization, it has been assumed that the synchronization policy within the region is broad in scope in that the policy addresses all the data atoms and their replicas within that region. Basically, this is a homogeneous synchronization policy (see Figure 10.3). However, in terms of interregion synchronization, this assumption is not valid. Data within a data region can be generated by either the application or the services that are in the region supports, or it can be imported or loaded into the region from any number of external data sources.

Therefore, the synchronization policy for interregion synchronization, at minimum, must have the flexibility to be individualized to each of the external data sources that the data region exchanges data with. So we have moved from a homogeneous synchronization policy to the requirement of a heterogeneous synchronization policy (see Figure 10.4) for external or interregion synchronization.

Certainly, a homogeneous synchronization policy for intraregion synchronization is valid. However, it will not support more sophisticated applications and the requirements for data management. Therefore, extension of the data region to support heterogeneous synchronization for external or interregion synchronization should also be brought into the intraregion synchronization policies as well (see Figure 10.5).

A wiser definition of synchronization policy granularity will extend beyond the individual data atoms from an external data source to any logical grouping of

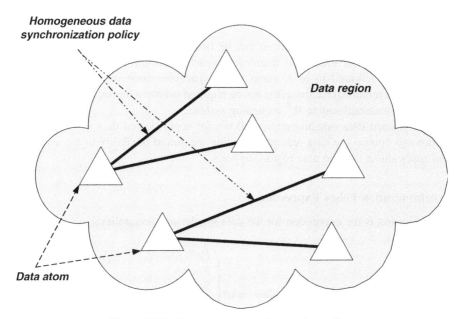

Figure 10.3. Homogeneous synchronization policy.

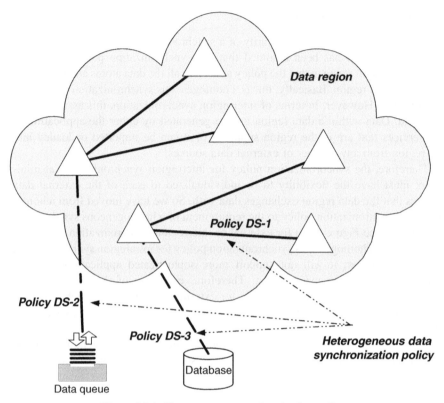

Figure 10.4. Heterogeneous synchronization policy.

data atoms. Therefore, a data atom can be tied to one or more synchronization policies for both for intra- and interregion synchronization. For example, a data atom may be required to be a transactional synchronization to "external source A," such as a relational database, but not be required to have a transactional synchronization to "external source B," a queuing system.

Fine-grained data synchronization allows for sophisticated data behavior both within and outside the data regions providing maximum flexibility to the services and applications that the data region supports.

Synchronization Policy Expression

The following is the expression for the data synchronization policy:

$$
SynchronizationPolicy = SP \begin{pmatrix} PolicyName, \\ Region, \\ Scope(), \\ Transactionality(), \\ LoadStore(), \\ Events() \end{pmatrix}
$$

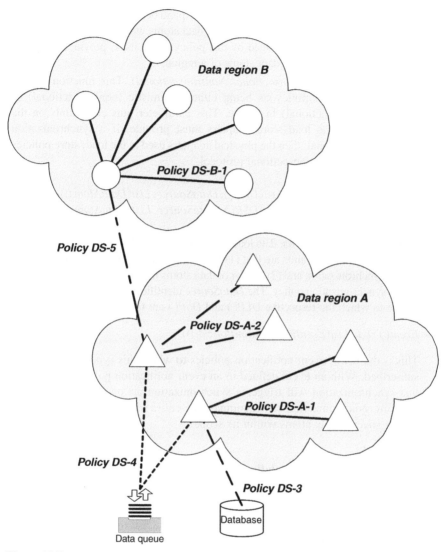

Figure 10.5. Heterogeneous synchronization for both inter- and intraregion synchronization.

where *SP* is the synchronization policy function with the following parameters:

- *PolicyName* = logical name for this policy. This is the logical name for this instance of a data synchronization policy. Depending on the implementation of the data grid, this name may or may not be unique.
- *Region* = primary region name. This is the primary data region to which this data synchronization policy is applied.
- *Scope( )* = *F(Boundary(Intra, Inter), List(DataAtoms)* = *NULL)*. The scope of the data synchronization policy is defined by its boundaries. Is the synchronization

local to a data region (intraregion), or does it expand beyond the data region (inter-region)? The second parameter defines the data atoms within a data region whose synchronization is to be managed by this policy. If no list is provided, then this policy encompasses all the data atoms of a region.

- *Transactionality = F(Transactional, Nontransactional)*. This function defines the synchronization policy as being either optimistic (nontransactional) or pessimistic (transactional) in nature. This parameter puts constraints on the QoS level that the load/store adapters must provide. If a synchronization policy is transactional, then the physical adapters used in the load/store policies must also support a transactional protocol.

$$LoadStore(\ ) = F\left(\begin{array}{l} List(DLP(\ ), DataSource, List(DataAtoms)), \\ List(DSP(\ ), DataSource, List(DataAtoms)) \end{array}\right)$$

This is a complete list of the data load/store policies required for this synchroniza-tion policy. The constraints are that (1) this parameter is valid only valid for inter-region synchronization and (2) the list of data atoms must be inclusive to the scope of this synchronization policy. The *DataSource* identifies the type name of the data source to which the respective *DLP(\ )* and *DSP(\ )* are to be applied.

- *Event(\ ) = F(List(EventNotificationPolicy(\ )))*.

This is the list of event notification policies to which this synchronization has subscribed. With an event defined in an event notification policy trigger, then this synchronization will trigger a synchronization action. The scope of the resulting synchronization can encompass the entire scope of this synchroniza-tion or specific data atoms within its scope.

Synchronization Pattern Simulations

There is active research in the area of data locality and access in distributed shared memory (DSM) architecture. There are various techniques of optimization patterns or overlays of data across nodes.[22] The assumptions are that there are synchronized "copies" of a data atom active in multiple nodes in the data grid. The objective is to find the fastest route to a data atom in the data grid, and thus figure out how to opti-mize the data query speed. There is no presumption to how data are organized across the data grid. The data are just there, randomly dispersed with no forethought as to how they are being used.

We will base a set of hypotheses on the fact that we do know how the data can be distributed and synchronized efficiently to reflect the needs of an application. The deterministic policies of synchronization and distribution allow for optimal query access. Business applications are inherently deterministic. Earlier, we offered an equation set that describes the characteristics of applications with regard to how those characteristics affect the data management policies of a distributed data man-agement system such as the data grid. These characteristics can be presented in mathematical form, although most likely not in simple representations since the systems can be complex. However, they are deterministic systems. The data grid, in reality, is not infinitely wide and dispersed. It has a boundary. The application traverses or operates over subsets of the data grid boundary. Some of the conditions defining this boundary are the characteristics of the application and application operations (operating systems, linked libraries, etc.) and so on. All these conditions set forth a deterministic pattern to data locality and data frequency. Therefore, if the deterministic nature of the application can be expressed in a mathematical form, then the data synchronization and data distribution policies required to support the application can be similarly expressed.

SYNCHRONIZATION POLICY AS A STANDARD INTERFACE

When the scope of the data requirements for an application is contained within the single data region—for example, when there are no interactions with other external sources, whether they are legacy systems or other data regions within the data grid—then the policies that we have discussed (synchronization, replication, distribution, load/store, and event policies) fully describe the data behavior within that region of the data grid. However, as scope of the application demands the integration of data from other sources external to the data region, the interaction and movement of data between those regions and other sources need to be defined. These interactions need to be defined in such a way as to maintain the QoS level, thus keeping it at an acceptable level for a constant and reliable business and system behavior. Of the data management policies, the synchronization policy can extend beyond the boundaries of the data region and define how the data region interacts with external data sources and other data regions. The other data management policies of distribution, replication, load/store, and event notification are all self-contained and describe data management within the region. They have no public interface defining the interaction with that region and the external sources. It is only the synchronization policy that defines this external or public interface.

Use of the synchronization policy as a standard public interface to a data region addresses the maintenance of or elimination of the fluctuation of QoS level between a data region and other external sources. This can include other data regions within the data grid, but also eliminates variances in QoS levels between different implementations and data grid versions. Defining a clean and concise interface of data movement and how the data are to be exchanged isolates mechanics (including the implementation) of any of the data regions involved in the sharing of data. We will delve into this topic further in a later chapter.

11

DATA INTEGRATION

ENTERPRISE APPLICATION/INFORMATION INTEGRATION (EAI/EII) IN GRID

In the chapter on Web Services, we will discuss an evolution to Web Services, starting from the point-to-point integration of standalone systems, to the client/server topology, to distributed computing [straight-through processing (STP)] and finally to the grid topology and the compute utility. This is a long progression of new and very different compute topologies that ushered in their own distinct operational environments, creating an intertwining that exists today. To better understand information integration within the grid, let us take a brief look at the evolution of enterprise information integration, better known as EII.

Straight-through Processing (STP), EAI, and EII

As client/server evolved into distributed computing, new buzzwords emerged. In the early days, enterprise application integration (EAI) was very common, and as time went on, achieving straight-through processing (STP) by leveraging EAI became the trend. Today, the more commonly phrase *enterprise information integration* (EII) has come to the fore. We would like to provide a level of understanding associated with each of these three commonly used acronyms:

- *Enterprise Application Integration (EAI).* The enabling of data sources and applications to communicate with each other via a network without custom

Distributed Data Management for Grid Computing, by Michael Di Stefano
Copyright © 2005 John Wiley & Sons, Inc.

process and point-to-point connectivity software, often referred to as a "spaghetti mess." The resulting infrastructure replaced the spaghetti mess with "middleware pipes." Through middleware, information flows among the applications throughout the business units of an enterprise.

- *Straight-through Processing (STP).* Like EAI, STP is designed to provide end-to-end business processing automatically and with little or no manual intervention. Each application sends the information to an infrastructure that allows for data processing, including data extraction, data parsing, data manipulation, and data reformating. In addition, this infrastructure is required to provide intelligent data routing and business processing to whatever end system or application requires the data. This infrastructure, or hub, as it is commonly termed, will provide the downstream applications with the data that they require in an automated fashion.

- *Enterprise Information Integration (EII).* The purpose of EII is to provide access to data from multiple sources, making the request transparent to the application. Thus, the data are automatically aggregated from the various sources and the requesting application does not have to deal with determining which source will provide which data, and with connecting to each source directly. EII allows all back-end information to be seen as if it came from one comprehensive, global database.

STP and EAI tend to go hand in hand; application integration is required to achieve a near-real-time enterprise or STP. The progression to STP is a direct response to various business drivers:

- In the financial industry, STP was driven by the initiative of moving trading to clear in one day, a process commonly referred to as $T + 1$.
- Too many manual processes, which increased costs, errors, and processing time.
- The high cost of implementing computer systems.
- The high cost of maintaining computer systems.
- The business shifting focus to a customer service model.

Prior to the emergence of EAI and STP, the predominant system architectures were "stovepiped" (see Figure 11.1), designed to run independently with no interaction. Examples are inventory control, human resources, and sales automation. Over time, more and more lines of business required these systems to share information, to get systems to share tasks and data and to eliminate the need for custom code that is normally written. Typically, these were one-off efforts quite often duplicated by different development groups supporting their respective business units. This normally resulted in many versions of code performing the same or very similar tasks and functions. Maintaining such point-to-point communication was very costly and yielded very few functional benefits. Companies started looking at product solutions that would solve these problems and eliminate the custom development that was in place.

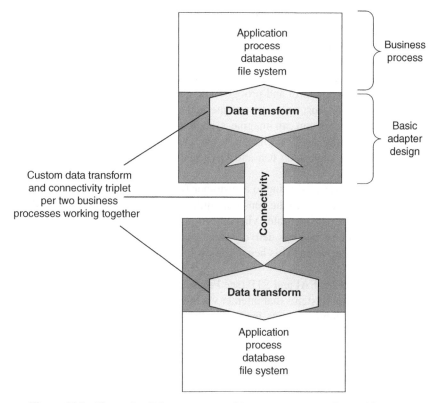

Figure 11.1. "Stovepiped" interprocess and intersystem connection architecture.

What began to emerge was a common process of separating how the applications communicated, for involving data transformation and data representation. Connectivity encompassed the physical hurdles of how the two processes or systems connected to each other, which was typically via a network socket or through file sharing, a more common process than one would expect. The second layer to connectivity was the protocol. The protocol defines the logical interaction between the systems, things such as how to establish a connection, how to terminate a connection, message headers and footers, message counting, how to identify missed messages, and how to request a retransmission of missed messages. In regard to file sharing, the functions included the FTP function, file checksums, and file ready for processing flag. This process employed specialists for each system, network programming specialists, and reams of specifications documenting every aspect of the process.

In conjunction with the system protocol were each system's data formats. This included message bodies, message headers and footers (separate from the communication protocol headers and footers), and field definitions. The message formats ranged from some delimited format (the delimiters could be anything that the developer of the system desired, typically a comma or any other character that was not part of the information being sent), or an offset of field bit position and size (analogous to a pilot's method of dead-reckoning navigation of an aircraft). The developer knew the starting point of each field since specific sizes were sizes associated with the fields. By counting fields and field sizes, the developer had a good idea of where the next field started and ended.

This process needed to be repeated for each system pair that wanted to communicate and share information and process. The end result was a rat's nest of intertwining systems that cost more to operate and maintain than did the respective systems themselves. As you can imagine, system maintenance and regression testing were a nightmare; the smallest change in one system impacted other systems and caused a cascading regression test and QA (quality assurance) cycle for all other connected systems.

The business driver of shifting to a customer-focused view requires the ability to deliver business processes to the consumer quickly and efficiently. Stovepiped data centers and applications integrated via point-to-point custom code do not lend themselves to this level of business delivery, thus leading to new techniques of system and application integration. This began the evolution to enterprise application integration (EAI).

The architecture for EAI and STP (see Figure 11.2) deals with the abstraction of system conductivity. Systems that interact via the sharing of events and information should be able to publish events leading to the sharing of information associated with the respective events without having to worry about direct point-to-point communication of any type, such as sockets. This concept describes one of the core functions of what was termed "middleware."

The EAI and STP architectures simplified matters, eliminating the complexity of connectivity by ushering in a new technology (and family of jargon) of middleware. The generic definition of middleware is software that connects two separate applications. It is sometimes referred to as "plumbing" or the "glue" that holds or connects applications together and passes data between them. In practice, middleware performs some wondrous feats. It provides a standard method and protocol for all applications to communicate; it completely disconnects any one system from all others that need its information to perform its own tasks; conversely, it can get to any other systems' data that it may need. This disconnect of systems allows for system maintenance without adversely affecting every other system in the information sharing chain simply by requiring a QA test with the middleware product. Note that the data side of the system integration equation is still not addressed. This is where we start to get into the wide variety of and differences in middleware products. At the highest level, there are basically two types, messaging-oriented middleware (MOM), and Common Object Request Broker Architecture (CORBA). The former has an entire family tree of brothers, sisters, and distant cousins, while the latter is attempting to fill the broader scope of service-oriented architecture (SOA), which has seen better days.

Messaging middleware has three basic flavors: simple queuing, where applications have "well known" inbound and outbound queues that anyone can access; message routing features that will automatically deliver "published" messages to all "subscribers" to that message; and data translation tools that will translate data

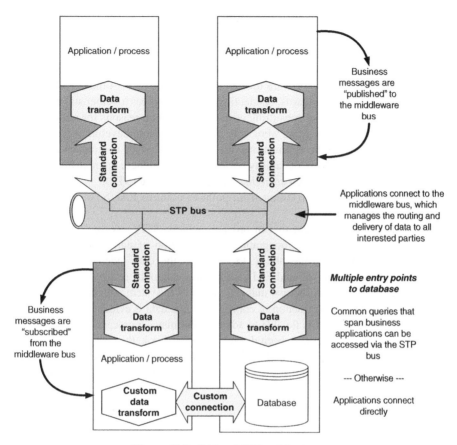

Figure 11.2. EAI and STP architectures.

from the originator's format to the recipient's format while it transports the data between the two systems.

CORBA, on the other hand, encapsulates systems as a "service" and publishes its services for other systems to access. The services include both data and function. Data representation in a CORBA environment is common to all applications to understand independent of hardware platform, implementation, and operating environment. CORBA's data representation is accomplished by using the Interface Definition Language (IDL). A service "publishes" its interface by defining it in IDL and then compiling it for source-level inclusion into the implementation of the service code. Any CORBA service can be "located" simply by making a request to the CORBA service broker. The requesting application has to know something about the service it needs and through a series of inquiries can find out all the details of the service in order to use it. As you can see, it can get quite complicated, and we are only skimming the surface.

CORBA's complexity and closed nature ultimately have led to its filling niche markets only. However, the base technology and lessons learned have led to today's current generation of service-oriented architecture, namely, Web Services (see Figure 11.3 for a comparison of the two architectures).

As you can see, all the different versions and flavors of MOM and CORBA still result in a complex network of stovepipes of middleware integration (see Figure 11.4) since each vendor's software did not communicate to the other vendor software. Without industry standards, connecting these stovepipes together still required tremendous effort. That and consulting costs were the main reasons for middleware vendor failure. Consulting costs were very high, and custom development was not eliminated even though the applications did not have to worry about such tasks.

One of benefits of EAI is the ability to achieve zero latency, the real-time enterprise via a methodology called *straight-through processing* (STP).

Figure 11.5 shows the evolution from point-to-point to EAI/STP, the service-oriented grid infrastructure.

It quickly became apparent that in order to achieve STP, a second front had to be opened up on information integration: the evolution of enterprise information integration (EII). Without the ability to represent the data independent of their source, the full benefit of STP and EAI architectures cannot be realized. This leads to fulfillment of the second of the two main components to system integration data. The fundamental concept of abstraction of connectivity and data is evident in the service-oriented architecture. SOA is flexible to adapt to and manage process-level and data-level integration, or, as we have been discussing in this book, the compute grid plane and the data grid plane. Grid technology is the evolution of middleware; it is the evolution to the distributed computing environments given birth to by EAI, STP, and EII.

EII IN GRID

Data integration with grid computing builds on the concepts of EAI and EII, which we have touched on in an earlier section. The data grid plane provides the

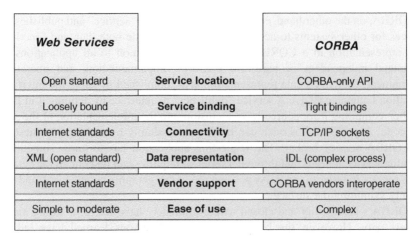

Web Services		CORBA
Open standard	**Service location**	CORBA-only API
Loosely bound	**Service binding**	Tight bindings
Internet standards	**Connectivity**	TCP/IP sockets
XML (open standard)	**Data representation**	IDL (complex process)
Internet standards	**Vendor support**	CORBA vendors interoperate
Simple to moderate	**Ease of use**	Complex

Figure 11.3. Web Services versus CORBA.

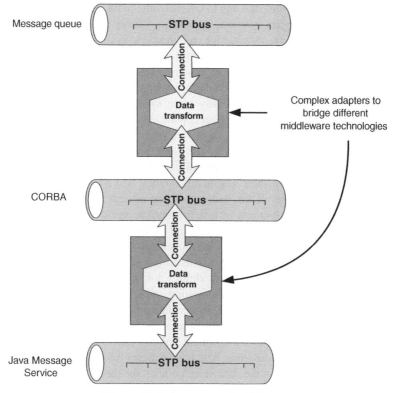

Figure 11.4. Integration of middleware.

focal point for data integration at the business service level. The core principles for data integration in the data grid leverage the same "adapter" techniques from STP; systems join the data grid in methods similar to those which they would attach to an STP bus.

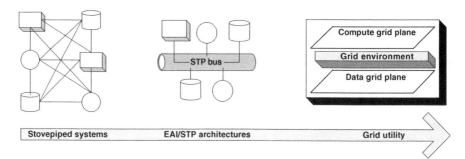

Figure 11.5. Integration architecture evolution.

One of the primary hurdles that had to be overcome in the EAI and EII evolution was the integration of legacy systems, numerous systems that were built across a long timeline. The people responsible for creating these systems—managers, architects, and programmers—have most likely migrated on to different groups or organizations. The technology on which these legacy systems were built can be different from the ones we are using today, technology that may not even be supported by the vendor in the form in which it is used. How many systems have we come across that are compiled against a third-party package, operating system, or an in-house library that is no longer supported because upgrading one vendor's version release will cause integration failure or conflicts with other packages also linked into the system? The inherent knowledge that is still part of the original project team may have migrated with them in their advancing careers. Any system documentations most likely do not capture all the nuances of the system, or the documentation itself may be lost. The investment in time, resources, and cost in the adoption of EAI, STP, and EII cannot be pushed aside, but rather leveraged in order to foster quick adoption of the grid technology and movement to service-oriented offerings. The adapter methodology, technology that is tested and working in production at data centers, must be reused. The methodology for bringing the systems into the STP-EII environment applies to grid computing and data grid integration.

We will see that the evolution of EII into the data grid goes beyond the mechanics of EAI, STP, and EII simply for data integration. In order to provide services in a quick and flexible manner, data management policies must be in place to describe and manage data load and data store: data load policies for the import of data into the data grid plane as well as the data store policies for the data export out of the data grid plane. These data load/store policies must orchestrate with the other policies such as data synchronization policy. We will build on this relationship, which has been introduced in earlier chapters.

EII within the data grid plane adds a layer of abstraction so that data movement decisions are policy-driven rather than being programmed into the business applications and adapters that attached them to the data grid. We will look at the architectures of data load and data store as well as the interaction between these policies and the other data management policies of distributed data management.

Natural Separation of Process and Data

Grid computing offers a natural separation of the process and the data. The compute grid plane manages the execution of the business logic of a process, service, or application. The data grid plane manages the data access, distribution, quality of service, and availability of the business data used by the business logic executing in the compute grid plane.

Let us start from the perspective of a developer—specifically, a developer using object-oriented methodologies to implement a system. This is simply a tool enabling us to visualize the separation of process and data management. Applications written in non-object-oriented paradigm follow the same separation of process and data separation in the grid. The point is more easily visualized in the following example.

This is a fair assumption as most applications written since the mid-1990s use this paradigm. Java, C++, C#, and SmallTalk are object-oriented programming languages, so the assumption is that if your application is written in one of these languages, it uses object-oriented design principles. This statement may make some people's hair stand on end, as C++ does not enforce object-oriented principles. This is a topic of discussion for another time. Please allow this indulgence for the scope of this discussion.

The structure of business objects takes the form of methods and attributes. *Methods* are the program or the business logic implementation of the object. The *attributes* are the data with which the business logic operates in order to perform its function. The following pseudocode shows a typical declaration of a business object:

```
1   public class FooBar
2   {
3   //NOTE TO THE READER
4   //A little Object Ease, Anything that is Public anyone can
      access. Anything that
5   //is Private ONLY this business object can access.
6   //
7
8   //===== Declare the Business Data Attributes of the
      Business Object =====
9   //declare the object's Private Attributes
10  //
11  private String thisProcessName;
12  private Integer thisProcessState;
13
14
15  //===== Declare the Business Processes (Methods) of the
      Business Object =====
16  //declare the object's Public Methods
17  //
18
19  //===== Public Method - Constructs the Object =====
20  public FooBar()//Object Constrictor - used to put the
      object in a well
21              //known state at its inception
22  {
23    thisProcessName="FooBar";
24    thisProcessState=0;
25  }
26
27  //===== Public Method - Change State =====
28  public void ChangeState()//Simple add one to the counter
29  {
30    thisProcessState = thisProcessState + 1;
31  }
32
```

```
33  //===== Public Method - Show the Business Process's State
    =====
34  public void HelloWorld()//prints out the object's name and
    state
35  {
36  print(``Process Name is:''+thisProcessName);
37  print(``Process State is:''+thisProcessState);
38  }
39
40  }//End Object Decloration
```

As is seen in this example, the data attributes are declared separately from the business logic methods; however, the data are used, read, and modified in the business methods. In a traditional compute environment, where *FooBar* executes on a single machine, we do not think of this as two separate compute and data management environments. The operating system creates a separate processing and memory space for the executing program and manages both for us. In a grid environment, it is the compute grid plane that acts as the grid operating system for resource and process execution and the data grid plane serves as the data management system for the grid operating environment.

The compute grid plane keeps track of the compute nodes capable of executing our business process *FooBar*. It also knows which of *FooBar*'s methods need to be executed. It will make the best possible match of task and resource; therefore, it can execute the "HelloWorld" method on compute node 1001 and the "ChangeState" method on node 1275.

It is the data grid plane's job to ensure that the data attributes of *FooBar* are available and in a consistent and correct state, accessible on both nodes 1001 and 1275 when needed.

Figure 11.6 shows the natural separation of compute and data management within a grid.

Note that we will reference the *FooBar* code example throughout the remainder of this chapter.

Data Load Policy

In Chapter 9, we discussed the basic principles of both data load and data store policies. Here, we will tackle the mechanical and operational aspects in data integration and EII of the data grid through the data load and store policies.

From the application's perspective, there are two ways to load data into the data grid. First is the do-it-yourself approach. In the *FooBar* example, *FooBar's* constructor initializes the state of the business object by setting the name to *FooBar* and stage to zero. In the *ChangeState*( ) operation, it modifies the state by adding one to the data attribute. Basically *FooBar* loads and changes its data attributes itself. Specifically, it loads in static values into the attributes. However, it could have just as easily have connected to a database, queuing system, or file system to load in the value on construction or leveraged some other external data source to change its state.

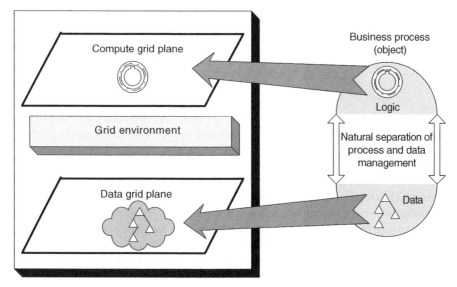

Figure 11.6. Natural separation of process and data.

The data load policy comes into play when *FooBar* relies on the data grid for loading some or all of its data attributes for it. For example, we can establish a data load policy for *FooBar* as follows

$$
DataLoadPolicy = DLP \begin{pmatrix} FooBar\_DLP, \\ ExampleRegion, \\ Granularity(Grouping(1), Frequency(500)), \\ FooBarFileAdapter() \end{pmatrix}
$$

with a data synchronization policy of

$$
SynchronizationPolicy = SP \begin{pmatrix} FootBar\_SP, \\ ExampleRegion, \\ Scope(Boundary(``inter"), List(``foobar\_ProcessStage")), \\ Transactionality(``transactional"), \\ LoadStore(List(``Foobar\_DLP"), List(``FooBar\_DSP")), \\ Events(NULL) \end{pmatrix}
$$

Given the policies set above, *FooBar* can be modified as follows. Obviously this omits details such as establishing a connection to the data grid and using cumbersome get and set methods. The code snippet is for showing the concept only. Working code examples are provided in a later chapter.

```
1  //===== Public Method - Constructs the Object =====
2  public FooBar()//Object Constrictor - used to put the object
   in a well
```

```
3                   //known state at its inception
4  {
5    thisProcessName = "FooBar";
6    thisProcessState = dataGrid.get("ExampleRegion",
                        "foobar_ProcessState");
7  }
```

Here, we are creating a "local copy" of the "FooBar" process state contained in the data grid. This local copy can be used elsewhere in the "FooBar" business process and saved to the data grid when necessary.

Let us step through what happens when line 6 of the sample code above is executed. First, we are assuming that we have a connection to the data grid, done earlier in the program, which is represented by the "dataGrid" object. The "dataGrid.get( )" call has two parameters; one is the data region, which in this example is "ExampleRegion." The data region is where the data atom "foobar_ProcessState" and the name of the data atom is resident, the second parameter to the "dataGrid.get( )" call. Since we have already defined policies for synchronization and data load, the data grid will do the following:

```
if (``foobar_ProcessState'' Data Atom is resident in the Data
Grid)
then check to see if another process has a lock on it
      if (``foobar_ProcessState'' Data Atom is locked)
      then wait till lock is released
      endif
      Read and return value of ``foobar_ProcessState'' to the
        business process
else
    //The Data Atom ``foobar_ProcessState'' is NOT resident in the
    //Data Grid
    //As defined by the Data Load Policy use the Adapter
    //``FooBarFileAdapter()''
    //that knows where the file resides, external to the Data
    //Region, access the file
    //and get the value for ``foobar_ProcessState'', translate it
    //to the proper data
    //representation and populate the Data Atom
    //``foobar_ProcessState''
    Create and Lock the Data Atom ``foobar_ProcessState''
    rawDataFormat = FooBarFileAdapter().load
    //(``foobar_ProcessState'')
    foobar_ProcessState = FooBarFileAdapter().translate
    //(``foobar_ProcessState'')
    Return the value of ``foobar_ProcessState'' to the business
    //process
    Release the lock on ``foobar_ProcessState''
end if
```

The end result of the business process *FooBar* is that the data it needs to perform the function "foobar_ProcessState" are physically retrieved from another data source, stored in a foreign format in a transactional manner without any working knowledge or code to do so. The entire process is defined by the data management policies and managed by the data grid on behalf of *FooBar*.

Simple changes in the synchronization policy can have a major impact on the behavior of the data grid and *FooBar*. For example, the data load policy can use a different adapter, which will get the data from a completely different source and data representation. Or the data synchronization policy can be switched to nontransactional, which will eliminate the need to lock data atoms, thus speeding up the entire process.

Figure 11.7 shows the separation of process and data management, the interaction of policy and adapters to achieve true enterprise information integration in the grid through the data grid's distributed data management policies and function.

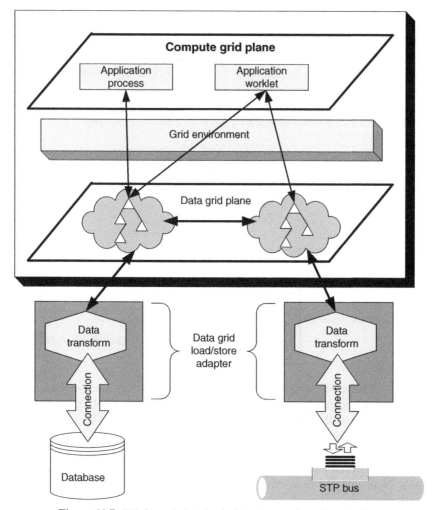

Figure 11.7. EII through data load, data store, and synchronization.

Figure 11.7 shows an application process "joining a data region" that has synchronization policies with a database and a second data region that in turn has a synchronization policy with an STP message queuing bus. Also, there is an application worklet that has joined both data regions. Both the application process and the worklet can share and interact with data sets in the first region without requiring any knowledge of where the data originate from, how the data are represented, or any other mechanical aspect of data region integration.

Data Store Policy

The discussions on data store policy are very similar to those of the data load policy. The differences are evident in the interaction with data sources and the effects of data synchronization policy on the system behavior.

Note, as with the data load process—which has two choices for loading data into the data grid—that an application can only save or store data out of the data grid through its data management policies and procedures. In the *ChangeState( )* operation, it modifies the state by adding to the data attribute. The result is then saved to the data grid through the *dataGrid.set( )* operation.

FooBar relies on the data grid to save some or all of its data attributes. For example, we can establish a data store policy for *FooBar* as follows

$$DataStorePolicy = DSP \begin{pmatrix} FooBar\_DSP, \\ ExampleRegion, \\ Granularity(Grouping(1), Frequency(500)), \\ Operation("store"), \\ FooBarFileAdapter( ) \end{pmatrix}$$

with a data synchronization policy of

$$SynchronizationPolicy = SP \begin{pmatrix} FooBar\_SP, \\ ExampleRegion, \\ Scope(Boundary("inter"), List("foobar\_ProcessStage")), \\ Transactionality("transactional"), \\ LoadStore(List("FooBar\_DLP"), List("FooBar\_DSP")), \\ Events(NULL) \end{pmatrix}$$

The data store policy as defined above defines the data region as *ExampleRegion* with a granularity of one grouping and 500 frequency. The operation to be performed is a "store" function and the adapter being utilized is the *FooBarFileAdapter( )*.

The synchronization policy again is for the same data region *ExampleRegion* and the *Scope( )*.

Given the policies defined above, the code for *FooBar* can be modified as follows. Note that the code snippet is for showing the concept only. Working code examples are provided in a later chapter.

```
1  //===== Public Method - Change State =====
2  public void ChangeState()//Simple add one to the counter
3  {
4   dataGrid.set(''ExampleRegion'',   ''foobar_ProcessState'',
   (thisProcessState+1));
5  }
```

The "local copy" of the *FooBar* process state is being changed by incrementing the state by one or adding one to it and then being stored into the data grid's data region, *ExampleRegion*'s data atom "foobar_ProcessState."

Let us step through what happens when line 38 is executed. Please note the following:

- First, we are assuming that we have a connection to the data grid, established earlier in the program, which is represented by the "dataGrid" object.
- The "dataGrid.set( )" call has three parameters.
- The data region *ExampleRegion* is where the data atom is found.
- "foobar_ProcessState" is the name of the data atom to set and the value to which it is set.

Since we have defined policies for synchronization and data load, the data grid will do the following:

```
if (''foobar_ProcessState'' Data Atom is NOT resident in the
   Data Grid)
then create the Data Atom ''foobar_ProcessState''

if (''foobar_ProcessState'' Data Atom is locked)
then wait till lock is released
endif
//Place a lock on the Data Atom ''foobar_ProcessState'' so no one
//else can access
//it while the update is being performed.
//As defined by the Data Store Policy use the Adapter
//''FooBarFileAdapter()''
//that knows where the file resides, external to the Data
//Region, access the file
//and save the value for ''foobar_ProcessState'', translate it to
//the proper data
//representation
  Lock the Data Atom ''foobar_ProcessState''
  source_FormattedValue = FooBarFileAdapter().translate
  (''foobar_ProcessState'')
  FooBarFileAdapter().save(source_FormattedValue)
  Release the lock on ''foobar_ProcessState.''
```

The end result to the business process *FooBar* is that the data it needs to perform the function "foobar_ProcessState" are physically stored to the data grid and the transition required to update an external system is performed without any working knowledge or code in the business process. The entire process is defined by the data management policies and managed by the data grid on behalf of *FooBar*. This allows for configurable changes to the policies without affecting any code in the business processes.

Simple changes in the synchronization policy can have a major impact on the behavior of the data grid and *FooBar*. For example, the data load policy can use a different adapter that will save the data to a completely different source and data representation. Or the data synchronization policy can be switched to nontransactional, which will eliminate the need to lock data atoms, thus speeding up the entire process. These kinds of policy changes are external to the business process, thus allowing system changes to occur through the change of policy definitions.

Load, Store, and Synchronization

Interaction of the data load/store policies with data synchronization policies defines the behavior of the data region and the exact QoS level required by the business service that it supports. These policies in combination determine the transactional behavior or transactional depth levels of a data region, which in turn determines the performance of the region.

What are the "depth levels" of a transaction? The data grid, its data regions, and its interactions with other data regions and external data sources have inherent levels of depth. Are the data synchronized in a data region limited in scope to the boundaries of that region (i.e., intraregion synchronization)? This is the first level of depth, internal to the data region. The next level, for example, applies if the data region interacts with external data sources and is transactional; is it transactional to the delivery of the data from the data region to the external source? The next-depth level applies if the transaction has completed accessing the external data source and reported the status back to the data region. Is the data atom/data region interacting with more than one data source for a transaction, and are these transactions processed independently of each other or grouped as a single unit?

Figure 11.8 highlights different depth levels, as an example.

This cascading effect—of pinpointing where the data delivery process occurs within the chain of data sources, and whether the business service is satisfied that the data are delivered—is referred to as the "depth levels" of a transaction. Obviously, the data management policies of a data region can extend only so far down into the behavior of an external source's management of a transaction. However, they can define the upper or closest levels to the business application as it interacts with the data grid.

The data load, data store, and synchronization policies in combination all define whether the data are to be managed in a best-faith delivery, data region transaction delivery, or fully fault-tolerant delivery. Let us look at what each of these data delivery modes are, what types of applications they support, and exactly which parameters in the respective policies affect these desired behavior.

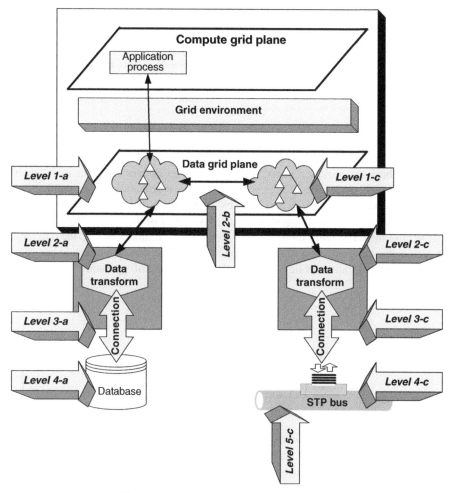

Figure 11.8. Level of depth of a transaction.

Data management policies for load, store, and synchronization from the earlier chapters where expressed as

$$DataLoadPolicy = DLP \begin{pmatrix} PolicyName, \\ Region, \\ Granularity(\,), \\ Adapter(\,) \end{pmatrix}$$

$$DataStorePolicy = DSP \begin{pmatrix} PolicyName, \\ Region, \\ Granularity(\,), \\ Operation(\,), \\ Adapter(\,) \end{pmatrix}$$

$$SynchronizationPolicy = SP \begin{pmatrix} PolicyName, \\ Region, \\ Scope(\,), \\ Transactionality(\,), \\ LoadStore(\,), \\ Events(\,) \end{pmatrix}$$

With the policies defined above, we will discuss the different delivery modes and what they mean:

1. *Best-Faith Delivery.* This is the most "optimistic" of all delivery modes. Here, the business service "trusts" the data grid to deliver the data in its own good time. It is optimistic with respect to the data grid's ability to deliver the data. This mode of delivery is best used by applications that are dealing with data that are time-critical and transient in nature. Examples of the types of applications that require such a delivery mode include Monte Carlo simulations, and the delivery of both news and quote data to trading applications. The data management policies for the synchronization policy for this delivery mode of operation can be set as follows:

$$SynchronizationPolicy = SP \begin{pmatrix} BestFaith\_SP, \\ ExampleRegion, \\ Scope(Boundary("inter"), List("foobar\_ProcessStage")), \\ Transactionality("nontransactional"), \\ LoadStore(NULL, NULL), \\ Events(NULL) \end{pmatrix}$$

2. *Data Region Transactional.* This is where the data atoms within a data region are transactional with their replicas distributed within the data region. This is important for instances when a level of resilience to hard failures (e.g., failure of compute nodes, or partial network outages) is required but 100% fault tolerance is not essential. In this instance, parts of the data grid can fail but there will be no data loss as part of this mode of delivery. This is best for applications where the volume of data in a region is large and the cost of reload in the case of a failure is too great, especially from an operational window perspective. In addition, applications that are mostly read-only or query-intensive are ideal for this type of mode delivery. Examples are datamart, data warehouse, and OLAP applications. The data management policies for both the load and the synchronization policies in this mode of operation can be set as follows:

$$DataLoadPolicy = DLP \begin{pmatrix} DRTransLoad \\ ExampleRegion, \\ Granularity(Grouping(1), Frequency(500)), \\ DRTransAdapter(\,) \end{pmatrix}$$

$$SynchronizationPolicy = SP \begin{pmatrix} DRTrans\_SP, \\ ExampleRegion, \\ Scope(Boundary("inra"),NULL), \\ Transactionality("transactional"), \\ LoadStore(List("DRTransLoad"), NULL), \\ Events(NULL) \end{pmatrix}$$

3. *Fault-Tolerant Transactional.* This is the most pessimistic mode of operation of all the delivery modes. In this mode, the business service has no faith in the data grid's ability to deliver data on its own and must confirm receipt of data delivery for all transactions all the way from the final destination. The data atoms within a data region are completely transactional down to and through the external data source, where the external source confirms that the transaction is complete. The type of applications for which this mode of delivery is best suited is where data delivery is paramount and system performance is not. Examples of applications requiring such a delivery mode are ATMs (automatic teller machines) and accounting and banking systems. The data management policies in this mode of operation for the load, store, and synchronization policies are highlighted below:

$$DataLoadPolicy = DLP \begin{pmatrix} FTTransLoad \\ ExampleRegion, \\ Granularity(Grouping(1), Frequency(500)), \\ FTTransAdapter() \end{pmatrix}$$

$$DataStorePolicy = DSP \begin{pmatrix} FTTransStore \\ ExampleRegion, \\ Granularity(Grouping(1), Frequency(500)), \\ Operation("store"), \\ FTTransAdapter() \end{pmatrix}$$

$$SynchronizationPolicy = SP \begin{pmatrix} FTTrans\_SP, \\ ExampleRegion, \\ Scope(Boundary("inter"), NULL), \\ Transactionality("transactional"), \\ LoadStore(List("FTTransLoad"), List("FTTransStore")), \\ Events(NULL) \end{pmatrix}$$

Enterprise Data Grid Integration

The buzzwords of *enterprise application integration* (EAI) and *enterprise information integration* (EII) describe how applications and information from various sources can be integrated into a larger, more purposeful, broad, and deep view of an organization's information at a business level. In these types of integration, we are discussing how to manage data within a distributed computing environment, which is just one system within an enterprise. As we have seen in the past with various database and middleware products, each of these products has its own advantages and disadvantages. On the basis of these advantages and disadvantages, an enterprise will have products from more than one vendor, thus creating the need for EAI and EII. There may be queuing system products from IBM or Tibco, for example. In addition, there may be database products from Sybase or Oracle; therefore, it is reasonable to expect that there will be various data grid products throughout an enterprise. The combinations and permutations of data grids can be as great as we have seen with database/middleware products. The same thing holds true for the compute grid. Some grid vendors may have a metadictionary, while others may be distributed-memory-based. There can be products from more than one grid vendor at any one enterprise implementation. For example, a distributed-memory-based data grid product from company A is used in one area of the organization while a different area can use a data grid from company B. The reason for choosing a respective product within the various areas within the organization is dependent on the business and how the products support the business.

It is reasonable to expect that multiple data grid products will be employed throughout an organization. Therefore, if we do not clearly define an interface for how data grids, specifically data regions within data grids, can interact with each other, then all we will have done is create larger data silos and a chasm that must be crossed in order for those organizations to share data with each other. So let's create a new buzzword; if enterprise information integration deals with the integration of information across an entire enterprise, and if data grid is a single product or single methodology for data integration within a grid, then *enterprise data grid integration* (EDGI) refers to the interoperation of data grids across an enterprise. EDGI is a subset or subcategory of EII. Armed with our new buzzword, let's review some of the data management policies for the data grid:

- *Data distribution policy* describes the distribution of data within the data grid or the distribution of data atoms within a data grid.
- *Data replication policy* describes exactly how the data atoms are to be replicated within a data region.
- *Data load* and *data store* define the mechanics, the adapters for moving data in and out within a data region and the granularity of the data movement process.
- *Event notification policies* notify the registered synchronization policies (and any other registered process for that event) that something—for example, a data atom—has changed state and an action needs to be taken.

The synchronization policy, on the other hand, depends on these policies to perform the mechanics of data movement within and between the data region and external sources. Therefore, the data synchronization policy must deal with the public interface for integration of data regions.

This raises an interesting question as to the definition of a data atom when the boundaries of the data region are crossed. For the situation where the data atom is identical between the two regions, synchronization is straightforward and any update of the data atom within a single region is replicated to the other region. Therefore, part of this public interface is the definition of the data atom that needs to be synchronized. There are two approaches to exactly where the data atom definition resides. In the traditional STP/adapter approach, the data representation inherently was addressed through the data load and data store policies. These policies leverage mechanics of the adapters, which know not only how to get data in and out of a region but also the external data interface for the data atom.

An alternative approach would be to define a public interface or method for data atom definition and have it either rolled into the synchronization policy or consumed not by a policy of data management but rather by a query or data access method for the data grid. The latter suggests that the definition of a data atom (for interregion synchronization) is defined externally to the data management policies of the data grid. It is defined as part of the "Service" the grid or data grid supports. In the case of Web Services, XML is the standard method for defining a data atom. Thus, if the data load and data store policies bind the physical adapter to the data movement process, it is that adapter that "understands" the Web Service definition of the data that are being moved. Therefore, data atom definition for interregion synchronization is the responsibility of not the data region but rather the "Service" that the data grid supports and the responsibility of the adapter to manage the mechanics of data translation as part of the data movement process.

12

DATA AFFINITY

Up to this point, our discussion has centered on data regionalization, data synchronization, and data distribution. All are important and necessary data management features within the data grid. Combined, they provide the tools that enable the data grid, in particular and grid computing in general, to expand beyond simple computational problems to the broader category of the data-intensive applications typically found in private industry and government agencies.

But there is another important feature of a data grid that must be addressed: data affinity. This, in short, addresses the maximum usage of the most precious and costly resource within the grid—the network. Minimizing the movement of data across a network increases the efficiency and pliability of the grid on both processing and cost bases. Data regionalization, data distribution, and data synchronization each provides a necessary component that, when managed in synchronization, achieves the broader objective of data affinity.

There are breakeven points, points where it simply becomes too expensive to move data within a grid in comparison to the cost of performing the operation locally without using a grid. Efficient data management within a grid, or data affinity, can lower the breakeven point for a broader and more complex application set. The more applications the grid can support, the broader the acceptance and the more relevant the technology becomes—a spiraling cycle that feeds on itself, expanding the technology beyond critical mass; in essence, a paradigm shift in computing.

Distributed Data Management for Grid Computing, by Michael Di Stefano
Copyright © 2005 John Wiley & Sons, Inc.

A MEASURABLE QUANTITY

The cost-basis components of grid computing are processing power/capacity (e.g., CPU), disk storage, and network bandwidth. The first two are orders of magnitude more economical than the latter, the network. Network bandwidth is by far the most costly resource. It costs more to move data across a network than it does to store them on disk. For example, it costs more to move data across a network than to spend additional CPU cycles to regenerate the data over and over again.

A paper written by Jim Gray, on distributed computing economics,[23] categorizes some of these costs. Included in the costs of distributed computing are database access and disk storage; our discussions will not take these parameters into consideration. Long-term data storage is a constant, independent of the compute topology used in grid computing or client/server computing. In the situation where the data grid is file-based (e.g., GridFTP, distributed file system, or some other variant), the local node storage is disk, which is inexpensive in comparison to other resources. In the case where the data grid's memory is used for data storage (e.g., RAM), this, too, is fairly inexpensive. Therefore, the result is a drop in the ocean compared with the overall cost of operating an efficient grid architecture. The two variables we will examine are the costs of computation—that is, the associated cost of different grid nodes (e.g., tens, or hundreds, or thousands of computational nodes)—and the cost/efficiency ratio of the nodes in performing calculation-type tasks. The second resource that will drive the cost analysis is network bandwidth, the cost of moving data between the nodes of the grid to perform a task.

A useful metric is the ratio of computational cost versus the cost of data movement on the network. This parameter defines the point where it becomes too costly to perform an operation over a grid because of the required movement of data. A paper written by Hewlett-Packard[24] discusses the dynamics of distributed computing (see equation below). An important part of this is minimizing the overall network traffic by locating the tasks or services closest to each other. A quantitative analysis metric is proposed in the paper is the "partial objective function (POF)." POF is a way to measure the cost of moving data between nodes alongside the computational cost or processing capacity of the nodes

$$f_{POF} = \frac{\beta}{\beta + (\alpha C_T + (1 - \alpha)u_T)}$$

where C_T = sum of traffic costs between the services on a pair of servers weighted by the distance between these servers, u_T = variance of the processing capacity usage among the servers, α = balancing factor between 0 and 1, and β = chosen according to the maximum possible values of C_T and u_T in order to ensure a relatively uniform distributions of the POF values.

Therefore, in order for a data grid to be effective, it must be able to provide metered data, metrics (i.e., POF or something similar), and data management policy controls (both manual and dynamic), and externalize data locality information to

- Allow the scheduling of a task or service to take into account data locality so as to move the execution of tasks to where the data reside in an effort to reduce network traffic.
- Enable the data grid to migrate or redistribute data to nodes where the task is most often performed, based on data movement patterns due to task execution.

What to Expect from Data Affinity

What improvement in performance can be expected by smartly routing task to data locality or by routing data to most probable task locality? Ian Foster conducted a study on just this topic,[25] where the task performance was measured both with and without an efficient data grid that takes into account data locality with task scheduling. The results with every aspect indicate that the performance of the grid increased. Metrics included the average response time per job, the average data transferred per job, the average idle time of processors, and the average response time. In each case, when data locality was factored in, the performance for each metric improved anywhere from one to two orders of magnitude.

HOW TO ACHIEVE DATA AFFINITY

In general there are two ways to achieve data affinity. The first uses the *compute grid*, where information is provided to it by the data grid so that tasks are routed to the data. The second uses the *data grid*, by observing data movement patterns, migrating (caching) data to those nodes where the tasks seem to be the most frequently computed. Individually, each technique will increase the data affinity levels. Optimally, combining the compute grid's routing task to data and the data grid's data migration techniques will yield higher data affinity levels, thus minimizing network traffic and increasing the performance of the grid.

Regionalization, Synchronization, Distribution, and Data Affinity

The objective of data affinity is to have the data and task collocated as closely as possible to eliminate network traffic and to increase performance by reducing latency. This can be achieved in two ways. The first method is proactive, whereby tasks are routed to the data by giving the compute grid's task scheduler the required information on data locality so that it can make smarter task routing decisions with regard to data location on the physical nodes of the compute grid. Keep in mind that this method may not always be 100% successful. This does not always mean that the node selected to perform the task is the best choice, since it may not have the data needed for the task already cached, thus forcing the data grid to move the data to that node.

The data grid manages the second method of data affinity. The following analogy highlights the role of the data grid as both predictive and reactive in nature and contrasts it to the task scheduling function of the compute grid. As the compute grid's task routing function is to the offensive unit of a football team, the data grid's data migration efforts are to the defensive unit of the opposing team. The defense, given all it knows about current situation of the game and history of the opposing team's offensive capability, will predict what the next play will be, and set up the appropriate defensive strategy. However, even before the ball is put into play, the defense has to react to the play as it unfolds. The same philosophy holds true for the data migration efforts of the data grid. The data grid is predictive; thus it anticipates the compute grid's task routing patterns and migrates data to the physical nodes ahead of it. The data grid is also reactive by making real-time adjustments to data migration as the "play unfolds." As the tasks are routed to the physical nodes, the data grid must react by routing the data to nodes where the data do not yet exist. The data grid can accomplish its predictive data migration objectives through the combinations of its data regionalization, data distribution, and data replication policies.

One interesting side note is the effect of the physical size of the data grid on the data migration efforts of the data grid. In the case where the grids are of small physical size, the data grid becomes less effective in its role of achieving data affinity, leaving the compute grid's task routing via data locality as the primary method. As the physical size of the grid increases, the effectiveness of data migration by the data grid increases its contribution to data affinity.

The following functions describe data affinity with regards to physical size of the grid. For grids of small physical size

$$DataAffinity = ComputeGrid(Task\text{-}to\text{-}Data)$$

As the physical size of the grid increases, the data grid's data migration efforts play an ever-increasing roll towards data affinity:

$$DataAffinity = ComputeGrid(Task\text{-}to\text{-}Data) + DataGrid(Data\text{-}Migration)$$

The data grid's management policies work together to achieve data affinity. The outermost container for data affinity is the data region, which is a logical partition of data within the data grid. The data region has a physical boundary within the grid, as discussed earlier. This boundary consists of the specific nodes that are allocated to a data region and contribute their physical resources to that data region. It is possible for any one physical node to be an active part of multiple data regions. If the compute grid is to route tasks to where the data are resident, it must be one of the nodes that physically support the data region and that contains the data necessary for the task to perform its operation. Within a data region's physical boundary, the individual data atoms are replicated. The data replication policy determines the exact replication pattern or the number of required copies. Each data atom, including all replicas, is distributed throughout the data region, based on the data distribution policy of the data region. The data synchronization policy determines how all the data atoms and all the replicas coordinate with each other within the data region.

Synchronization can be tightly bound, where a change in state of one data atom is transitionally reflected in all replicas, or loosely bound, where a change in state of one data atom is reflected in the replicas, but in a nontransactional manner. The data synchronization policy has increasing importance as the data region starts to span the following:

- Areas of varying network bandwidth; should the data region span across a wide-area network (WAN), then the coordination of the replicated data atoms distributed across the data region becomes necessary for data accuracy and performance of the system. These two aspects must be weighed against each other when setting the policies of synchronization and distribution within the data region.
- Nodes of the compute grid support applications or services of different, noncoexistent hardware and/or software configurations (applications that require different operating systems, libraries, or other software configurations that cannot be shared on a single machine). This forces the creation of subregions within a single data region of the data grid. Within each subregion, data affinity must be maintained. This is done through data synchronization between the subregions, and within each subregion separate data replication and distribution policies are also required. An alternative approach is to have separate data regions, each spanning a configuration set and leveraging interregion synchronization to keep the group of data regions cohesive and in a well-known steady state.

Through the combination of data regionalization, data replication policy, data distribution policy, and data synchronization policy, the data grid performs both proactive and reactive data migration methods to contribute to data affinity within the data grid.

Other considerations include *macro events*. From the macro level, the size and shape of a data region can contribute to a slow-moving data grid, and the distribution of data within the region can be equally slow to change. Macro events cause changes in the data region's size, shape, and data distribution. The macro events are usually peak and off-peak service loads that occur at various intervals, including daily, weekly, monthly, and yearly. However, there are external forces to the grid that affect data regions at the micro level that cause smaller changes to the region. Such events are hardware failures, the addition of new hardware to the grid/data region, and variations in service demand. Macro changes are predictable and can be planned for, while micro changes are not predictable and are harder to plan for. Thus, continual adjustments to data regionalization, distribution, replication, and synchronization policies must be made to maintain peak data affinity levels within the data region.

Data Distribution is Key to Data Affinity

Earlier, we discussed what the data grid could do to assist in achieving data affinity. Among the data management policies of synchronization, replication,

and distribution, the latter has the most impact. The data distribution policy determines on which nodes the data atoms will physically reside. Should the data grid
via its data distribution policy estimate correctly the nodes of the grid where tasks
are most often performed, the movement of data across the data grid will be minimized. This area of data management in the data grid is one that will receive a great
deal of attention by computer scientists, mathematicians, and engineers alike going
forward. Similarities can be drawn to the exotic derivatives sectors of the financial
markets. Mathematical models are under constant flux to predict market conditions
and volatility in the markets, and ultimately determine instrument pricing and risk
exposure. In each area, certain assumptions are made. For example, to price an
option, one has the choice of using the Black–Scholes, binomial (Cox–Ross),
Adesi–Whaley, or a host of other models. The Black–Scholes model assumes
that the price of the underlying instrument follows a lognormal distribution. The
binomial model is based on the probability that the price of the underlying
instrument has an equal probability of going up or down. The Adesi–Whaley
model establishes a differential equation between the estimated and actual prices
of the modeled instrument. Today, the area receiving the most attention is the
prediction of market volatility, a key input parameter to all the pricing models
mentioned.

Prediction of how to best distribute data in a data grid has the same characteristics
as pricing an investment in the derivatives market. Assumptions will be made on
many of the variable parameters of data distribution, and quantitative models will
be derived on the basis of these assumptions. For example, one can assume complete
randomness. Any task has an equal probability of being executed on any given node
of the grid at any given time; therefore the data can be randomly distributed across
the data grid. Or one may make the assumption that tasks will center around the
physical "hot spots" in the grid but will dissipate or radiate outward like a bell
curve, and therefore a data distribution bell curve with two, three, or four standard
deviations will be required. An engineer—your author is one—will establish a feedback loop and dynamically adjust the physical location of each data atom, based on
past data movement patterns that have been collected and analyzed. As you can see,
the possibilities are bound only by our minds.

In Part IV of this book, we propose a hypothesis that data distribution patterns
occur at two levels: namely, data atom distribution within a "data body," and a
second distribution pattern of the "data bodies" themselves. A data body is a grouping of a single data type, such as market pricing data or a customer portfolio. Looking at the larger system of a business service or application, data bodies will exhibit
natural forces of attraction toward each other within the space of the data grid. The
data grid will in turn exert a resistive force on the two data bodies. When the resistive force equals the attractive force of the data bodies, an equilibrium distance is
established. The point of equilibrium distance represents the point of minimal
data movement within the data system (all the data bodies of the business service
or application) of the data grid. This suggests a system model where data distribution
describes data bodies in a fashion similar to those found for the most fundamental
laws of nature and physics.

Regardless of the assumptions one makes and the resulting data distribution model, the objectives are the same. How best to predict data usage patterns within a data grid in order to minimize the data movement during the normal operation of a system within a grid? The better the prediction model, the faster an "equilibrium" or "steady state" can be reached for data distribution, thus resulting in the most efficient use of the precious resource of the grid, the network.

Data Affinity and Task Routing

The compute grid's task scheduling function for data is one tool for achieving data affinity. This is done by making the compute grid aware of the data locality so that it can be used as part of its formula for routing a task to a grid node. Armed with the knowledge of what data are required for what task and physically where in the grid those data are localized, the task scheduler can make a smarter decision on where to send the task for execution. The first choice is to eliminate network traffic by routing the task to where the data are already cached. If this is not possible, then a node with the network proximity closest to those where the data reside is selected, which again will minimize network traffic. The number of "hops" that the data must take from the node A where the data reside, to node B where the task is routed, will affect network traffic.

What is the task scheduler of a compute grid? The task scheduler is the logical unit of work in the overall work flow of the compute grid that maintains an active inventory of

- Task—work to be done by the compute grid
- Dependencies required to complete the task; some examples are
    Operating system
    Compiled libraries
    Task/service type dependencies (e.g., Web server, queuing systems)
- Resources capable of executing the task
- Determining which capable resources are available at the point in time when the task is to be executed

According to this inventory, the scheduler matches the best available resource to execute each task and distributes the task to the compute node.

INTEGRATION OF COMPUTE AND DATA GRIDS

The data grid can monitor usage and data movement patterns within regions and adjust the data distribution policy in such a way as to minimize the movement of data within the region. For example, if the compute grid routinely routes tasks to a node where the data are not local, the data grid needs to move the required data to that node. If the data grid notices this pattern occurring often enough, the data distribution policy should be adjusted so that the data reside locally on the node in question in order to limit movement of data. Thus, readjustment of the data distribution policy will increase performance by estimating future data locality needs. However, this becomes more of a reactive approach to solving the problem of data affinity. One way of being proactive is to give the compute grid's scheduling algorithms the additional information about data locality. Armed with this additional information, should the scheduling algorithm have a choice between two nodes to route a task—one node where the data are local and a second node where the data are not local—the smarter decision would be to route the data to the node where data are local. In this way, the compute grid, through its task scheduler with the knowledge of data locality, can increase the level of data affinity by scheduling tasks to data locality.

Recalling the diagrams of a compute grid environment consisting of parallel compute and data grid planes, interaction between the planes is nonexistent and they can run and operate independently of each other (see Figure 12.1).

However, we have just made a case for improved performance and broader application sets that a grid environment can support through data affinity. This will force sharing of information or an interaction between the data grid and the compute grid (see Figure 12.2). The type of information that needs to be shared is data locality from the data grid to the compute grid, which identifies the physical nodes where the data atoms are located.

Even though data affinity is not necessary for operating a grid environment, the overall benefits outweigh the extra effort required to establish a link between the compute and data grids. Currently, there is no standard interface between the compute and data grids, so in the absence of a standard, some of the minimum requirements of such an interface—all of which will require the cooperation of both the data grid and compute grid providers—are listed below:

- The compute grid will require an open interface to the task scheduler to which the data grid can publish.

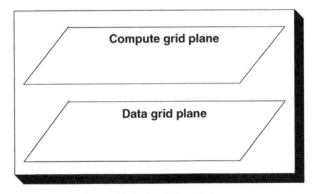

Figure 12.1. Parallel grid planes.

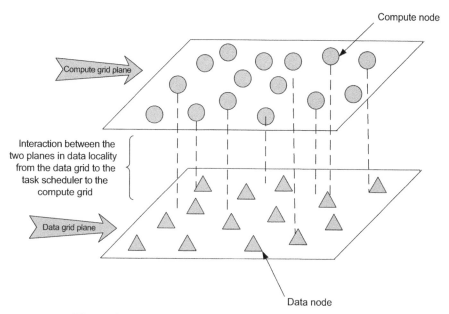

Figure 12.2. Interaction between compute and data grid planes.

- The data grid must provide a pull-based public interface, or a query capability so that the compute grid's task scheduler can query the location of data types, as well as and specific data atoms.
- (*Note*: This is an advanced method at the programmatic level.) At the application/task level integration (a programmatic API used to grid-enable an application), the data grid API can feed the specific data information required by the task via the compute grid public API, where the information is supplied into the compute grid, thus prepopulating the data locality requirements to the task scheduler.

EXAMPLES

Earlier, we discussed the separation of data management from the underlying engine of the data management system. Some implementations of the data grids can be metadata-dictionary-based, distributed-file-based, or distributed-cache-based. Each type of data grid is supported by its own unique engine. The separation of data management from the engine allows for the data management principles of regionalization, synchronization, distribution, and data affinity. The following are some examples of data grids that support data affinity:

- OceanStore: a project run at Berkeley, CA; distributes data (as files) across any number of servers in such a way as to promote data locality, robustness, and fault tolerance. It analyzes usage patterns, network activity, and resource availability to proactively migrate data toward areas of use.

- A common query interface for individual data sources through the use of a shared metadata dictionary.
- Integrasoft's Grid Fabric, a data grid that establishes a federated cache space that spans the entire grid. Supports the distributed data management principles discussed in this book.

Part III

PRACTICAL APPLICATIONS OF GRID COMPUTING

13

WHICH APPLICATIONS ARE GOOD CANDIDATES FOR THE GRID

During my research for a book, presentations to clients, and discussions with colleagues, I discovered that each introduced a new and impressive use case for the practical application of grid computing. The common thread was the increasing importance of robust data management systems tailored for the grid topology. It is my own optimistic opinion that as more people are exposed to the lower cost and high performance of grid computing with a robust data grid, a new class of applications will emerge that will be bound only by our indignation.

What I have discovered is a realistically achievable set of use cases given the current state of grid computing and its supporting technologies. The early applications address longstanding business problems, which are not solvable with the current commercially available technology in some sort of reasonable manner. I have categorized these use cases in the following sections.

GRID ENABLING APPLICATION CHARACTERISTICS

Let us focus on the characteristics of an application and distinguish which of these characteristics make the application a good candidate for a grid environment.

Atomic Tasks

One of the most basic characteristics of applications is atomic task. Is the application's task a repeatable task that can be executed independently of any type of interaction, whether direct or indirect, between other operations or tasks within the same applications. Such atomic tasks can be run independently of each other in a parallel environment of the grid. Applications of this nature were among the first to be moved into a grid environment.

Complex Data Sets

An application whose function is to perform complex analysis over large data sets is a candidate for a grid environment. The analysis process does not need to be atomic, but it does need to operate over large data sets with the goal of identifying patterns of behavior. Some data manipulations functions can include

- Pivoting of the data
- Creating new data views
- Creating various derivative data sets
- Cross sections analysis
- Identifying data intersections points

Data Collection

Many applications are designed for data collection because of the large data requirements by business. There are many flavors of data collection. The most basic examples are in the collection of information from a wide variety of disparate systems within the data center or across data centers. In addition, there is another class of data collections where the data producers are sensors monitoring external conditions (i.e., seismic data). These types of applications are good candidates for the data grid, thus requiring the collection of analysis of large volumes of data in real time.

Operations

From an operational perspective, there is the need to increase the performance, scalability, and reliability of data centers as well as how to manage data centers more efficiently. To operate a data center efficiently is synonymous to knowing the state of the data center at all times. Therefore, there is a requirement to collect *metered data* in order to get an accurate view of what is happening in the data center as it is happening. To operate systems more reliably, the data must be available to a system's redundant backup in real time so that one can achieve "hot standby" versus "warm" or "cold standby." The collection of metered data, small bits and pieces of data from large numbers of dispersed devices across a network, form a large body of information that must be analyzed in its entirety in order to determine the state of the data center. Such data requirements make data centers good candidates for a data grid. The data grid offers efficient mechanisms for the collection of metered data as well as for the real-time analysis of the larger body of data that it forms.

GRIDABLE APPLICATIONS

Highlighted above are a handful of generic applications for a wide range of areas that lend themselves well to a grid infrastructure. The most common class of application now found running on a grid are calculation-intensive types of applications. However, both the economics and businesses force the use of grid computing in commercial industry to go well beyond these classes of applications. They extend into data mining, system administration, and command-and-control types of applications, all leading to a compute utility for the purpose of providing Web Services. I foresee a steady progression of applications, each moving closer to Web Services architecture and demanding higher levels and qualities of service from the data grid. Figure 13.1 highlights the various functional applications and the movement to the compute utility services.

The examples presented throughout this book are far from a complete list of all the applications that will and can use the data grid; in fact, they are just the tip of the iceberg. As more people look at and apply data grid technology and the technology proves its purpose, more and more new use cases will emerge.

Compute-Intensive Applications

Computation-intensive applications are naturally "gridable," for lack of a better term. The calculations in this class of applications are pretty much the same, iterations through a looping procedures where each iterations through the loop varies in its input and output data sets while the work within each loop is a constant. Thus, this inherently allows an application to be split up and run in parallel across a grid. It also allows the building and distribution of the input and output data sets for each iteration through the calculation loop to live across the data grid so that they can be managed without the overhead of data transport or some crude version of localized cache. We find that in most cases, the data inputs and

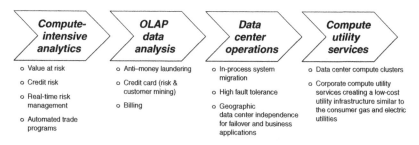

Figure 13.1. Applications of grid computing.

outputs to this applications class are fairly small in size. However, there is also a characteristic of a ballooning of interim data or "data surfaces" during the calculation state en route to achieving the end result(s). This combination of input and output data sets to atomic units of work generating a ballooning of interim data required to achieve a final result renders these applications good candidates for grid computing.

When analytical applications of this nature are integrated into the data grid, other applications can leverage or reuse both the intra– and inter–data sets. These interim services offer the potential of being reused, such as in the case of a Monte Carlo simulation. The ability to offer the reuse of these interim data surfaces from one simulation to another or from one application to another improves the performance of these computation-intensive calculations, thus resulting in more efficient compute resources. Having these interim data surfaces persist in a data grid can eliminate the need to continually rebuild them, which in itself is a timesaver and a performance to a boost of the simulation for the business users. Now, applications that normally run overnight and where the outcome is not known until the end of the process is completed can be viewed as the data are being processed to determine whether the model is performing as expected.

OLAP Data Analysis

The OLAP data analytical processing of large and complex data sets is a major category for the data grids. The ability to look and pivot large data sets that have intersections in various dimensions is an application that lends itself well to the data grid. However, not all implementations of a data grid fit this class of application. The closer one brings data to the in-memory computational resource of a grid node, the more efficient the OLAP process becomes. Thus, in-memory-based data grid implementations will yield higher efficiencies than will disk-based data grids. The ability to bring in large amounts of data and distribute the data across the data grid in order to perform the analysis directly against the data grid (as opposed to the manipulation of data on physical disks) will yield faster performance and permit more complex data analysis. This type of architecture offers new classes of datamarts, where the marriage or intersection of a traditional data warehousing with data grids allows for faster and more complex data analysis.

Data Center Operations

Adding additional capabilities for data center operation is a category in which data grids can improve issues normally faced by an operational staff and the required support of running these applications. Offering the use of the data grid in the operational environment will increase the level of system availability offered by a data center from today's "high availability" (HA) and bring it closer to a fault tolerance level of reliability. In this example, the data grid technology will directly maintain the application's state, thus enabling nearly instantaneous failover to the backup systems. There is a second operation area in which data grids can offer improvement for the migration of applications and testing of new versions of software across environments. For example, opening a read-only window to production data for the QA environment allows for real production testing. This enables QA tests to run not in a simulation environment but against the real production environment data set. This enhances the quality of QA testing, thus reducing production risk. Static data testing and simulation requirements will be reduced or eliminated depending on the environment. The result is a production release thoroughly tested against production data, thus eliminating the usual production issues that arise with any new release. The outcome is a greatly enhanced product quality released out of QA into production.

Compute Utility Service

The ultimate outcome of this new technology is the compute utility. The evolution to the compute utility where data grids are an integral component will begin in one of two ways: (1) an intentional outcome in the form of companies exploring enterprise-wide adoption of grid computing or (2) unintentionally as more and more business units begin to migrate their applications over to a grid environment. Companies will begin to see that data centers composed of inexpensive networked machines are capable of supporting multiple business applications and effectively scale as the business need demands more compute power. The type of data center operation that would be required to support the compute utility services does not exist today; one key missing component is the area of command and control. In the situation where the management and operations of large grids are required, it will become necessary to generate, record, and make decisions on information that we do not require in the data center today. This information is metered data at the various levels. The required metered data for the compute utility infrastructure starts from the physical systems, to the policy layer, to the service layer, and ends at the application layer of the utility. All the layers of the utility must interact and coordinate within and between each other, forming what is similar to a foodchain, a command-and-control or feedback control loop. These foodchains are the small bits of data from large numbers of machines creating large data sets to be traversed and analyzed in real time, thus requiring the high performance of the data grid.

USE CASE PRESENTATIONS

The use cases presented in this section will tie in the data management concepts addressed in earlier sections. Each will address a practical application of grid computing with specific focus on data management as the overall theme for the solution. The "data grid analysis" will consist of the following:

- Application definition equation for a distributed environment:

$$Application(Work(\ ), Data(\ ), Time(\ ), Geography(\ ), Query(\ ))$$

where the following are the driven parameters of the functions:

Work(batch/atomic, synchronous/nonsynchronous)

Data(overallsize, atomicsize, transactional, transient, queryable)

Time(Real-Time, Not Real-Time, Near Real-Time)

Geography(Topology, NetworkBandwidth)

Query(basic, complex)

This application is a function of *Work( )*, *Data( )*, *Time( )*, *Geography( )* as well as *Query( )*.

- The various data management policies can be defined as illustrated in the following equations:

$$
DataDistributionPolicy = DDP \begin{pmatrix} PolicyName, \\ Region, \\ Scope(\ ), \\ Pattern(\ ) \end{pmatrix}
$$

$$
DataReplicationPolicy = DRP \begin{pmatrix} PolicyName, \\ Region, \\ Quantity, \\ Scope(\ ) \end{pmatrix}
$$

$$
SynchronizationPolicy = SP \begin{pmatrix} PolicyName, \\ Region, \\ Scope(\ ), \\ Transactionality(\ ), \\ LoadStore(\ ), \\ Events(\ ) \end{pmatrix}
$$

$$
DataLoadPolicy = DLP \begin{pmatrix} PolicyName, \\ Region, \\ Granularity(\ ), \\ Adapter(\ ) \end{pmatrix}
$$

$$
DataStorePolicy = DSP \begin{pmatrix} PolicyName, \\ Region, \\ Granularity(\ ), \\ Operation(\ ), \\ Adapter(\ ) \end{pmatrix}
$$

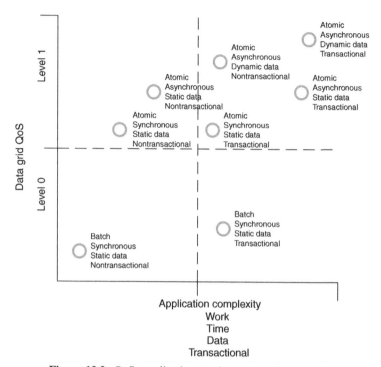

Figure 13.2. QoS–application requirement quadrant graph.

$$EventNotificationPolicy = ENP\begin{pmatrix} PolicyName, \\ Region(\ ), \\ Scope(\ ), \\ Operation(\ ) \end{pmatrix}$$

• The graph in Figure 13.2 shows how the quality of service (QoS) changes in association with the application requirements.

Note that level 0 QoS in Figure 13.2 is associated with batch type of static data for both transactional as well as nontransactional applications. Level 1 QoS deals with most of the other types of applications.

14

CALCULATION-INTENSIVE APPLICATIONS

DESCRIPTION

As I identified in an earlier chapter, many applications naturally lend themselves to the grid architecture. These applications are classified as being very computation-intensive and where the computational paths are data-dependent, they therefore can be run in parallel across many of the compute grid's nodes. The ability to run pieces of the computational process in parallel is where the first class of use case for grid computing comes into play. The use cases are responsible for defining the compute grid and the early stages of the data grid.

Today, many areas of research that use the grid technology, including

- Various engineering disciplines using computer-aided design[26]
- Genome research[27]
- Physics research: high-energy physics[28] and fusion research[29]
- Earthquake research[30]

The data sets for these applications are, for the most part, static in nature. For example, DNA sequences, seismic data, and collision patterns of high-energy beams in a particle beam accelerator, do not change once the data are recorded. In the commercial industry, an area of interest is risk management. There is one distinct difference between the risk management analysis and the abovementioned applications, which is that the data are far from static and tend to be dynamic.

Distributed Data Management for Grid Computing, by Michael Di Stefano
Copyright © 2005 John Wiley & Sons, Inc.

The data continually change on a real-time basis (at varying time intervals: seconds, minutes) to more batch-type updates, which can be daily, monthly, quarterly, and so on.

Regardless of whether the application processes static and/or dynamic data, there is one commonality in all these applications: that all these application produce interim state data sets, during the analysis process where large temporary data sets are generated, used, and ultimately deleted. We can see that performance optimizations can be gained by smart data management of these interim data sets, independent of and in addition to any programmatic and procedural optimizations.

USE CASES

Calculation-intensive applications tend to naturally process the same algorithm repeatedly at varying iterations where only the input data set differs between all the iterations used to perform calculations. A large set of financial service applications fit this paradigm, including Monte Carlo simulations, binomial approximations, and Black–Scholes models, for example. Thus, parallel processing (parallelizable) can be easily achieved for these types of applications.

What does it mean for an application to be parallelizable? An example would be an identical unit of work that is typically run inside a processing loop and given a different data set to operate over for each iteration of the loop wherein each pass through the loop is independent of the ones that came before it; such a unit of work can be parallelized. Figure 14.1 illustrates how such applications can be parallelized through worklets running at the same time independently of each other in a grid compute environment.

We will start out be identifying each unit of work as a "worklet." Worklets can be assigned to execute on different machines in the compute grid depending on capacity levels. Applications that consist of these worklets are parallelized applications.

Worklets executed in parallel in the compute grid take advantage of the inherent nature of the compute grid, where a large numbers of machines are available to execute computational tasks. Worklets, via the compute grid, are assigned to the numerous compute nodes of the grid to be run in parallel, transforming a serial process into a parallel one and therefore reducing the overall time of execution and leveraging ideal resources. This feature is becoming increasingly essential in today's business. The window of operations continues to decrease, therefore mandating more and more near-real-time results as soon as the data are available and with the lowest latency possible.

In the early 1990s, universities and other areas of research found themselves with large complex computational analysis problems to solve without a supercomputer on which to run these computations. Necessity is the mother of invention; then came grid compute, since the objective was to make the most of what was available. All systems, including networked computers in labs, student unions, libraries, and classrooms, were utilized to perform such tasks. The hardware resources that were used in such research environments can be classified as represented in the

```
for (int i = 0; i < m_timeStep-1; i++)
{
```

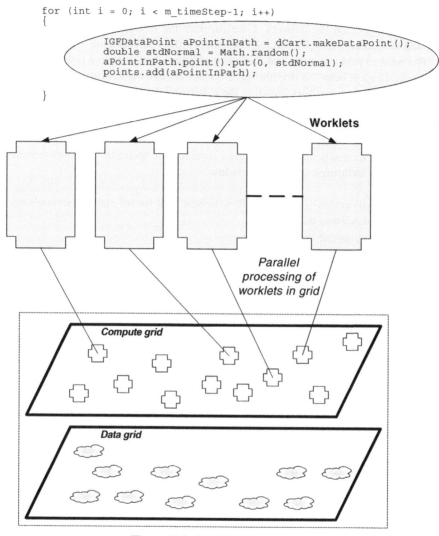

```
        IGFDataPoint aPointInPath = dCart.makeDataPoint();
        double stdNormal = Math.random();
        aPointInPath.point().put(0, stdNormal);
        points.add(aPointInPath);
```

```
}
```

Figure 14.1. Parallelizable processes.

following formula:

$$TotalComputationalResource$$

$$\cong \sum_{1}^{computers-on-campus} NetworkedComputerComputationalResource$$

The total hardware resources were a function of all the available resources in the whole facility. With this, they were able to divide the overall problem into atomic work units or worklets and parallelize the workload across all the available and capable machines on the network. Glue together the results into a cohesive data set, and the effect is a high-powered computer or the compute grid.

The need to perform more and more complicated, data-intensive tasks and limited resources has been the driving force behind the evolution of grid technology. Very similar forces are also found in the commercial enterprise and are causing widespread interest in further developing grid computing. The first commercial grid applications are similar in nature to those that gave birth to grid computing, where intensive analytical applications needed to perform with greater speed and the number of data sets that they required continued to increase. The applications spanned many industries, as indicated below:

- *Energy exploration*—where and how to best drill for oil and gas through the analysis of seismic data
- *Biopharmaceutical*
    Protein folding
    Clinical trials—drug interactions with the human body through simulation
- *Government*—various types of government applications for the analysis of large data sets and pattern detection
- *Financial services*—quantitative analysis to accelerate risk reporting
- *Computer-aided design*—aerospace, chip design, and other applications

The common thread connecting these diverse industries is that the business applications require complex data analysis over increasingly larger data sets. The analytical process that traverses and mines these data sets can require execution times spanning days. Time is our most precious and irreplaceable commodity, so any reasonable effort to maximize its utilization is well spent. Shortening the analysis times yields more available time and resources to perform increasingly complex analysis. Grid technology offers a reasonable solution to not only maximum utilization of time but also to provide a powerful, flexible, fungible, and cost-effective computing environment.

GENERAL ARCHITECTURE

The general architecture for this class of applications in the compute grid has focused on the management of computer resources and task distribution, which is the compute grid, and less on data management or the data grid. Historically, grid vendors have been perfecting and commercializing the core of the compute grid technology. The compute grid is used to manage compute resources—which machines are currently available and of these, which are capable of executing the worklet; the management of task assignment, data assignment, and retrieval for each worklet; and finally the assembly of the individual worklet's result data set into the larger application result data set format. The final job of the compute grid is to perform data packaging from each worklet since each has been assignment to a different compute node. Figure 14.2 illustrates this data assembling processes and final storage of the data to some data store, such as a database or a file on disk.

In the workflow shown in Figure 14.2, the compute grid manages data retrieval and distribution along with the worklets across the compute grid. This is a six-step process starting with data retrieval required by each compute node; this main process retrieves the necessary data from the various external data sources either before or during the worklet creation/assignment process of the compute grid. The compute grid management process then packages the input data necessary for the worklet to perform its task and ships it along with the worklet to the respective compute node to perform the task. However, before shipping the data–worklet combination, the data must be packaged. Part of this packaging is data marshaling. Once the compute node receives the worklet, it must unpackage the input data before it can start to process the tasks as defined in the worklet. The unpackaging process involves reversing the data marshaling process to enable the compute node to read the data in a format that it understands and can operate on. Once the task is complete, the resulting data sets must be packaged (and marshaled) before being sent

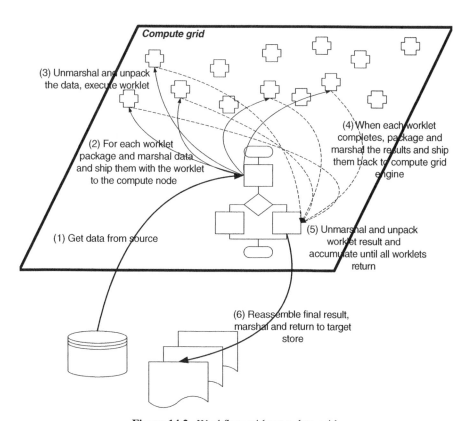

Figure 14.2. Workflow without a data grid.

back to the compute grid management process. The compute grid management process receives the resulting data sets from all the worklets that it dispatched, unpackages each one (again, part of the unpacking process consists in unmarshaling the data), and assembles them back together to form one cohesive data result set for final storage in some sort of persistence.

As can be seen, this process of packing, marshaling, sending, receiving, unmarshaling, and the unpackaging of data must happen twice, once for the input data to the worklets and once for the resulting data set of the worklets. This process must occur for each worklet followed by a data assembly process so that the worklet results can be understood at the application level. The more worklets that the compute grid dispatches, the better the parallelization of the overall process will be, but this, too, has a price. The efficiency gained by parallelizing the work is counterbalanced, either in part or in whole, by the overly complex data packaging/marshaling work.

Some level 0 data grids mitigate this performance consequence by creating a distributed file system across the compute nodes of the compute grid or via GridFTP. Each transfers the responsibility of data packaging and transport from the compute grid to the level 0 data grid; however, there may still be data marshaling involved by either the data grid or the worklets–application combination. However, these solutions do not address performance enhancement techniques such as data affinity.

The current commercially available grid solutions are tailored to these calculation-intensive applications with the static data sets. However, as corporate America adopts grid technology and begins to leverage it throughout the organization to encompass tasks beyond those of static data sets, compute grid solutions will need to be augmented with a data grid that also manages dynamic data, a level 1 data grid.

Unless running overnight batch processes, the majority of business applications is dynamic in nature and requires level 1 data grids. Some of the examples listed earlier for risk management, in either financial services or government security, are characteristically real-time and dynamic data sets. Figure 14.3 illustrates the integration of the data grid into the compute grid architecture, where many worklets perform their defined tasks in parallel.

Level 1 data grids inherently lend themselves to the transient data sets produced by calculation-intensive processes such as a Monte Carlo simulation. These processes generate and leverage vast amounts of interim data that are used throughout the running simulation to produce an end result but are not part of the end result itself. A comparison of the quantity of data input and output from a Monte Carlo simulation to that of the interim data generated by the running simulation is analogous to an iceberg, with the input and output data representing the tip of the iceberg and the interim data as the majority of the iceberg that you do not see.

In the specific case of a Monte Carlo simulation used in the financial markets, the interim data sets can be, but not limited to, random-number surfaces and yield curves. Worklets produce and consume these interim data on a regular basis. Some produce the random-number surfaces; others produce the yield curves, while others will use parts of each to produce other interim data surfaces, all leading to the final resulting data surface. In a later chapter an example of the code for part of

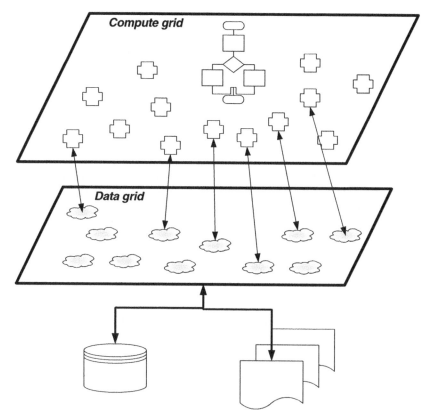

Figure 14.3. Workflow with the data grid: level 1 data grid.

a Monte Carlo simulation is provided using a level 1 data grid. One of the main objectives in creating and maintaining a Monte Carlo simulation is performance tuning. There are various methods of increasing the performance of a simulation. Here I will introduce performance enhancement techniques that a level 1 data grid offers above and beyond that gained by traditional computational performance enhancement techniques.

Data enhancement techniques take two forms: data reuse and data affinity. For some simulations, many of the interim data surfaces can be reused from one simulation to another. Keeping these surfaces active in a data grid eliminates the need to continually regenerate them from one simulation run to another. While a level 0 data grid can address data reuse, it may not yield any performance benefits as it may be faster to regenerate on a local node than to query, locate, transport, package, and marshal the data out of the data grid and to the compute node where they are needed. A level 1 data grid inherently addresses many of the data accessibility issues inherent into a level 0 data grid, thus minimizing much of the work and performance bottlenecks to such an extent that it would be cheaper to reuse interim data surfaces than to regenerate them from one simulation to another.

Data affinity is addressed by level 1 data grids. *Data affinity* is the ability to group interim data sets to the compute nodes that most often generates and uses them, thus further reducing data movement. With this strategy, data are locally resident on the compute node, eliminating the entire data packaging–movement process overhead. Between data reuse and data affinity in the data grid, the overall processing time of a Monte Carlo simulation can be dramatically reduced by as much as half.

DATA GRID ANALYSIS

In order to analyze calculation-intensive application with the data grid, I will leverage the Monte Carlo simulation as a model. The first step is to start with the application definition expressions as presented in an earlier chapter.

The application definition equation for a distributed environment is

$$Application(Work(\ ), Data(\ ), Time(\ ), Geography(\ ), Query(\ ))$$

where

$Work(batch/atomic, synchronous/nonsynchronous)$

$Data(overallsize, atomicsize, transactional, transient, queryable)$

$Time(Real\text{-}Time, NotReal\text{-}Time, NearReal\text{-}Time)$

$Geography(Topology, NetworkBandwidth)$

$Query(basic, complex)$

The "interim" data surfaces of a Monte Carlo simulation can be prebuilt and subsequently used to produce the final result surface (the output result set of the simulation). However, some of the interim result surfaces may be dependent on other interim surfaces being partially or completely built. For the purposes of this discussion, we will consider the building of an interim data surface as a "batch" process even though in reality it is a completely parallelized grid process. There exists an interdependency of interim result surfaces that prevents all interim result surfaces from being simultaneously generated independently of each other. Figure 14.4 represents an example of such interim dependency.

Therefore, when there is an interdependency of two surfaces as illustrated in Figure 14.4 for A and B, where B is contingent on A being in place before the building of B can start, then coordination of the two processes is necessary. Further complexities will exist when only parts of a surface are dependent on parts of another surface. For instance, to continue with our example illustrated in Figure 14.4, not all of surface A must be completely built before construction of surface B can start. Therefore, this will result in creation of a partial dependency between the two surfaces. In both instances there exists an element of synchronization of processing with regard to start building interim surface B only when "$X\%$" of surface A is complete, where the internal processing of both A and B are completely atomic and

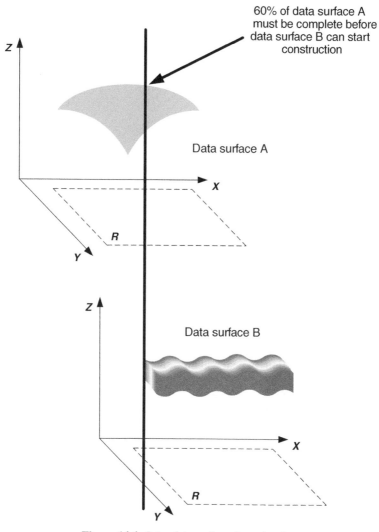

Figure 14.4. Inter data surface dependencies.

nonsynchronous. In this case $X\%$ represents some variable of completeness. From the Monte Carlo expressions in the earlier chapter, the Monte Carlo simulation was represented as

$$MonteCarloSimulation \begin{pmatrix} Work(W\_T1(\,),W\_group1(W\_T2(\,),W\_T3(\,))\ldots,W\_Tn(\,)), \\ Data\_input(\,),Data\_output(\,),Data\_S1(\,),\ldots Data\_Sk(\,), \\ Time(\,), \\ Geography(\,), \\ Query(\,) \end{pmatrix}$$

where

> *"W_Tx" represents a task that has no dependencies on another task;*
> *"W_group" represents a grouping or tasks where interdependency exists,*
> *thus an element of synchronicity.*
> *W_T1(atomic, nonsynchronous)*
> *W_T2(atomic, nonsynchronous)*
> *W_T3(atomic, nonsynchronous)*
> *W_Tn(atomic, nonsynchronous)*
> *W_group1(batch, synchronous)*

The input and output data surfaces are small in comparison to the interim data surfaces that will be necessary to derive the final output data surface.

> *Data_input(1kbits, 100bits, nontransactional, transient, nonqueryable)*
> *Data_output(1kbits, 100bits, transactional, transient, nonqueryable)*
> *Data_S1(3Gbits, 100bits, nontransactional, transient, queryable)*
> *Data_Sn(3Gbits, 100bits, nontransactional, nontransient, queryable)*

The ability to run simulations in near real time enables business decisions to be made with accurate and timely data. This simulation is to run in the confines of a single data center and the applications requirement to analyze (complex queries) any of the data sets is not essential to the business.

> *Time(Near-Real-Time)*
> *Geography(DataCenter, 1GbitEthernet)*
> *Query(basic)*

The data management policies that need to be imposed are represented as

$$DataDistributionPolicy = DDP \begin{pmatrix} MonteCarlo\_DDP, \\ MCRegion, \\ Scope(ALL), \\ \\ Pattern \begin{pmatrix} Automatic, Random \begin{pmatrix} MCDDPPattern, \\ WhiteNoise(), \\ NULL, \\ NULL, \\ NULL, \\ NULL \end{pmatrix} \end{pmatrix} \end{pmatrix}$$

$$DataReplicationPolicy = DRP \begin{pmatrix} MonteCarlo\_DRP, \\ MCRegion, \\ 7, \\ Scope(ALL) \end{pmatrix}$$

$$SynchronizationPolicy = SP \begin{pmatrix} MonteCarlo\_SP, \\ MCRegion, \\ Scope(Boundary(``intra"), NULL), \\ Transactionality(``nontransactional"), \\ LoadStore(List(``MarketFeed\_DLP"), NULL), \\ Events(NULL) \end{pmatrix}$$

Use if Events to coordinate interdependencies between data surfaces

$$EventNotificationPolicy = ENP \begin{pmatrix} W\_Group\_SurfaceCoordination, \\ MCRegion, \\ Scope(List(W\_Group\_Atoms)), \\ StartDependentSurfaceBuilds(\ ) \end{pmatrix}$$

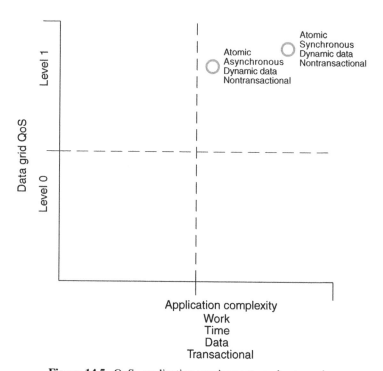

Figure 14.5. QoS–application requirement quadrant graph.

$$DataLoadPolicy = DLP \begin{pmatrix} MarketFeed\_DLP, \\ MCRegion, \\ Granularity(Grouping(1),\ Frequency(50)), \\ MarketDataAdapter(\ ) \end{pmatrix}$$

$$DataStorePolicy = N/A$$

The graph in Figure 14.5 shows nontransactional application characteristics; however, some, but not all, of the application's data surfaces are dependent on each other, thus creating a dual characteristic of nontransactional for data surfaces with no dependencies and transactional where the data surfaces are interdependent.

15

DATA MINING AND DATA WAREHOUSES

DESCRIPTION

Analysis of large data sets comes at a cost. The cost:benefit ratio is the level of complexity of the analysis versus the compute infrastructure (hardware, software, network, etc.) required to support the analysis. As the complexity of the analysis increases, more extensive infrastructure is required. I will present data warehousing as a use case study to emphasize that the business is not realizing the full potential of the data in the data warehouse. This is due to many reasons, including the physical limitations imposed on the warehouse's ability to perform queries and/or analysis. Examples are in the areas of fraud detection and customer pattern analysis.

There are many ways to construct a data warehouse and methods in which to perform analysis. One method is to query and extract data out of the warehouse and perform the analysis on a system external to the data warehouse. Traditional methods for increasing performance may require the thin distribution of data across increasing numbers of disks or require custom hardware and software combinations that are proprietary to the data warehouse vendor. These alternatives contribute to the increase in both the cost and risk.

The data grid architecture offers an alternative to traditional data mining and warehousing infrastructures. Not all data grid implementations lend themselves to this use case, only those that meet specific criteria, the details of which will be discussed in the following sections.

Distributed Data Management for Grid Computing, by Michael Di Stefano
Copyright © 2005 John Wiley & Sons, Inc.

USE CASES

The topic of data warehousing is rich in research, products, tools, and methodologies. The purpose of this section is not to include all aspects of the topic but to foster a new perspective on the subject that will evolve into new data warehousing techniques so as to increase value with both lower cost of ownership and risk reduction.

At the highest level of the block diagram, a data warehouse is a collection of servers and disks. Data are distributed across multiple disks for storage capacity and can be arranged in specific patterns to increase speed of access. Via the data warehousing servers, a client application can query, perform some level of analysis, and receive the results. Figure 15.1 highlights this high-level process.

The following discussions will focus on business applications querying the data warehouse and performing further analysis on the data. The purpose of data grids in a data warehousing solution is not to replace the data warehouse but to augment it in such a way that will increase the query and analytical performance of the overall process. Therefore, I will not address EAI- and EII-related issues of how the data warehouse is initially populated and updated from the raw datastreams throughout an enterprise.

For this discussion, the workflow model is simple. We will have two branches of processing for this example, with one branch making some level of analysis performed within the data warehouse and the other branch with minimal to no analysis performed in the data warehouse. This processing difference defines the following two use cases:

Use Case 1. Business logic/analytics are performed in the data warehouse.

Use Case 2. Business logic/analytics are performed outside the data warehouse.

These two cases are illustrated in the flow diagram in Figure 15.2.

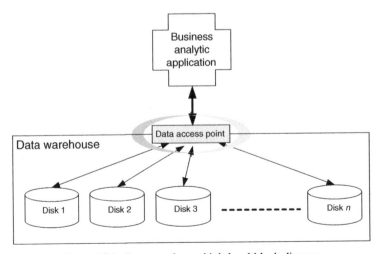

Figure 15.1. Data warehouse high-level block diagram.

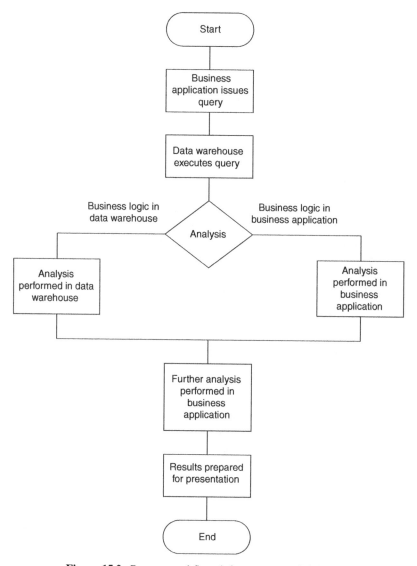

Figure 15.2. Process workflow defines use case definitions.

The type of implementation of the data grid will determine its viability to augment a data warehouse. Data grids that support the following features are candidates, for example

- Bringing the data close, in a networked proximity, to the compute nodes where the business application is running
- Offer full data grid management support
- Data query capability

Certainly level 0 data grids do not meet these criteria and thus will not apply. Some types of level 1 data grids will not apply, either.

An example of a level 1 data grid that will dovetail with a data warehouse is one whose implementation is an "in-memory model" that spans a compute cluster or the compute grid. The benefits of such data grids are performance since the data are kept close to the processing and must offer a distributed memory space that increases capacity as the number of machines in the grid increases.

The economic and logistical concern of staging large volumes of data in a data grid are not daunting hurdles to jump. Both concerns center on the number of machines or nodes required in the data grid to hold large volumes of data. The physical size of the data grid or the number of nodes in the compute grid is dependent on the memory capacity of a single machine of a node and the total data size extracted and analyzed from the data warehouse. Since one of the economic driving forces behind grid computing is to reuse the large numbers of inexpensive machines, the cost of large grid infrastructure is comparatively low in comparison to the large servers that they will be replacing.

The logistical concerns are addressed via new generations of provisioning and management software that automates much of the system administration processes. Therefore a data grid infrastructure is an economical means to dramatically increase the performance and analytical complexity of large data sets.

GENERAL ARCHITECTURE

In both use cases the general architecture is the same. The data grid sits in between the business application and the data warehouse. The business logic operates directly against the data grid. Independent of the use case, the architecture and business application's workflow is the same; the only change is to the capacity (therefore the size) of the data grid. As data capacity requirements increase, the size of the data grid must also increase. The new architecture with the data grid is illustrated in Figure 15.3.

The data grid spans the compute space of the business application, thus bringing the entire scope of the data warehouse (depending on the use case) directly into one continually addressable and ready-to-access data space. The advantages for time to process are realized in the ability to pivot data in complex structures and hierarchies in near-in-memory speed, without having to swap data in and out of a local memory space and files system/database, and independent loading of data from any one or multiple data sources.

In this context, the term "data warehouse" refers to the traditional data warehousing infrastructure in place in most organizations today.

First Use Case

In this use case, the data need to be loaded into the data grid. Most if not all of the data of the data warehouse are reflected in the data grid. Thus, any query and

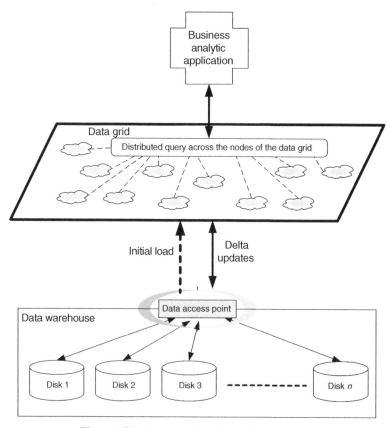

Figure 15.3. Data warehousing with a data grid.

subsequent analysis of the data are run directly against the data grid, not the data warehouse. This implies a one-time data load with periodic data synchronization between the data warehouse and the data grid. Any data integration from external sources into the data warehouse can remain as is (into the data warehouse) or loaded in parallel to both the data warehouse and the data grid. For our discussion, we will assume the former. The EII data load into the data warehouse and subsequent synchronization process into the data grid is independent of and transparent to the business applications. The result is two copies of the data warehouse, one in the data grid for analytics operation and the other in the data warehouse for long-term persistent storage.

As discussed earlier, the class and implementation of the data grid for this use case yield benefits to the business from a cost perspective, reduced processing time, and increased OLAP complexity. Specific potential areas of benefit are increased query speed, savings on analysis processing time, increase the number of business analytics that can be run, and increase the next level of complexity of the analytics that could otherwise not be achieved. However, as with all things, there are tradeoffs. This architecture will expose the risk of large data loss within the data grid. Should enough of the data grid "go down," full or partial data loads could occur, therefore requiring the need to perform data upload from the data warehouse. On such a failure, the required time to reload and recover the system is dependent on the amount of data to be reloaded, the network bandwidth between the data warehouse and the data grid, as well as the network bandwidth within the data grid itself.

The architecture of the data warehouse and data grid transfers the responsibility for direct data access and querying from the data warehouse to the data grid. Therefore, this minimizes the requirements for the expensive data warehousing infrastructure and augments it with a lower cost, faster, and more powerful data grid infrastructure. The cost–benefit difference lies in the data grid's ability to support large quantities of data with an infrastructure that is inexpensive to grow and maintain.

Second Use Case

Whereas the first use case is a dual data repository of data warehouse and data grid, this use case is more of a hybrid approach. The initial queries are run against the data warehouse, returning a small subset of data (as compared to the total size of the data warehouse), which is then loaded into the data grid. Once these data are loaded in the data grid, the same benefits of the data grid are realized in the first use case. These benefits include savings on processing time, increase in the number of business analytics that can be run, and increase in the complexity of analytics. On the other hand, the disadvantages of this approach are the increase in the overall time to perform the business application since the data warehouse is involved in the initial query and load of the data into the data grid as business requests occur. However, the downsides are minimized; a catastrophic failure of the data grid will not require a costly reload of the entire data warehouse. Also implied is the size of the data grid infrastructure required to support the OLAP process since an increase in data capacity implies an increase in the number of nodes of the data grid. In summary, the first use case implies a large data grid infrastructure just to support the data warehouse as compared to the second use case, where only a subset of the data warehouse must be stored in the data grid.

The data load process of this use case can be managed in a number of ways: (1) by the business application/data warehouse, (2) by the data grid/data warehouse, and (3) using a method similar to that used in the first use case. If multiple business applications require similar data sets, then keeping those data continually loaded and synchronized with the data warehouse makes sense. If data loss occurs in the data grid, the data load and recovery time is not as catastrophic since it is a subset of data that is required from the data warehouse.

The shifting of fast data access and querying for the data warehouse to the data grid are not as dramatic as in the first use case, but are present nonetheless. In addition, other architectural, processing, and financial benefits are realized from the business application perspective. If the analytic process runs outside the data warehouse and in the memory/processing space of the business analytic, then the data extracted from the data warehouse must be stored somewhere else. When using traditional methods (non-data-grid), there are only a few alternatives; try to fit the data set into the RAM (random access memory) of the user's machine or put the data into a file on the user's machine. Depending on the size of the data, they may not fit in the available RAM, thus eliminating this option in many cases. File sizes also have their limitations. Data may have to be split across multiple files and be swapped in and out of RAM as the business analytics requires. This adds an upper bound to the amount of data that can be extracted. In addition, engineering will need to be involved for managing and splitting the data across multiple files.

The use of a data grid eliminates the need for engineering efforts around large data sets. The data that are extracted out of the data warehouse would easily fit within the data grid, circumventing the need for the application to perform the extra file loading, splitting, and swapping. As a result, the analytics in turn would simply run faster and be available for other nodes and applications if required.

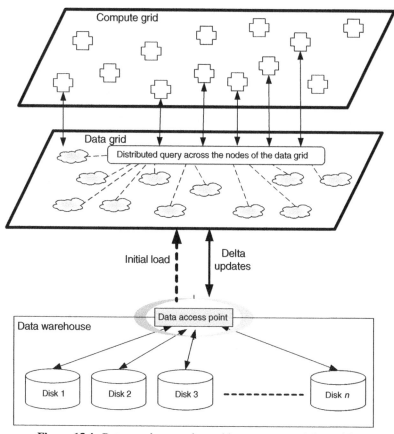

Figure 15.4. Data warehouse enhanced by commute and data grids.

Enter the Compute Grid

Up to this point we have discussed how the data grid can benefit an analytic application. The performance of the business application can be enhanced even further by running the OLAP process in a compute grid. The benefits gained will depend on how well the OLAP process of the business application can be parallelized across a compute grid (recall the discussions in Chapter 14, on calculation-intensive applications). In these instances the benefits are manyfolds: (1) the benefits of the data grid–data warehouse combination as described above, (2) the ability to split a serial process into worklets running in parallel across the compute grid, and (3) the turboboost (if you will) of adding data affinity to the mixture. Figure 15.4 illustrates the new architecture that evolves with the compute grid and the data grid for the data warehousing solution.

DATA GRID ANALYSIS

For the data grid analysis of data mining and data warehouses, I will use the application definition expressions as introduced in Chapter 5. For both use cases discussed above, the general architecture is very similar; thus the general equations will also be similar. However, within each use case there are numerous variations on implementation that are dependent on the specific environment in which the use case is to be deployed. These differences in environment and implementation will appear in subareas of the application definition expressions and in the data management policies. Therefore, the expressions shown below are a template; it is left to the reader as an exercise to architect in each case given the variations in definition and policy expressions:

- The application definition equation for a distributed environment is

$$
OLAPProcess \begin{pmatrix} Work(\ ), \\ Data\_output(\ ), Data\_S1(\ ), \dots Data\_Sn(\ ), \\ Time(\ ), \\ Geography(\ ), \\ Query(\ ) \end{pmatrix}
$$

where

$$Work(atomic, nonsynchronous)$$

The output data surfaces are small in comparison to the data surfaces that will be analyzed from the data warehouse.

$Data\_output("x" kbits, "y" bits, transactional, nontransient, queryable)$

$Data\_S1("z" Tbits, "k" Mbits, nontransactional, transient, queryable)$

$Data\_Sn("z" Tbits, "k" Mbits, nontransactional, transient, queryable)$

The ability to run complex analysis over large data sets in short periods of time provides the business with a better view into the prevailing economic forces and consumer demands of the current environment. Armed with better and in-depth quality views of the "bigger picture," the business can target specific consumer groups and manage manufacturing and supply chain in finer detail otherwise not possible. This OLAP process is to run in the confines of a single data center and the applications requirement to analyze (complex queries) of any of the data sets is not essential to the business.

$$Time(NearReal\text{-}Time)$$
$$Geography(DataCenter, 1GbitEthernet)$$
$$Query(complex)$$

- Data management policies are expressed as

$$DataDistributionPolicy = DDP \begin{pmatrix} DataWarehouse\_DDP, \\ DWRegion, \\ Scope(ALL), \\ Pattern \begin{pmatrix} Automatic, Random \begin{pmatrix} DWDDPPattern, \\ WhiteNoise(\ ), \\ NULL, \\ NULL, \\ NULL, \\ NULL \end{pmatrix} \end{pmatrix} \end{pmatrix}$$

The data replication policy shows a lower number of replicas per data atom since the overall size of the data in the data grid is quite large. Each replica increases the overall storage capacity requirements of the data grid by the size of the data loaded from the data warehouse. The downside to a lower replication size per data atom is resilience of the data in case of failure. These tradeoffs must be considered in each use case and architecture variation.

$$DataReplicationPolicy = DRP \begin{pmatrix} DataWarehouse\_DRP, \\ DWRegion, \\ 3, \\ Scope(ALL) \end{pmatrix}$$

$$SynchronizationPolicy = SP \begin{pmatrix} DataWarehouse\_SP, \\ DWRegion, \\ Scope(Boundary("intra"), NULL), \\ Transactionality("nontransactional"), \\ LoadStore(List("DataWarehouse\_DLP"), NULL), \\ Events(NULL) \end{pmatrix}$$

Below are three scenarios for data integration (EII) and data consistency between the data warehouse and the data grid. Starting with the data source it can update both the data warehouse and the data grid simultaneously. Assuming that there is already an integration of data source to the data warehouse, this would imply a second integration path into the data grid. If EII is achieved via a middleware bus, such as a queuing system, this may be the preferable path. Alternatively, the EII into the data warehouse remains unchanged, leaving the data warehouse to manage synchronization with the data grid, possibly via event/trigger mechanisms. The third alternative is to have all data sources input directly into the data grid, and leverage the data grid's event processing to manage synchronization with the data warehouse. The example presented here assumes that the EII functions of the data warehouse remain within the data warehouse. Should one choose to transfer the EII responsibility from the data warehouse to the data grid, then the data grid event notification policies will need to be established to maintain data consistency to the data warehouse.

$$EventNotificationPolicy = N/A$$

The data load policy is required only in the second use case, and if the implementation offers the business application the data grid as the medium to instantiate queries to the data warehouse. Then the data load policy will manage the data warehouse interface for data query and loading result sets into the data grid as defined in the equation below:

$$DataLoadPolicy = DLP\begin{pmatrix} DataWarehouse\_DLP, \\ MCRegion, \\ Granularity(Grouping(1), N/A), \\ DataWarehouseAdapter() \end{pmatrix}$$

$$DataStorePolicy = N/A$$

The QoS–application requirement quadrant graph in Figure 15.5 shows application characteristics of nontransactional complex data analysis that are large in size.

BENEFITS AND DATA GRID SPECIFICS

The benefits of applying data grid technology to a data mining/data warehouse application are twofold: the speed of processing and the complexity of the process. The use of the data grids and the compute grids enable complex analysis to be performed in a comparatively shorter timeframe. Therefore, this opens the door for the feasibility of creating increasingly sophisticated analysis programs and running more of them. These advances in business possibilities and sophistication are not

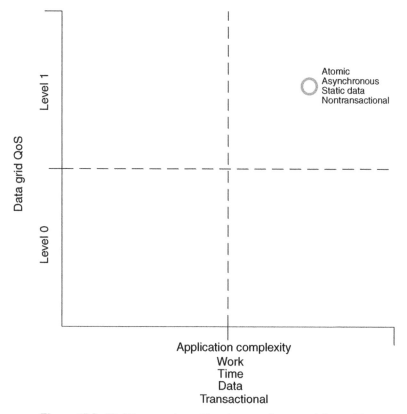

Figure 15.5. OLAP processing with a data warehouse and data grid.

possible without a data grid infrastructure. Using an implementation without the data grid architecture would expand to your traditional data warehouse with more disks and CPUs to perform queries and/or analytics but would still be unable to achieve the levels of complexity that you would desire and need with the ever-increasing business requirements.

16

SPANNING GEOGRAPHIC BOUNDARY

DESCRIPTION

There are a wide range of applications that the data grid addresses where geography poses chasms to be crossed. In this chapter, I will touch on some examples and their respective technical issues.

Grid computing, a network of machines collaborating together to perform tasks, are bound by network bandwidth and not geography. Geography does not factor in the performance of the grid irrespective of physical locality and proximity of the machines:

- Local within a data center
- Distributed within a building
- Across many buildings on a campus or diversely separated by geography

Are there other attributes that impose physical boundary limits in the larger equation for the grid? The other attributes to the equation include application behavior; overall data size, atomic data size (data required for atomic units of work), application transactional behavior, and finally the available network bandwidth of the grid region.

Distributed Data Management for Grid Computing, by Michael Di Stefano
Copyright © 2005 John Wiley & Sons, Inc.

BUSINESS USE CASES

There are many practical examples of geographic boundary problems in today's systems. Here, I will focus only on the current problems faced in the financial services industry, data center operations, and customer service.

Financial Services

Following the September 11, 2001 attacks, the Securities and Exchange Commission (SEC) released the following guidelines:

> Interagency Paper on Sound Practices to Strengthen the Resilience of the U.S. Financial System Federal Reserve System [Docket No. R-1128]; Department of the Treasury Office of the Comptroller of the Currency [Docket No. 03-05]; Securities and Exchange Commission [Release No. 34-47638; File No. S7-32-02] (http://www.sec.gov/news/studies/34-47638.htm)

One of the recommendations in the paper establishes a minimum distance requirements between sites for operations and data centers that do not depend on a common infrastructure; thus this targets the reduced risk in situations of tragic measures. Earlier drafts of this paper suggested a physical minimum distance of 200–300 mi. Figure 16.1 illustrates how this separation can be achieved.

In response to the SEC's requirements, the industry cited that there are logistical issues that include high costs prohibiting this from happening even if it is technically feasible. In addition to the added cost of maintaining separate physical facilities, there are the nontrivial human workflow difficulties of coordinating a physically separated staff that must work as well as if they were sitting together on the same floor.

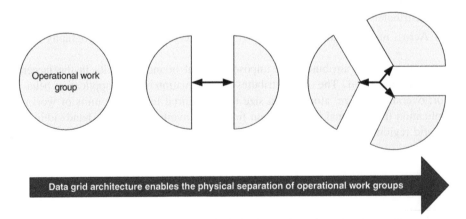

Figure 16.1. Physically separated work groups that operationally act as one.

The technology question that needs to be addressed is how you get people who are geographically separated to work, coordinate, and share data in such a fashion that is seamless to the customers that the group services.

Continuity in human workflow across geography is dependent on continuity of communications, data, and business applications across the same geography. Looking at the micromodel of fault-tolerant data servers will offer a platform to see how a proper compute and data grid environment can address workflow continuity across geographic boundaries. Sophisticated data servers (the physical server machines) have multiple CPUs running in synchronization; should one fail, the operation runs uninterrupted as the workload is continuously running on the other CPUs [This is also referred to as "high availability" (HA)]. Within the server, the CPUs are connected via an internal "bus" architecture that enables them to commutate and coordinate tasks with each other. The same concept is extended to the distributed computing systems. In the distributed compute architecture there are multiple compute nodes (CPUs) that are interconnected via a network. The compute grid is similar to the operating system that controls the processes running on the server; it coordinates task among the compute nodes. The data grid manages the data sharing operations between the CPUs. Similar to the fault-tolerant server, a grid architecture enables levels of fault tolerance to applications that run on the grid; operations can be split, running in parallel across the grid. Should any operation fail, the grid will restart it on another compute node until the overall operation successfully completes. Thus, the grid can provide the required fault tolerance or HA to the applications that the business units require. The difference between a fault-tolerant server and the grid is the physical separation of the CPUs. In a server, the CPUs are in very close proximity, literally inches apart. On the other hand, the grid architecture is bound by the network, and the physical separation between CPUs can be 10 ft of cable, for example, or across a building via a local-area network or across the country via a wide-area network. The efficiency of the grid is less dependent on the compute power of each individual compute node and more dependent on the bandwidth and latency of the network connecting the nodes. Therefore the amount, quality, and efficiency of the work that can be performed on the grid are in direct correlation to the network and the management of data movement in the grid.

With sufficient network bandwidth and proper data management in the data grid, the grid architectures can deliver varying levels of fault tolerance to the applications running on the grid independent of physical geography, thus adding the required fault tolerance to the applications. Extending this concept to the human workflow and interaction, the data grid allows the data to be shared in real time with the workers irrespective of geography. Geographic independence of the data grid effectively bridges the physical distance of the employee work groups. They can be sitting next to each other, one on the north side of the floor and the other on the south side, or with one in New York City and the other in Chicago. The grid architecture with a data grid enables work groups to be distributed across the grid in much the same way as the grid delivers fault tolerance to their business applications that are running on it. The grid delivers fault tolerance across geography for the business applications, including the people that use them and their workflow. A power outage in New York will yield no interruption of service to the customer as the workload is distributed across from the New York site to the Chicago site and San Francisco site in real time, for example.

Operations

The data center operational procedures are different when the compute center is distributed across disperse geographic areas. Tactically, there are tools to monitor networks and the status of the individual compute nodes that compose the grid. There are provisioning tools that will, with little to no human intervention, bring a machine from the "out of the box" bare metal to a database server, application server, or whatever it needs to be in order to run the specific business application. The compute grid offers tools to give an in-depth view into the compute nodes, including their status and availability to perform tasks, and provide status on tasks that are running and those that are queued to be run. In addition, the data grid must provide information on data statistics such as data movement, frequency of access and update, and size. I will not look into the nuts and bolts of the operational management of a grid architecture. Instead, I will be addressing areas of improvement that the presence of a data grid enables from an operations perspective.

Described below are two areas of operation that can be improved with the use of a data grid. These are provided as example; they are not the only operational areas that a data grid can enhance. It is left to the reader to build on the concepts presented here and foster thought in the area of application of the data grid to data center operations.

Areas of operation improvement can include the following:

1. *Application Migration from Older Systems to Newer Systems.* Compute systems in a data center, both hardware and software, are in continual flux. Servers can be upgraded, networks expanded, application software changed, software applications supported, and the current systems completely replaced with a new hardware–software environment. Each type of change requires regression testing to ensure that there is no change in the QoS to the business. The scope of regression testing is not limited to the system in question but all the other systems it touches and that touch it. Often this means working "after hours" (late nights and long weekends) by all involved, including the developers, operations staff, and managers. Deadlines need to be set, as does a point of no return, where, if the rollout of the new system is not completely up, running, and tested, the changes need to be rolled back and the old system put back in place. Let us look at the simplest event that can trigger such chaos. One common cause of a business application moving from one version to another is a third-party software vendor discontinuing support for an older release of its product, thus forcing its customers to "move" off an earlier release to the latest and greatest version. Let us assume that there are no business logic changes to the application, so this should be a simple port and/or recompile of the code. However, from a QA operations standpoint, there is no difference between this simple change or a major application rework. Both instances

require regression testing on this system and all other systems that it touches. The data grid in this instance provides a platform where quality assurance (QA) and regression testing can occur in parallel to production during normal business hours, thus minimizing or even eliminating the after-hours work involved in a roll-out. The QA data region can be synchronized with the production data region such that as data become available to the production data region, those same data updates are reflected in the QA region. As the production systems change state, the QA system should mirror the same state changes. Once this occurs, the QA system is ready to be cut over to production. The compute and data grid planes make the switchover from QA to production, and, if need be, the fallback procedures are equally transparent as system rollout and rollback are both a matter of provisioning the machines to the respective configurations. The ability to use the data grid to provide the same information state as available in production minimizes the risk since the QA environment is similar to if not completely the same as the production environment for regression testing. This kind of architecture is represented in Figure 16.2, where the production environment is feeding the QA environment.

2. *High Availability (HA) and Fault Tolerance.* The objective is to move an HA environment from a loss of service spanning minutes to a loss of service that spends

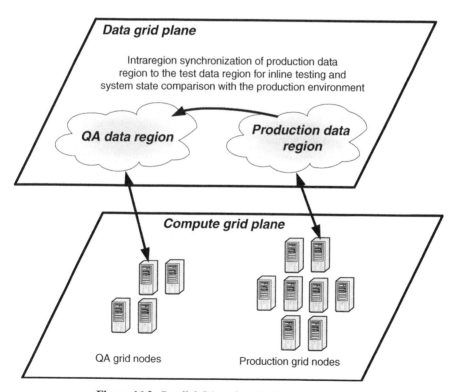

Figure 16.2. Parallel QA and production environments.

seconds, regardless of whether these services and servers are physically next to each other in a data center or are diversely separated by geography.

In the early 1990s Risk/Unix platforms were gaining popularity in the commercial industry, playing the role of both servers and clients in the client/server evolution. The drawback to this platform in the early days was that Unix was emerging out of universities and research facilities such as AT&T (where the operating system was invented); thus few people were experienced in the operating environment and even fewer tools for development and administration/operations existed. One of the largest hurdles that the platform had to overcome in order to cross into a mainstream technology for mission-critical systems was automatic monitoring so as to ensure reliability and availability of the systems and the software running them. The expected reliability at that time was not up to par with today's demands on fault-tolerant systems (fault-tolerant systems had 99.999% reliability). A new term emerged to describe a reliable but not fault tolerant environment; "high availability" (HA).

HA software monitors the hardware and the software services running on it in order to detect a failure; it monitors the health or the state of the system. Should a service fail, the HA system would take the appropriate action to resolve the problem. The time that elapses between failure detection and problem resolution can range from seconds to minutes depending on the software solution and the configuration. From the customer/user prospective, the system was simply slow to respond when in reality a hardware failure, for example, caused the software that was running on the failed box to be restarted somewhere else on the network (typically a spare or "warm" backup machine). This process is called "service failover." In order for the service failover to work, the "state" of the service has to be carried over to the backup machine. In the case of a database service, the physical disks of the database had to be connected to both the primary and backup servers. This way, when the backup server started the database engine, it was accessing the same physical disks that the primary server was using.

How can the data grids improve the reliability of HA, moving it even closer to hot-standby fault tolerance? There are two methods for achieving this; the first is to use the data grid as the primary user access plane. Note that I did not use the term "access point." Unlike client/server applications, grid computing is by nature a multiple access plane for the business users. Node failures will not bring the grid "down." (Only large or catastrophic failures can bring the grid to a total failed state.) The second method involves one of the key necessities of HA: service state maintenance. The data grid can maintain the state of a service so that any node on the grid can act as the backup to the primary node. With the combination of the data grid acting as the primary user access plane and maintaining the state of the services, the user should experience no "sluggishness" of the system during a failover process. In addition, data loss will be eliminated, ensuring high data integrity. Figure 16.3 highlights the architecture of how this would work between the two environments.

One instance where the data grid not only improves system reliability but also improves performance and increases over all server utilization rates is with the

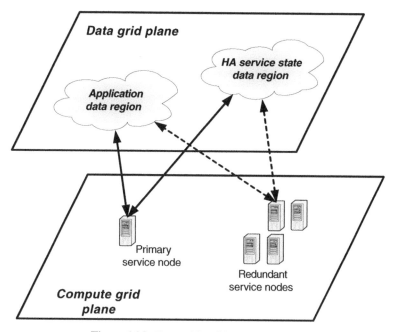

Figure 16.3. Data grid and high availability.

use of Internet application servers. The state of the incoming requests from the Internet are maintained in the data grid; therefore the responses to a specific request no longer need to be routed to the same server that processed the incoming request. Rather, any available server can process the response since the complete state of the request/response is maintained in the data grid where all the application servers have access to it.

Following the Sun

"Following the sun" refers to the ability to shift the business responsibilities from one region to another as the resources of the next region become available. As a business wants to maintain a 24 × 7 × 365 infrastructure, grid computing enables business units to "follow the sun across the globe" with a smooth transition of service, from a customer perspective, as responsibilities shifts from the U.S. East Coast to the U.S. West Coast to Asia, to Europe and back to the U.S. East Coast, for example. In addition, where there are overlaps on time zones between geographic regions (e.g., New York and Chicago), day processing or load processing during heavy usage periods in New York could leverage Chicago's, which could leverage Denver's compute environments, and so on (see Figure 16.4, on grid infrastructure spanning geographic regions).

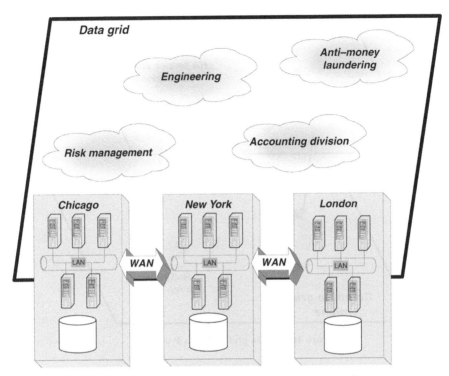

Figure 16.4. Grid infrastructure spanning geographic regions.

GENERAL ARCHITECTURE

Applying traditional technology and methodology to solve the use cases described above would yield custom solutions that would vary greatly from one use case to another. Also, within each use case, one implementation can be vastly different from the others. I will illustrate what the data grid offers as a common architecture that addresses each use case with specific customizations to match the specificities of each business requirement.

I will start by assuming that the base architecture of a data grid is consistent across all use cases. For geographic boundary problems, the variances factor to consider is in the network bandwidth both within and between data regions. This will directly affect the various data management policies for synchronization and transaction as well as some design chrematistics with respect to data granularity.

Like a close-up camera shot panning back so to see the panorama, we start with a close-up of the general architecture and expand the view back to a higher level, reducing what was once detail to larger functional boxes. Panning back even further, the boxes represent geographic regions until the entire global grid infrastructure is revealed. Whether it is a geographic region such as a city or simply a group of buildings within a city, each have their own grid infrastructure. As the scope expands to include multiple regions, larger data grid infrastructure forms, connecting regions with each other across the wide-area network. The global grid infrastructure now encompasses each of those regions as seamlessly as encompasses the infrastructure within a single region. Figure 16.4 illustrates this concept.

When it comes to data management within a grid environment that spans different geographic regions, you have to factor in the following parameters:

- Available network bandwidth
- Application chrematistics
- Application data requirements

The data grid must supply the proper data management tools to allow effective and efficient sharing and movement of data between the regions, across a pipe such as a WAN that may not have the bandwidth you have at your local backplane and in the blade center.

Proper analysis of the application and its data requirements is essential to defining and configuring the data regions and how to best bundle and synchronize the data between the data regions. This data synchronization needs to be performed in such a way that is efficient and workable to enable the application to span the data regions. This will involve the definition of data granularity within the application. *Data granularity* is the packaging of data to its most fundamental element. For example, within a high-bandwidth backplane it's very reasonable to have a very fine granular view of the application data, down to the most basic data elements of an integer, float, or byte. However, if your application does not have a high-speed backplane, it will not be worthwhile to try to move and synchronize data in such small grains. Therefore, it becomes necessary to have a more coarse data granularity for movement and synchronization across a slower bandwidth to ensure that the application will meet the business requirements. Figure 16.5 illustrates the data view as associated with the regions and various applications.

In addition, Figure 16.5 also illustrates the data regions from the logical and physical prospectives. The data regions are logical groupings of data, which is visualized as a cloud in the diagram. As time passes, these clouds move across the sky or the data grid and assume new shapes. Similarly, data regions will change shape as the business requires and the usage dictates. These clouds may physically span multiple data centers, and the shape of the data region may expand and contract throughout the day depending on data needs spanning across one or more data centers. The data management facility must provide the proper tools to permit data region shaping and manage data availability to match the physical demands imposed by the business.

DATA GRID ANALYSIS

Even though the general architecture for the geographic boundary use cases is similar, most of the application definition expressions and data management policies are very application-specific and thus cannot be expressed as one set of general expressions. The most general settings to span the data regions across the WANs

The logical grouping of data in a data grid can be viewed as a "data cloud"
with fluid changes in shape and motion across the data grid plane

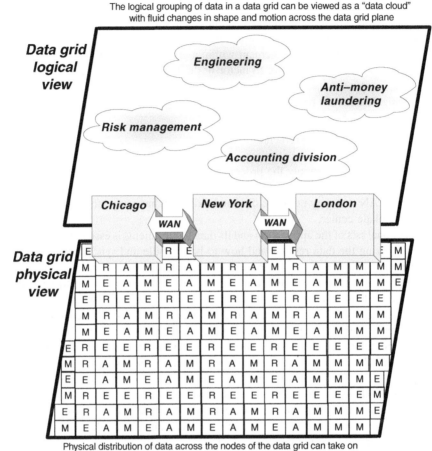

Physical distribution of data across the nodes of the data grid can take on
properties of a statistical pattern (e.g., chaotic, Gaussian)

Figure 16.5. Data regions across a data grid.

are presented below. Therefore, it is left to the reader as an exercise to architect in
each use case the variations in definition and policy expressions.

There are many ways to express the applications and data management policies for
the geographic boundary use cases. Some possible scenarios are one business data
region spanning the geographic space that addresses data affinity. Data affinity is
addressed through data distribution and replication policies to ensure that data
atoms are sufficiently represented across the entire region. Additional scenarios include

- Moving data atoms across the geography only on being requested to do so
  without any considerations for data affinity
- Combination of data affinity for data atoms that are often used across geography
  leveraging data distribution and replication policies with an as-requested data

distribution and replication policy for data atoms that rarely span the geography of the region.

A separate option is to establish "local" data regions for each geography with a series of "bridging regions" that span or connect the local regions to form one large region that spans the global geography space. This bridging region simply holds the data atoms that need to be synchronized across the geography, thus allowing each local region to have specific data management policies to maximize performance and data affinity specific to its local usage patterns.

As can be seen, the possibilities are numerous and need to take into account the physical limitations of the network, business requirements, data set analysis, and the resulting data atom granularity, among many other factors. The performance requirement for both local and global usage also needs to be considered. Since the parameters are too great and the scope is too broad, and without specific application requirements, the expressions for the various data policies are too difficult to represent in general terms. Specifically, the *Data( )* expression is so dependent on all the parameters mentioned above that it cannot be defined at this stage. The following expressions and policies assume a single data region supporting a business unit that spans the geographic boundary expressed as an example:

- *The Application Definition Equation for a Distributed Environment.* This equation can be expressed as follows:

$$
GeoBoundaryProcess \begin{pmatrix} Work(atomic, nonsynchronous), \\ Data(\ ), \\ Time(near\text{-}Real\text{-}Time), \\ Geography(WAN), \\ Query(Basic) \end{pmatrix}
$$

- *The Data Management Policies.* The data distribution and replication policies ensure that the data atoms are sufficiently robust across the entire region to maximize data affinity within a geographic space of a data region and are expressed as follows:

$$
DataDistributionPolicy = DDP \begin{pmatrix} GeoBoundary\_DDP, \\ GBRegion, \\ Scope(ALL), \\ Pattern \begin{pmatrix} Automatic, Random \begin{pmatrix} DWDDPPattern, \\ WhiteNoise(\ ), \\ NULL, \\ NULL, \\ NULL, \\ NULL \end{pmatrix} \end{pmatrix} \end{pmatrix}
$$

The Data Replication Policy shows a slightly high number of replicas per data atom since the data must span geographic boundaries.

$$DataReplicationPolicy = DRP \begin{pmatrix} GeoBoundary\_DRP, \\ GBRegion, \\ 12, \\ Scope(ALL) \end{pmatrix}$$

$$SynchronizationPolicy = SP \begin{pmatrix} GeoBoundary\_SP, \\ GBRegion, \\ Scope(Boundary("inter"),NULL), \\ Transactionality("nontransactional"), \\ LoadStore(NULL,NULL), \\ Events(NULL) \end{pmatrix}$$

$$EventNotificationPolicy = N/A$$
$$DataLoadPolicy = N/A$$
$$DataStorePolicy = N/A$$

The QoS–application requirement quadrant graph in Figure 16.6 shows application characteristics that are nontransactional but large in size and complex in data analysis.

BENEFITS AND DATA GRID SPECIFICS

The application of the grid to resolve geographic boundary problems is manyfold. Here I touched on some simple and powerful examples of geographic boundary problems that the grid directly addresses and resolves efficiently. In the following paragraphs I will discuss both the business and technical benefits of the geographic independence of data access in a reasonable near-real-time paradigm.

The business benefits of geographically dispersed business units are many. Evaluation at each use case yields its own unique benefits. Examples are the ability to take a single business unit and disperse the people across geographic boundaries and to have people in one city seamlessly coordinate and interact with their colleagues in another city or even other countries. A scenario in which geographically disperse or "distributed" individuals work on the same data allows for an efficient use of skill sets, providing workforce redundancy and business resilience; it allows the best available resources working and coordinating to achieve a common task. The result yields a high utilization of resources best fit for the task, time efficiency, and a high-quality product or service based on a very cost-effective basis.

The use case of "following the sun" includes the ability to provide a wider range of service for your clients by expanding the time window of service without having

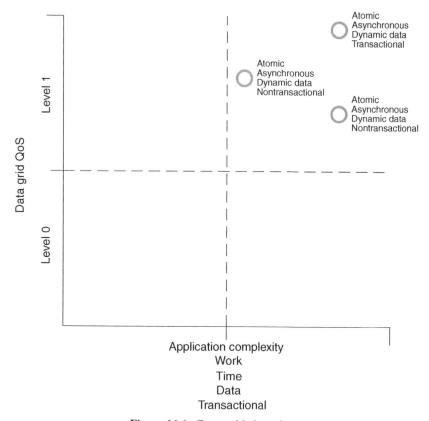

Figure 16.6. Geographic boundary.

to maintain the second or even third shift of people working through the night. The data grid enables seamless accesses to data independent of geography, thus yielding the ability to smoothly and effectively pass the baton from one group of people located in one place to another group of people in another time zone in an efficient and cost-effective manner.

The use case for "application migration" or the migration from one version of the application to another is also a good example. Typically these rollout operations have to occur during system downtime, such as overnight or on weekends. This results in

- Time constraints to when rollouts can be done
- Limited frequency of new features into a production environment
- Additional pressure on the staff (from users, to developers, to administrators)
- Overhead to the rollout process
- Higher risk in production since the QA environment might be limited in capability

Tasks have to be scheduled and cutoff periods have to be monitored and coordinated among many groups within an organization, sometimes on a local basis and other times on a global one. Should a rollout not occur successfully by a certain time, then everything needs to be rolled back to the original systems and software, which also is not easy, depending on the rollback plans.

The use of a data grid allows for application and system rollouts to occur in parallel. The migration from one version of release to another can be done during business hours, allowing for the ability to test against production data and to be able to release into production flawlessly, eliminating the need to wait for downtime before such rollout events can occur. This allows organizations to better leverage their staff and eliminates the long hours and overtime costs associated with having the staff working extended hours during the rollout period.

In the "high availability" (HA) use case, the more bulletproof a service needs to be, the greater the need for the level of fault tolerance within systems to be directly related to the financial cost in service, hardware, and network. For example, in a Unix environment, levels of fault tolerance are achieved through HA software. HA is a means to switch from a failed service to its replacement in a relatively short time, typically minutes. Problems arise when a failover takes longer than the "reasonable" time window expected for the service or if the failure does not successfully recover. In the latter case, there is no quick or immediate solution. In typical situations the recovery time is several minutes, but in the few rare occasions the recovery time for the service could take hours.

The use of a data grid to span primary and redundant systems and having user groups access its business data through the data grid brings high availability closer to the higher levels of fault tolerance that can be achieved only through an extensive hardware–software approach. High availability with the data grid allows for more resiliencies in your systems and operations, and better support for your business at a very reasonable cost structure.

17

COMMAND AND CONTROL

PROBLEM DESCRIPTION

Command and control is the classic feedback control loop that is seen in most engin-eering applications. A *feedback control loop* is a continuous process of state measurements, analysis, decisions, and commands in an effort to change the state of the system. Typically the goal of the analysis and commands is to keep the system in a stable, well-known state commonly referred to as a "steady state."

I will discuss two basic applications that share one common characteristic; the systems consist of many devices (e.g., computers, sensors) with the requirement to collect information from the dispersed devices and perform an analysis on the col-lected information. Command-and-control loops continue the process of immedi-ately processing and analyzing the data, with the resulting adjustment of the system state as the final outcome. Figure 17.1 illustrates this state management process for the command-and-control loop function.

We can consider a subset of command-and-control loops to exist when the control commands of the feedback loop are not needed. Monitoring weather, for example, utilizes a vast network of sensors, weather stations, and other facilities. The information from the sensors is recording weather conditions for analysis. The speed with which the data are collected and analyzed has a direct impact on the required actions that need to be taken depending on the final results. However, in some cases the resulting actions may not necessarily be to issue a command back to the sensors but rather to issue a storm warning to the public.

Distributed Data Management for Grid Computing, by Michael Di Stefano
Copyright © 2005 John Wiley & Sons, Inc.

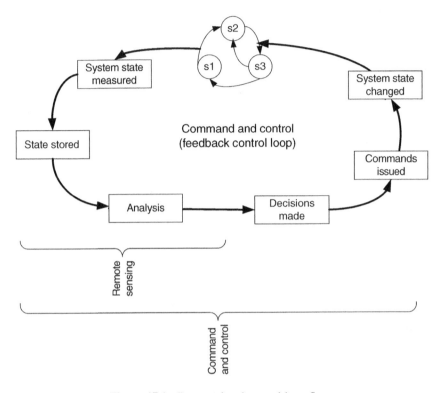

Figure 17.1. Command-and-control loop flow.

In the following discussions, the terms *sensor*, *device*, and *computer* are used interchangeably.

SOLUTION ARCHITECTURE

There are two possible architecture implementations for the command-and-control (command/control) loops that will be discussed and compared. In the first case, I will analyze the process where there is no data grid and then expand to the use of the data grid in the second case. The procedural steps in command/control loops are independent of the implementation, therefore enabling a direct comparison to the efficiency gained by using a data grid. The procedural steps normally outlined for the command/control loops are as follows:

1. Collection of data from the remote devices
2. Preparing the data for analysis, formatting, and inserting the data into storage
3. Analysis of the data
4. Decision process with input from the analysis process
5. Formulation of commands supporting the decisions of step 4

6. Issuing of commands
7. Delivery of commands out to the respective remote sensors
8. Repetition of the process, thus looping back to step 1

Command and Control Without a Data Grid

In step 1 as identified above, the collection of data from the sensors is always a good place to start. In a homogeneous sensor environment, the sensors are supplied by the same manufacturer or have a standard interface on which all manufacturers agreed. Therefore the data collection processes are uniform. However, in the more realistic scenario the sensor environment is heterogeneous and for each sensor type, manufacturer, and interface there are multiple sensor interfaces and data collection processes. The sensor collects data that need to be shared with other parts of the system for processing. To extract the data, one must know how to physically connect to the sensor, understand its communication protocol, and understand its data format. With this information and the knowledge of the larger systems networking characteristics, "adapters" must be created to collect the data from the sensor and deliver them to a common storage for analysis. Conversely, this same process must be done in reverse in order to send commands (if necessary) back to the sensors. Most likely, the input data process to the sensor will be different from its output process. For the purposes of simplifying this discussion, the physical connectivity for input data is the same for output sensor data. However, there could be a separate protocol and data format for the input process and data stream. Keep in mind that

- Data are moved from one system to another; the message that is transported over the network must be marshaled before transmission and then unmarshaled on receipt.
- In a heterogeneous environment, the input/output data process must be duplicated for each different sensor type, manufacturer, and interface.

Once the sensor connectivity is established, the collected data must be stored somewhere on their receipt. For example, the storage facility can be a file system, database, or even the memory space of the analysis process itself. Odds are that the data format from the sensor will not be the same as the input data format required by the analysis process. Therefore a level of data translation must take place. If the data are to first be placed in a file system or database for later retrieval by the analysis process, then it is safe to assume that the data representation of the storage medium is different from that of the analysis process. Therefore the sensor data must go through two data translation processes: sensor to file and file to analysis. As the process continues, one can see the large number of required data transformations that take place. Figure 17.2 shows this process without the use of the data grid.

In Figure 17.2, the triangles represent the sensors that interface to the data collection process and command distribution process. Once the data are collected and stored, the analysis process begins, followed by the decision and finally the

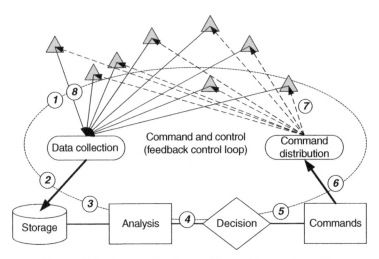

Figure 17.2. Command-and-control loop without a data grid.

formulation of the command. The command is than sent out to the external sensor environment. Physically, the command/control loop system may be a single system that we are representing as three logical components. Analysis is performed directly against stored data. The analysis process extracts the input data from the data store and performs its operations with the resulting output feeding the decision process. Commands are then issued through a communication mechanism specific to the topology of the underlying communications network of the command center and the sensors. The process of issuing the commands to each individual sensor is similar to the one described for the data collection, which involves connectivity, protocol, marshaling and unmarshaling, and data format translations.

Command and Control with a Data Grid

Applying the same system as described above, the data grid architecture simplifies the process, eliminating the number of "moving parts." The data grid encompasses the sensors and the command center where the analysis/decision/command process occurs. The sensors place or put their data directly into the data grid, therefore making them immediately available to the analysis process, completely bypassing the storage step and many of the data translation steps required without the data grid as described in the other scenario. In addition, the data grid can also serve as the storage medium, unless the raw sensor data need to be persisted in a database for long-term or future reanalysis. Should long-term persistence be required, the data grid can assume the responsibility of persisting the data to the proper storage device (e.g., file, database), a process independent of the analysis and command paths.

The result is the elimination of the multistep process of collection, local store, packaging, download, unpackaging, storing, and finally reading into the analysis programs with a single step of "writing to a data grid." The issuing of commands

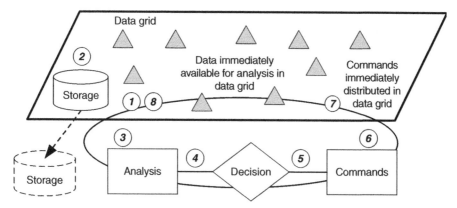

Figure 17.3. Command and control with a data grid.

can also be done via the data grid. Commands can be put into an area of the data grid from which the remote sensors can read. Again, taking the diagram of the command/control loops as represented in Figure 17.2 and architecting with the data grid results in the scheme shown in Figure 17.3.

Observations and Comparisons

The key points of differentiation between the data grid and non-data-grid implementations are data collection, translation, availability, and finally connectivity for transport of information to and from the sensors. Now the workflow process is simplified to the schematic representation in Figure 17.4, with the data grid as an integral part of the system.

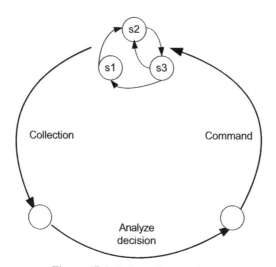

Figure 17.4. Points of comparison.

TABLE 17.1. Points of Comparison Between Data Grid and Non-Data-Grid Implementations

Point of comparison	Procedure steps	Non-data grid implementation	Data grid implementation
Collection	Collect data	Yes	Yes
	Translate data	Yes	Yes
	Transport data to central store	Yes	N/A
	Translate data for database	Yes	N/A
	Store in database	Yes	N/A
Analysis	Analyze	Yes	Yes
	Decision	Yes	Yes
Command	Store	Yes	Yes
	Forward	Yes	N/A

Without a data grid, the solution is highly customized and an artistic process. The variable parameters of the process are sensor type, location, data collection and storage at the sensor, and connectivity to the rest of the network. For example, if the sensor is a Unix computer and you are interested in its operational state, then the information in the "syslog file" is of value. Data collection for these data can be via a customized protocol or a well-known one such as a FTP. This is a non-real-time batch process where data are accumulated and periodically downloaded to a central repository.

Issuing of commands back to the sensors is a separate process but can leverage similar methods used in data collection. For example, the command files are FTPed so as to be read by the sensor; or command messages may be passed via a networked messaging or queuing protocol. The point is that these are all customized methods of collecting and issuing commands between sensors and the control center and are usually nonstandardized.

A side-by-side comparison of data grid versus non-data-grid implementations of command/control loops shows that there is an elimination of the complex moving parts once the data grid is architected in the solution. Thus, there is an increased efficiency since the time is drastically reduced from the point that data are available from the sensors for analysis. Table 17.1 identifies the various components that are needed in the two scenarios:

DATA GRID ANALYSIS

I will make some assumptions regarding the topology of the command/control system that we will analyze as part of this exercise. The complete sensor community is large in number and distributed across large geographic areas. At each location there is only one or a small number of collection sensors. The sensors are heterogeneous in nature as outlined in the earlier discussion in this chapter. The data atom size for sensor input and output is small in size, let us say on the order of

100 bits, and the data transfer intervals are on the order of minutes. However, this is just one part of the system processing requirements. The second part revolves around the data analysis and the command process. Even though each sensor produces a small amount of data per update, the sensors are large in number and the total sum of the data that needs to be analyzed, in sum, is quite large. The analysis process can be quite complex, thus making it very similar to the data mining and data warehouse use case as highlighted in earlier chapters. In this situation, the data collection aspects of the system are very similar to those of the geographic boundary use case of Chapter 16. Both are presented below with some customization for the particular case at hand, command/control loops.

The previous example for the data warehouse and OLAP analysis is as follows:

- *Application Definition Equation for the Distributed Environment*

$$OLAPProcess \begin{pmatrix} Work(\ ), \\ Data\_output(\ ), Data\_S1(\ ), \ldots Data\_Sn(\ ), \\ Time(\ ), \\ Geography(\ ), \\ Query(\ ) \end{pmatrix}$$

where

$$Work(atomic, nonsynchronous)$$

The output data surfaces are smaller for the command/control loops in comparison to the data surfaces that will be analyzed from the data warehouse.

$$Data\_output(``x" kbits, ``y" bits, transactional, nontransient, queryable)$$

$$Data\_S1(``z" Tbits, ``k" Mbits, nontransactional, transient, queryable)$$

$$Data\_Sn(``z" Tbits, ``k" Mbits, nontransactional, transient, queryable)$$

The ability to run complex analysis over large data sets in short periods of time provides the command/control process with a better view into the system state, demands on the system, including its current state, and its ability to meet the demands. Armed with better and in-depth quality views, the command/control process can target specific "in-time" adjustments to the system to meet the demands placed on it. This command/control OLAP process is to run in the confines of a single data center, and the applications requirement to analyze (complex queries) any of the data sets is not essential to the business.

$$Time(Near\text{-}Real\text{-}Time)$$

$$Geography(DataCenter, 1GbitEthernet)$$

$$Query(complex)$$

- *Data Management Policies*

$$DataDistributionPolicy = DDP \begin{pmatrix} DataWarehouse\_DDP, \\ DWRegion, \\ Scope(ALL), \\ \\ Pattern \begin{pmatrix} Automatic, Random \begin{pmatrix} DWDDPPattern, \\ WhiteNoise(\,), \\ NULL, \\ NULL, \\ NULL, \\ NULL \end{pmatrix} \end{pmatrix} \end{pmatrix}$$

The data replication policy shows a lower number of replicas per data atom as the overall size of the data in the data grid is quite large. Each replica increases the overall storage capacity of the data grid by the size of the data loaded from the data warehouse. The downside to a lower replication size per data atom is resilience of the data in case of a failure. These tradeoffs must be considered in each use case and architecture variation.

$$DataReplicationPolicy = DRP \begin{pmatrix} DataWarehouse\_DRP, \\ DWRegion, \\ 3, \\ Scope(ALL) \end{pmatrix}$$

$$SynchronizationPolicy = SP \begin{pmatrix} DataWarehouse\_SP, \\ DWRegion, \\ Scope(Boundary(``intra"\,), NULL), \\ Transactionality(``nontransactional"\,), \\ LoadStore(List(``DataWarehouse\_DLP"\,), NULL), \\ Events(NULL) \end{pmatrix}$$

Use of events to coordinate data consistency between the command/control loops and the data grid are managed via events or triggers from within the data grid to or from the sensors. This assumes that the EII functions of the system remain as part of the command/control loops. Should one choose to transfer the EII responsibility from the command/control loops to the data grid, then the data grid event notification policies will need to be established to maintain data consistency.

$$EventNotificationPolicy = N/A$$

The data load policy is required in this use case, and if the implementation offers the business application, the data grid as the medium to data loads and data pushes to the sensors. Then the data load policy will manage the sensors' interface of extract and load result sets into the data grid.

$$DataLoadPolicy = DLP \begin{pmatrix} DataWarehouse\_DLP, \\ MCRegion, \\ Granularity(Grouping(1), N/A), \\ DataWarehouseAdapter(\,) \end{pmatrix}$$

$$DataStorePolicy = N/A$$

Geographic boundary analysis may be applied to the command-and-control loops:
- *Application Definition Equation for a Distributed Environment*

$$GeoBoundaryProcess \begin{pmatrix} Work(atomic, nonsynchronus), \\ Data(MultiGbits, 100bits, nontransactional, \\ \quad transient, queryable), \\ Time(near\text{-}Real\text{-}Time), \\ Geography(WAN), \\ Query(Basic) \end{pmatrix}$$

- *Data Management Policies.* The data distribution and replication policies for this scenario may need to be a manual pattern as opposed to an automatic one. While each sensor is a node in the data grid, it is safe to assume that it will not be available to contribute storage capacity to the data grid, thus eliminating it as a possible data replication and distribution node for other sensor data. However, for this analysis, we will use the same white noise distribution policy as before. It is left to the reader as an exercise to determine the physical and behavioral characteristics of the overall system and to create a distribution pattern to meet the specific requirements:

$$DataDistributionPolicy = DDP \begin{pmatrix} GeoBoundary\_DDP, \\ GBRegion, \\ Scope(ALL), \\ \\ Pattern \begin{pmatrix} Automatic, Random \begin{pmatrix} DWDDPPattern, \\ WhiteNoise(\,), \\ NULL, \\ NULL, \\ NULL, \\ NULL \end{pmatrix} \end{pmatrix} \end{pmatrix}$$

The data replication policy for the commandcontrol loops as illustrated above shows a low number of replicas per data atom in order to meet the assumptions made in the data distribution policy expression:

$$DataReplicationPolicy = DRP \begin{pmatrix} GeoBoundary\_DRP, \\ GBRegion, \\ 3, \\ Scope(ALL) \end{pmatrix}$$

$$SynchronizationPolicy = SP \begin{pmatrix} GeoBoundary\_SP, \\ GBRegion, \\ Scope(Boundary(``inter"), NULL), \\ Transactionality(``nontransactional"), \\ LoadStore \begin{pmatrix} List(``DLP\_SensorTypeA",\dots), \\ List(``DSP\_SensorTypeA",\dots) \end{pmatrix}, \\ Events(List(``ENP\_SensorTypeA",\dots)) \end{pmatrix}$$

Event notification may not be necessary in this application for data gathering; however, it will prove valuable to notify nodes that there are commands waiting for them to be read in and acted on:

$$EventNotificationPolicy = ENP \begin{pmatrix} ENP\_SensorTypeA, \\ GBRegion, \\ Scope(``All"), \\ SensorCommandFunction() \end{pmatrix}$$

Similar load policies are needed for each sensor type. Only one example is illustrated below for all the possible types of sensors:

$$DataLoadPolicy = DLP \begin{pmatrix} DLP\_SensorTypeA, \\ GBRegion, \\ Granularity(Grouping(1),10000), \\ Adapter(``SensorA-OutputAdapter") \end{pmatrix}$$

Similar store policies are needed for each sensor type. Only one is illustrated below for the possible types of sensors:

$$DataStorePolicy = DSP \begin{pmatrix} DSP\_SensorTypeA, \\ GBRegion, \\ Granularity(Grouping(1),10000), \\ Operation(``store"), \\ Adapter(``SensorA\text{-}InputAdapter") \end{pmatrix}$$

- *Qos–Application Requirement Quadrant Graph.* As can be seen from Figure 17.5, the command-and-control loop falls into a level 1 zone and is atomic in nature.

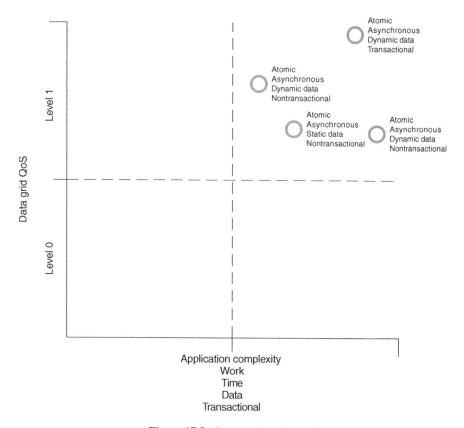

Figure 17.5. Command and control.

APPLICATION SPINOFFS

Command and control plays a key role in a compute utility service. In order for a computer utility service to be effective, the state of the service must meet the supply-and-demand curves of the user community. As the need for the computer services increases, the utility has to be able to adjust to the demand requests by changing its profile; thus, reallocation of the physical resources is necessary. This implies that information describing the state of the utility service including user demands is monitored on a real-time or near-real-time basis. Analysis must be done on this information and commands must be issued back to the utility service for it to change its state in a timely fashion in order to meet the demand on the system at that point in time.

Should the change in state of the utility service lag behind the demand, the utility service will be put into a state that does not meet the demand of the user community. If this happens repeatedly, the utility service will move out of a steady-state condition to one that adversely affects its quality of service to the customer.

A second example is the collection of information from remote devices, where the analysis needs to be performed in real time. However, no commands are issued back to the system to change its state; instead the results that have been analyzed are used elsewhere, for example, by another external system. Weather monitoring entails the ability to collect data from remote weather stations, analyze the raw data in near real time, and have the results available to people or other computer systems to generate weather alerts such as tornado and hurricane warnings.

18

WEB SERVICE'S ROLE IN THE SOA/SONA EVOLUTION

DEFINITION OF WEB SERVICES

Web Services is changing how businesses and customers interact. Through the use of common protocols and standards developed as a direct result of the Internet boom of the late 1990s, businesses can package internally used siloed business applications as a service available over the network (Web Services), making them available to their customers. A common conception is that "Web Services" is an "Internet"-only-based delivery. One must keep in mind that the Internet is a network; fundamentally the same base networking technology used in the public "Internet" is also used for private and internal networks. Many of the standards that define Web Services, such as XML, are not "Internet"-exclusive technologies. They are generic methods, XML specifically, that describe data (messages and state) of a service that can be used by any other system. The same "Internet Web Services" delivery protocols apply equally to private and internal networks. The changing force potential of Web Services determines how businesses interact with all customers, internal and external alike without any distinction.

The impact of Web Service technology on how information technology (IT) organizations operate is vast. For Web Services, allowing disparate systems to interact with each other by leveling the playing fields of protocol and data sharing therefore minimizes if not totally eliminates the human interaction that is required for many traditional (non–Web Services) system integration efforts. The "business–customer interaction radial effect of Web Services" (see Figure 18.1) encompasses intra- and interorganization business service offering for consumer

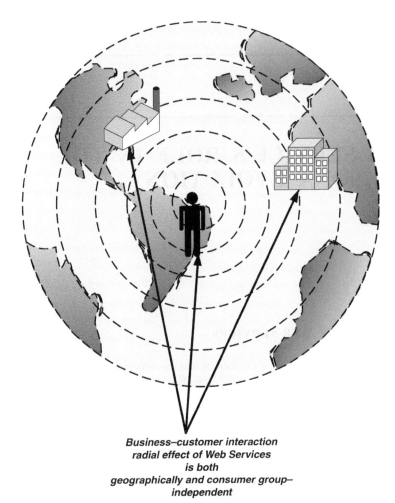

Figure 18.1. Business–customer interaction radial effect of Web Services.

service consumption. This is a "geographically independent" boundary of producer–consumer service relationship.

More and more buzzwords are seeping into our discussions, and it is time to step back and level the field of regarding we mean by producers and consumers when talking about service-oriented architectures (SOA) and Web Services. The *producers* of a service are those who manufacture the service and offer it for consumption or sale to others. It is the "who," the consumer of a service, that has a broad impact. If you are like me, the term "consumer" brings the image of someone purchasing a good such as groceries, clothing, telecommunications, or electricity. However, in the scope of Web Services, the consumer extends beyond the public market to encompass any person or group of people interacting within a business or businesses or with other businesses. This creates a new business interaction leading to new business opportunities and efficiencies not achievable otherwise.

I have provided two definitions for "Web Services" from leading organizations that are helping to shape the Web Services landscape:

1. The first is from W3C, The World Wide Web Consortium (www.w3.org). The W3C charter promotes evolution of the World Wide Web by developing common protocols (there are over 450 members of the W3C). The following excerpt is from W3C Working Draft 8, August 2003 (http://www.w3.org/TR/2003/WD-ws-arch-20030808/), *Web Services Architecture*, Section 1.5—"What is a Web Service":

A Web service is a software system designed to support interoperable machine-to-machine interaction over a network. It has an interface described in a machine-processable format (specifically WSDL). Other systems interact with the Web service in a manner prescribed by its description using SOAP-messages, typically conveyed using HTTP with an XML serialization in conjunction with other Web-related standards.

2. The second definition for Web Services is from: Dr. Bob Sutor, Director of Web Services Strategy, IBM, *The Definition of Web Services*, (source: Search-WebServices.com; available online at http://searchwebservices.techtarget.com/originalContent/0,289142,sid26_gci874060,00.html).

Web services provides standards for an electronic envelop, a language for describing how you talk to a service and what it says back, plus techniques for publishing and discovering these descriptions.

Now with our new understanding of what Web Services means to different people and how organizations and standards influence our thoughts, it will become evident that SOA consists of Web Services, the compute utility, as well as the command and control scenarios presented here.

DESCRIPTION

Real-life businesses are a connection of processes, from manufacturing, sales, delivery, and payment as examples. An event in any one part of this chain has major repercussion on the other events. Corporate business units in partnership with IT organizations are leveraging technology and its associated methodologies of distributed computing to create information systems that meet the business demand. Distributed computing is the transformation of manual, or silo-based processing of information into cohesive real-time information sharing of event-driven enterprisewide systems.

Methods to address information sharing between disparate systems start with file sharing or pipe (or sockets) communication protocols to establish connections between systems (in much the same way as we use telephones). The communication can leverage message queues, through the advent of "middleware" technology such as CORBA or messaging for the encapsulation of enterprisewide components and services. Figure 18.2 is a timeline showing the evolution of client/server communication to today's grid and Web Services.

The evolution of distributed computing continues as the encapsulation of services extends to the corporate infrastructure that delivers "business" services. For each new application a family of new hardware, software packages (i.e., databases), administrative policy and procedure, and human resources must accompany it. The next generation of distributed computing products and methodologies extract the physical process and the administrative layers of the applications into an enterprise service. This new area of distributed computing creates grid services (which consists of compute and data grids) in support of Web Services for the delivery of business services.

In other sections of this book we discuss the practical application of the data grid, for example, the feedback control loops and the compute utility service. These kinds of processes collectively constitute some of the key components that make up Web Services and the SONA architectures. For such services, flexible, fungible, and scalable infrastructures are essential.

DATA MANAGEMENT: THE KEYSTONE TO WEB SERVICES

Web Services brings together various software components, each individually built to deliver some level of service to the business, in such a way as to extend those services for a broader purpose and to a broader audience. This implies an infrasturcute that allows these components to interact and share information and provide process management, and requires a flexible underlying physical layer capable of provisioning its resources to meet the service demands. Key to most, if not all, aspects of delivering Web Services is the *data*. Some points regarding Web Services and its data are as follows:

- Web Services is close to the business, where business process implies business state; thus *state means data*.

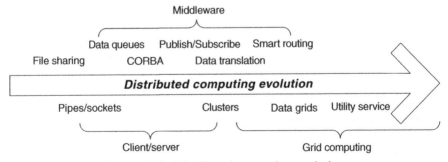

Figure 18.2. Distributed computing evolution.

- Since Web Service components interact with each other, they require *data sharing*.
- Components interacting with each other require a broader level of process management, which means the *management of state, which again implies data*.
- To deliver Web Services to broader audiences, flexible and fungible infrastructures are required. The goal of a compute utility is to become such an infrastructure through the collection of *metered (state) data* from all the nodes that make up the utility, therefore describing the *complete state of the utility*.

The common theme is that the closer one gets to the business, the more important data become, not just to the business application itself but also to the means of delivering the data to the application. Here we talk about data requirements as state management. Therefore state management is associated with two aspects: (1) the internal state of the business application being delivered as a Web service to the user community and (2) the state of the mechanisms needed to successfully deliver the Web Service. Figure 18.3 highlights the interaction of Web Services with business processes, state management, and the data management or data grid.

The compute utility service enables business compontents to be delivered anywhere on the network. With the data grid as an integral part of the utility, it also provides the means to deliver state management for the Web Services components as well as the process and infrastructure management. Figure 18.4 illustrates the relationship between the grid utility service and Web Services.

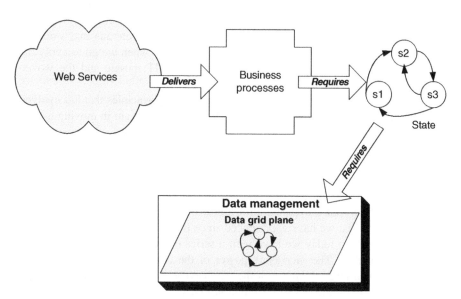

Figure 18.3. Business service, state management, and the data grid.

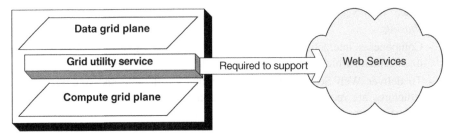

Figure 18.4. Grid utility service as a requirement for Web Services.

WEB SERVICES, GRID INFRASTRUCTURES, AND SONA

It is always beneficial to understand our own history so that we can see clearly where we need to head. Web Services, the grid, and service-oriented network architecture (SONA) are instances of importance of the past that lead us into the future. We will see that the direction of information technology closely parallels the evolution of other point-to-point services that have transformed the services into commodities such as telecommunications and electricity.

The Undiscovered Past

We all know about Moore's law and the fact that the Internet was created by Dr. Metcalfe but not how the Internet evolved from the works of the brilliant scientists and mathematicians of the twentieth century. It was not until authoring this book that I, too, came to appreciate the facts about the commoditization of information services into the consumer marketplace. All of us currently building our careers in information technology, like the seasoned veterans and students, should spend some time studying our rich history so that when we go to apply the Weiner process we can appreciate the beauty of our IT mosaic and the woven foundation on which it was built.

We will also see that the same fundamental laws and principles that has evolved the computing technology since the mid-1940s is just as relevant in moving us into the mid-2060s, including. Shannon's communication theory, the operational research and control processes of Weiner, Amdahl's law of locality of reference, Moore's law driving the cost of the CPU to zero, and Metcalfe's law of increased value of the total number of users. John Narghton's book, *A Brief History of the Future*,[6] does an excellent job in reminding us of just how we have arrived here. Below is just a brief look into the building blocks of the technological and communications evolution that we have experienced since the mid-1940s or so.

From the 1930s to today we have seen a series of progressive transition in the digitalization of data. The increasing power of the computer (i.e., Moore's law) has led to an even larger increase in the pervasiveness of information technology in our everyday lives. Access to information that was once limited is now almost transparent, creating a cycle of information creation and consumption and in some cases information overload, causing the value of the system to increase at exponential rates (Metcalfe's law). In the 1920s and 1930s computation power was limited as well as expensive; for example, telecommunication service was a manual point-to-point connection with a human switchboard establishing the physical circuit connection between two parties. During the 1950s and 1960s, as computation power increased and became more readily available, coupled with new areas of research such as *operations research* (a branch of applied math developed by scientists such as Norbert Weiner) and *agents* (an entity that has been empowered to make decisions on behalf of another entity), circuit switching emerged. After that, circuit switching, packet switching, and the Internet emerged in the 1970s. In the discussions later in this chapter it is important to understand the mechanics of the Internet. Thus the following points need to be highlighted:

- *Switching.* Switching is a signal that triggers the policy decisions that are required to commit resources to the connection. In this context, the term "agent" refers to the transmitting/receiving device—these, along with the switching infrastructure that is delegated decision making authority in terms of resource scheduling and prioritization. In computer-based communication, these transmitting/receiving devices are software-based; producing or consuming messages. These software agents may be realized as either a process or a component running on a thread in that process.
- *The Layers of the Internet.* The Internet is a layered architecture that inherited characteristics of Selfridge's "daemon" and OSI's reference model. The Internet protocol suite consists of four layers: application, transport, Internet, and data link. In the Internet architecture, these functions were purposely deferred to the application. This boundary is enforced via the "Berkeley socket API." Applications specify the configuration of port, host, transport, and so on via this API. The session layer (OSI's fifth layer) resides above the transport layer and is subsumed either by the application or the Internet's other three layers.
- *Destination Addressing.* Destination addressing is described by an IP address by either the destination's daemon process or the application service. The address also includes the use of a specific port number. Together, the IP address and the port number are analogous to a telephone number (another vast utility network).

In the 1980s and 1990s we saw an emergence of ad hoc "middleware" that started to form the initial concept of delivering a "service," but only to those producers and consumers who subscribed to the specific middleware's internal infrastructure. (*Note*: this progression of information technology also saw a progression of professional titles from applied mathematician, to system analyst, to system model architect.)

In the late 1990s the Internet craze left in its wake HTTP and XML as represented by DTDs and the likes of "Web Services." Web Services can be defined as the externalization of the service independent of its internal representation. At the same time, we saw the emergence of "grid computing," which is an evolution in distributed computing that virtualizes the physical computer and how it manages its resource and task processing. Together, grid computing, forming the "compute utility," and Web Services, externalizing the production and consumption of services, form the bridge necessary for us to cross the chasm from siloed business applications and data centers to a market-driven economy of supply and demand of IT services.

The SONA Model

The general problem of connecting consumers and suppliers of a product or service is one of logistics. The observation is that the logical connection between a consumer and supplier is point to point. In practice, a point-to-point connection does not scale, as the number of conusmers increases the complexity of managing and the associated costs to deliver the service increases. This does not allow for an efficient market for supply and demand. Considering how any commidity that is delivered over a logistical transport, (roads, telephone communication, energy, etc.), the supply of the product or service goes from multiple sources to some consumption field. This proven method of product/service delivery, connecting customer to supplier, increases the availability to better meet the demand, lowering the price and thus improving the efficiency of the market. See my discussion of supply and demand economics in Chapter 3.

In the world of computing, looking back to the 1950s and 1960s, the application was pointed toward distributed computing; the network layer was constrained primarily by the CPU. The cost of the CPU was high; therefore a limited amount of computation was available for data switching. This has been the case until relatively recently. The application of Moore's law has brought the cost of CPU mips (millions of instructions per second) to near zero in relation to the costs of the software and data movement across a network. Therefore, with the cost of computation near zero and the cost of data high, why not migrate the computation to data rather than data to computation. In effect, this would entail a shift back toward a centralized data center. The problem is that a point-to-point connection as implied by a physical centralized data center will not scale in today's Internet. Enter the data grid. The data grid, in essence, provides the virtual data center. The data grid today is about locational services and replication, how to move data effectively and efficiently, and how to find the best place to run a computation. This is similar to packet switching of the 1960s and 1970s. With packet switching, the intent is to move packets of data (scheduling of packets to an IP address) rather than today's data grid, which moves large amounts of data.

The key to any switching layer is source and destination, creating any number of paths and optimizing on the shortest path. Creating a virtual circuit of source and destination allows for choices and flexibility as to where data are serviced, thus requiring a service to locate data as well as a service to replicate data so as to put data proactively out near the consumption. The same is true for the data grid in creating a virtual data center; the data grid allows for data location independence and replication of data making them readily accessible when needed, with centralized management and control, yet enabling people to interact independently on ad hoc communications.

This bears repeating. The same fundamental laws and principles that have driven computing technology since the mid-1940s are just as relevant in moving us into the future to the mid-2060s.

Connecting the Dots of the Past into the Continuum of the Present. The history of technical communications is closely linked with the evolution of computing. The history of computing can be divided into two branches, one originating in the mainframe labs of IBM and the other in the network labs of AT&T. To understand the accelerated innovation of the present, one needs to look to the past. Specifically, the points in history in which we are interested which originated from the application of stochastics to networking and culminated with the present-day Internet. Each step of this evolution laid the foundation for a paradigm shift in our thinking. Claude Shannon originated the notion of stochastics applied to networking. Weaver, Bush, Weiner, and Dijkstra, building on Shannon's work; therefore the application of computing progressed to the command and control of technical communications. Selfridge and Licklieder (the founders of ARPANET, the original Internet backbone) followed with the publication of the application of daemons and agents and dynamic programming to technical communications. The influence of Licklieder and his predecessors can be seen in the architecture and implementation of the Internet as we know it today.

The Internet is based on a layered architecture that inherited characteristics of Selfridge's "daemon" and OSI's "reference model." Although OSI's layered model provides a well-defined mechanism for communications, it leaves one layer, the session layer, undefined. The session layer enables communication and session semantics between applications. It is this application-specific layer, called *middleware*, that received significant attention in the early to late 1990s and has led to a proliferation of nonstandard solutions (the progression of queues, CORBA, and the various flavors of MOM are illustrated in Figure 18.2). It is this layer that will be the focus of the paradigm shift of the 2000 decade. For it has already begun, the implementation of SONA is a nexus of grid computing and Web Services and can be seen in Figure 18.5, as well as at its early stages in Planet-Lab. PlanetLab[31] is a consortium of universities and research facilities establishing a worldwide network of hundreds of computers (connected via the Internet) forming a grid that can be "sliced" to run applications. (For more information on the Planet-Lab, refer to http://www.planet-lab.org/php/overview.php.)

Figure 18.5 shows the parallels between SONA and the OSI model. Included in the diagram are the policy-based control loops of SONA. The principles of the command-and-control loops were discussed earlier in this book and are a key part of SONA. There are three control loops: the uppermost loop, in the Presentation/Communication Protocol layer, is for "macroscheduling" of the grid. The lower two control loops in the data link/plant scheduling and transport/service delivery layers are for microscheduling of the grid facility. In brief, macroscheduling is

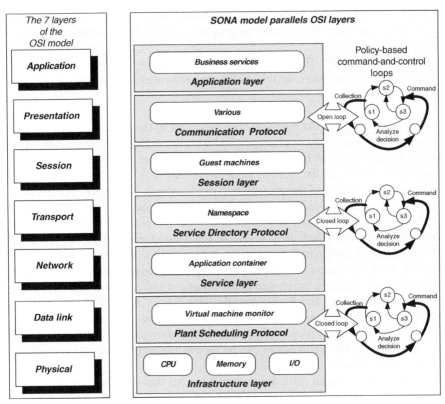

Figure 18.5. SONA layers parallel the OSI seven-layer model.

the long-term planning of plant resources and capacity looking forward for one or more years. Microscheduling involves shorter-term resource allocation, looking forward in periods of quarters, months, and weeks. Macro and microscheduling are discussed in Chapter 19. In fact, we will see that the SONA model is the foundation for the compute utility, forming the lower layers of the physical infrastructure, plant scheduling, service, and service directory.

Service-Oriented Network Architecture (SONA). SONA is an attempt to learn from our past and build on it. The basic principles that have built the infrastructures that we depend on so much today can and should be leveraged to evolve compute services into a consumer-based economic model supported by a utility infrastructure delivering quality product at an affordable cost. We will look at the drivers and the building blocks behind the SONA evolution. Please refer to earlier chapters for a description of SONA layered architecture.

The Drivers. The history and present-day state of technical communications are driven largely by three kinds of forces: macroeconomic, sociogovernmental, and technological. Furthermore, each of these forces is itself influenced by the emergence of new mediums and/or modes of communications. Figure 18.6 illustrates the interactions between such forces.

Economics has always played a major role in technical evolution. Markets drive innovation and are themselves affected by new technologies. Market economies, however, are unpredictable in nature and as such do not apply the same unidirectional force to innovations from decade to decade. At the time of this writing, in the early–mid-2000s, the macroeconomic picture is shaped largely by recession. In particular, uncertainty, dwindling profit margins, rapidly restructured business models, and increased reliance on (and thereby cost of) automation are all independent forces driving the economy.

The current economics impacts technology in several distinct ways. For instance, they place new demands on information technology (IT), including the requirement to satisfy variable demands in service levels, inventory, and people. They also require a greater transparency from IT for resource utilization and cost. The continuing economic uncertainty has generated pressures to rationalize technology investment. Elasticity of IT planning and fungibility of IT resources are two manifestations of economic pressures on information technology.

Societal and governmental pressures have played a major role in driving changes in technology. Computing devices have pervaded the very fabric of society, and as a

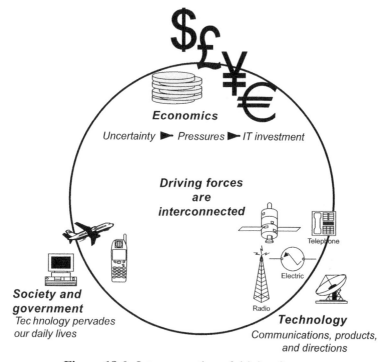

Figure 18.6. Interconnection of driving forces.

result their interconnections have increasingly driven society forward. What would happen if electricity were removed from our lives, for example? We have had very brief glimpses into this possibility with each power blackout. In the early 2000s the entire eastern U.S. seaboard went dark for hours and in some places even as long as days. Without electricity, we are without light, communication (computers, telephones, radio, television, cable, satellite, etc.), and transportation (cars, trains, motorcycles, trucks, airplanes, shipping, traffic signals, etc.), the foodchain is broken (refrigeration is gone, meat and produce cannot get from the farm to the stores, etc.), modern medicine, is disrupted, and the list goes on and on. All of these things are fundamentally dependent, or have become dependent on electricity. We humans have lived only since the late 1890s dependent on electricity, so in its absence we would continue on; however, we would be thrown into a minidark ages as most of the knowledge of simply how to survive without electricity has been lost to the masses.

Defense spending has significantly increased since September 11, 2001 and will as a result produce technology that would simply not be available because of market economics. Society as a whole plays a pivotal role in the evolution of technology. In addition to social forces that drive innovation, government involvement, particularly in research, contributes significantly to the evolution of technology. In the twentieth century, society focused and continues to focus on communications, particularly through the rapid adoption of pervasive interconnected devices. The U.S. government has focused significantly on research to enhance the nation's infrastructure and to more tightly integrate existing institutions. The resulting impact has led to an increased pace of innovation in the academic community. It has also led to an increased reliance on communications as a basic element of the social fabric.

Technological evolution has itself played a role in driving convergence and benefiting from it. Most notably, developers have taken advantage of the predictive power posited by Moore's, Metcalfe's, and Amdahl's laws. This has enabled the construction of more complex applications as well as the interconnections and communication paradigms between them. Communications has not experienced major fundamental shifts since the 1960s. All current systems have simply evolved as strata above the IP substrate. This stratum (middleware) has become heavily bloated with a variety of products, approaches, and directions without any clear winners. This in turn has led to an exponential increase in information, middleware bloat, and overprovisioning. Some of the main technological driving forces are described below.

Network Computing Power Explosion. Technical communications have been gated by the ability of the switch or router to process and route packets. Since the mid-1990s these routers and switches have become increasingly complex and have embedded more features. This network computing power explosion is enabling a higher degree of intelligence in the network layer. This will lead to a more complex routing/networking model, particularly as the previous models, which were built to take advantage of a significantly less powerful network switch fabric, reach the end of life.

Consequences of Moore's and Metcalfe's Laws. *Moore's law* states that the number of transistors on a chip (which implying an increase in compute power) doubles every 18 months and has brought us to the point of compute cycles since the most precious resource of the computer is now more of a commodity. *Metcalfe's law* observes an exponential increase in value of the network as the number of users on the network increase (specifically, the usefulness is the square of the number of users). This has led to the current computing resources that have been producing information above and beyond the ability of humans to process it, a trend that is not about to change. Thus more system power needs to be in place to address the overflow of this information.

Isomorphism to Evolution of Previous Systems. The isomorphism evolution is similar to the evolution of the telephone switch, as traced from Shannon, Weiner, and Dijkstra.

Grid and Web Services as Manifestation of State Transition. The grid addresses some of the key points dealing with this manifestation. Through the network power explosion that enables more intelligent resource management at the switch level, including not only network but other resources as well, the grid is the next solution. Combined with Moore and Metcalfe's laws, this will continue for some time; thus grid capabilities and network computing capabilities will be closely correlated. Web Services provides the ideal organizational mechanism for network services such as discovery, connection, and management.

Conclusion. The convergence of macroeconomic, Sociogovernmental, and technological forces is the fundamental driver behind the paradigm shift in communications. Macroeconomic forces are driving a demand for elasticity, fungibility, and granularity of service levels, resources, and IT planning. Societal forces are driving the emergence of novel communication mechanisms as well as the rapid adoption of such mechanisms within the basic social fabric. Coupled with the steady increase in CPU clock rates, these forces together have pushed modern communication to a breaking point, leading to a proliferation of point solutions, custom middleware, and overprovisioning.

Communication is a fundamental element of our social fabric. Technical communications is slowly beginning to attain the same status and as such is evolving through a set of paradigms. These paradigms are driven by the needs of society as well as the capabilities of technology and will eventually settle on a set of mechanisms that will become the lingua franca of our time. SONA and Web Services have the potential to become this lingua franca.

19

THE COMPUTE UTILITY

The evolution in distributed computing is leading us toward a business focus where we have to consider how systems are designed and delivered. This line of thinking is a shift toward service-oriented architecture (SOA). The philosophy of software packaging is taught in every Computer Science 101 class starting with a compartmentalization of logical units of work with a well-defined interface. Just about every programming language supports some form of macros, subroutines, functions, objects, and services. Each is a progression in granularity of function starting with fine grains of work in macros to a more coarse grain definition of objects with a service as the coarsest or broadest in scope. An example of a service is a payment system. The payment system can be composed of 10s or 100s of individual objects, each specific in scope and function to deliver a piece of the larger payment system service. Only the service made up of the user interface to the payment system is visible to the user or consumer, not the finer-grained objects of which the complete payment system is composed.

As businesses offer more and more services to the user community, a change in the way the services are delivered and packaged results. It is important to note, as mentioned earlier, that siloed data centers do not lend themselves to service delivery. What was once an application for a specific user group that maintained its own hardware within a data center (a silo) now becomes a corporationwide service to be leveraged across the business units on an on-demand basis as well as a client service available externally. The shift in offering services immediately implies a different business model for information technology. The technology is required to transform to a consumer–producer model. The user groups are the consumers purchasing the

Distributed Data Management for Grid Computing, by Michael Di Stefano
Copyright © 2005 John Wiley & Sons, Inc.

services that are offered by information technology. Therefore, the consumer satisfaction rating of the service is measured by the functions provided by the service and the availability/performance of the service as the service is utilized. This implies that the infrastructure required to deliver the service to the customer now becomes an integral part in defining the quality of the service. This requires a change in the way the services are delivered. With this model, in order to meet the supply/demand curves that the consumer will levy on the infrastructure and its ability to deliver the service, the data centers need to be

- *Flexible*—responsive to change
- *Fungible*—interchangeable, substitutable
- *Scalable*—growing with business demands

There has been an emergence of standards from various corporations and research groups for the definitions of how to deliver the business services. Some examples are IBM's On Demand Business,[32] Sun's N1-Grid, Stanford's Compute Utility Architecture, The Global Grid Forum,[33] "cluster on demand,"[34] and the HP Adaptive Enterprise.[35] All the standards describe the architecture required to deliver services and use buzzwords such as "the compute utility" and "the virtual data center." We will examine the basic architecture for a compute utility, including its components and objectives, the architecture, and the interaction of the components so that the compute utility can be as efficient as a manufacturing plant or factory. On the broad scale, the user demands on the manufacture of a product or to supply the services are known to the plant manager; however, like many things in life, the factory production line will undergo daily changes based on user demand that they need to be addressed.

The architecture that will be discussed in this chapter originates primarily from two sources: a white paper that was released by Hewlett-Packard in March 2001 on virtual data centers and their operating environments, and an extension of this architecture that was a derived by the partnership work of Integrasoft, Platform Computing, and Corosoft.[36] Each component or layer of the compute utility is vital to the compute utility as a whole and equally complex in function, deserving of more attention than can be provided in the forum of distributed data management. Our discussions will concentrate on the role of data management within the compute utility.

OVERVIEW

The compute utility has many objectives, which are reflected in its design. To summarize some of these objectives, one must consider the purpose of the compute utility, which includes

- Reduce risk exposure.
- Lower operational costs.

- Achieve controlled and predictable costs for new implementations and services.
- Improve responsiveness of information technology to the business units that they support.

These goals can be achieved without cannibalizing the current data centers, which will not be an option in any real scenario. Many companies cannot justify reinvesting and doing away with their current data center investments in order to build and offer utility services. Therefore, the new architecture needs to reuse as much of the existing infrastructure as possible by at least leveraging the computer servers to increase utilization rates and build on the intra/inter–data center networking infrastructure. The key milestones must be the reduced complexity in the data center from an operational and maintenance perspective through more and better automation, providing an elastic infrastructure support and cost transparency to the business units.

In order to meet these objectives, one needs to determine what is required in data centers. Well, the data grid is the answer. The role of the data grid within the compute utility is to provide visibility into the system. Visibility into the compute utility extends the current thinking of what visibility is in a siloed IT infrastructure. "Visibility" into the utility refers to the information infrastructure needed to deliver a service that has been perfected in industries other than computer software. Examples or models that IT can use when architecting the compute utility and considering visibility into the utility are the telephone line, power (electricity), and energy (natural gas). These respective industries have vast infrastructure for delivering service to the consumer on a supply and demand basis. A key ingredient in delivering the service is the *timely availability of accurate metered data.* So the key to a utility service is accurate metered data in order for that service to meet the demands. The system as a whole records and tracks information about itself, including its state, and feeds the data back to a control center. The metered data must include usage information. This information will allow the utility to change state in such a way as to accommodate the increase of demand as usage peaks occur. Similarly, as the usage decreases, the system can change its state to adjust to the lower service demand. The system will always be in the state to best offer the service to the customer on an as-needed basis.

Today in IT, data centers and the applications, that they support do not monitor or track any required metered data. The data grid implemented as part of the existing data centers architecture that can be used as the focal point to collect metered data and make them available to all users in a timely fashion, thus enabling broad and deep visibility into the state of the compute utility. For example, user demand is placed on the system by the consumer. With timely, accurate, and visible metered information describing the state of the compute utility, smart decisions can be made and appropriate actions taken to keep the compute utility in a predictable steady state. The steady state of a compute utility is just like the steady state of a factory, which I touched on above. It needs to be to efficient, in a time- and cost-effective manner, and to deliver service to the consumer when the consumer demands the service. The quality of the service is equally evaluated as to how well the service functions when the demand is imposed on it. The data grid is not only the collection focal point of metered data; it is also the event channel to deliver control commands issued by the command mechanism. The data grid will deliver the instructions to the various components within the compute utility to complete the command/control management loop.

ARCHITECTURE

The architecture for the compute utility consists of five basic components: the physical resource, the operational environment, the service environment, the data grid, and the measurement and management (command and control). Figure 19.1 shows the compute utility architecture in an arch rather than the traditional block

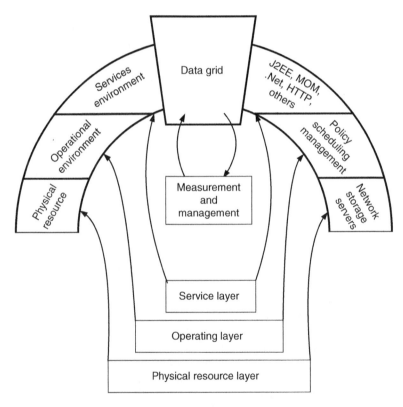

Four base layers supporting a SOA with the data grid as the keystone of the compute utility arch

Figure 19.1. Compute utility architecture.

diagram format. The arch is one of the oldest and strongest infrastructures known. Its beauty is in its simplicity.

The architecture for the compute utility mirrors the simplicity and strength of the arch. At the foundation, the physical resource layer, is the physical resource, which includes the network, the storage, and the servers. The next layer up is the operating layer or environment. The operational environment is a logical view of the physical resource layer. It is a management layer that is policy-driven to keep track of, allocate, and provision the physical resources. The next layer of the arch is the service layer or environment. These are the typical services that we have become dependent on in distributed computing such as message-oriented middleware (MOM), J2EE, microsoft.Net, and HTTP. As with any arch, the strength of the arch comes from the keystone; the keystone to the compute utility arch is the data grid. The data grid's primary function is to provide the mechanism for collecting the metered information from within each of these layers and deliver this information or data to the measurement-and-management component of the compute utility. It is the interaction between all the layers of the compute utility through their metered data that allows this utility to deliver services on a supply/demand basis. With the absence of the data grid, the collection of metered information becomes cumbersome and the responsiveness of the utility to the users diminishes, thus lowering the quality of service that is delivered to the customer.

We have already addressed the major aspects and components of data management of the compute utility in our discussions on geographic boundary problems and command and control.

Geographic Boundary

The beauty of the data grid to manage and meter data is such that the physical resources do not need to be contained within a single data center. The operational environment abstracts physical locality of the servers and data centers to the layers above it (the service environment and ultimately the consumer). Recall from previous discussions that the limitations of geographic boundaries are not distance but are rather the network bandwidth. The data grid and the compute grid are the tools in the operational environment that provide the geographic independence and establish a policy-driven view of the physical resource.

Command-and-Control Systems

In our use case for command and control, we discussed how the data grid is essential for the collection of vast amounts of data from numerous dispersed sources. Each layer of the compute utility (the physical, operational, and service environments) must generate metered information. Each subsystem, software program, server, router, hub, and other component is generating new bits and pieces of information that individually tend to be smaller in size but taken as a whole end up as vast amount of data moving very quickly in time. In the command/control analysis it is the data grid that provides the mechanism for the quick and easy collection as well as access to these data. The data grid can also provide the distribution backbone for the commands issued by the command and control. Figure 19.2 expands on the use of compute utility architecture for command and control.

In the architecture shown in Figure 19.2, the role of the data grid in the compute utility is twofold. The first part is getting the application to run in the environment. For example, some delivered services include credit risk and anti–money laundering. The services themselves rely on the data grid to distribute the data across the compute utility to the physical locations (the physical compute nodes of the compute grid) where the service is located. Please refer to the section on compute-intensive applications in Chapter 13 and Figure 15.3, on data warehousing with the data grid, for more in-depth discussion on how the data grid functions in these business leveling services.

The second area where the data grid plays a key role in the compute utility is in the management of the utility itself and in the command-and-control aspects of maintaining the compute utility. Figure 19.3 shows the interactions between the

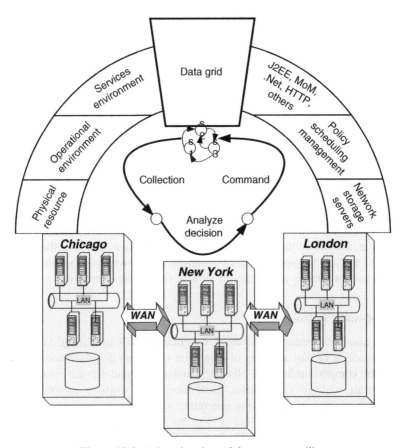

Figure 19.2. A broader view of the compute utility.

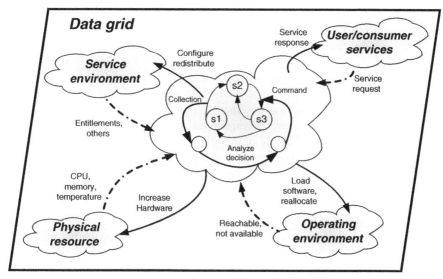

Figure 19.3. Compute utility interlayer data interaction.

various layers of the compute utility from the metered information that is generated by each layer and the command/control information that flows back to each layer.

Each layer has its own data region within the data grid: the physical resource, the operating environment, and the service environment, as well as the consumer services. The fifth data region is the command/control region. Each layer will generate metered information that flows into the command/control system via the data grid. At the physical resource layer, metered information can be CPU usage, memory utilization, temperature, and various networking statistics. The operating environments can tell us whether the physical resources are accessible or available. The service environment can give us information about entitlements. And, of course, the consumer services provide information usage such as workload, service, and user requests of the consumer community.

Macro/Microscheduling

Managers of an electric utility infrastructure or the power grid that delivers electrical power to the customer know that certain areas of the country have high usage during the summer months to deal with the hot temperatures. Similarly, natural-gas companies know that their peak usage periods are in the cold winter months. The managers can plan and adjust their utility infrastructures to handle the seasonal peaks and valleys of consumer supply and demand. However, even though electrical power demand in July and August is expected to be high in New York City, of brownouts and even blackouts still occur. Just the other evening, more than just the typical hot, hazy, and humid mid-August evening, by 10 P.M. it had managed to cool down to 90°F; I was at Yankee Stadium watching the Anaheim Angels shut out my beloved

Yankees (but that is another story) in the sixth inning, when parts of the Bronx experienced a blackout. The stadium scoreboard went dark, but for some reason, the stadium lights stayed on, allowing the game to continue. The point to note here is that even though the utility infrastructure is geared to deliver more power to places such as New York City in the summer, there are microscale peaks and valleys that augment tie macroscale peaks and valleys. Should the microscale peaks amplify or occur in such a way that exceeds even the best of expectations, the utility must respond. If it cannot respond quickly enough, or most likely if the demand peaks are above the ability of the infrastructure to deliver, circuitbreakers trip, causing brownouts or blackouts. The tripping of a circuitbreaker protects against wide-scale damage to the system. Remember that the entire northeast coast of the United States as well as parts of southeastern Canada lost power because the power grid tripped breakers to protect itself from a bigger potential danger. The only way this can occur is through measurement and analysis of metered data that describe the state of the utility. The metered data describe not only the state of the system but also the microscale peaks and valleys of user demand.

The command/control system of the compute utility performs a quick analysis of the metered information. The purpose of the analysis is not for macroscheduling but rather for microscheduling since the manager of the utility has a good idea of the larger cycles of consumer usage patterns on the utility. It is understood that there will be peaks and valleys for certain services throughout the day, the week, the month, and the year. However, as the user community's demand varies up or down (as a result of any number of reasons, e.g., variations in community size, external unpredicted events, local or global), you will see minipeaks and minivalleys, thus creating a microscheduling pattern that augments the macroscheduling of services. Think of macroscheduling as the carrier frequency of a radio signal and microscheduling as modulation of the carrier frequency. Figure 19.4 highlights micro- and macroscheduling and how to maintain a steady state for the compute utility.

Figure 19.4 shows three curves: the macroscheduling curve that the manager of the utility uses for long-term planning, the microscheduling curve describing unexpected peaks and valleys in usage demand, and a third curve that describes how the commute utility has to adjust to accommodate both the macro- and micro-scheduling demands. Both types of scheduling are needed to deliver the service.

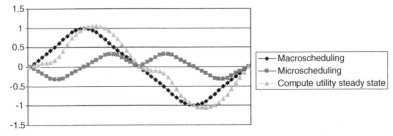

Figure 19.4. Macroscheduling, microscheduling, and the compute utility steady state.

The command/control system will issue commands back to the physical resource level to increase certain hardware components or reprovision servers with various software components. A top-down analysis starting from the customer service usage will show a chain of interdependence of metered information at each layer affecting commands to the next. The service environment will be issued commands to reconfigure or redistribute a service or services that will force commands down into the operating environments to load software or reallocate servers to supply the needed services, which will in turn cause commands to the physical resource layer to increase hardware or reprovision of servers.

We see two areas of information flow for the compute utility command and control. The two flows are metered information flowing up within each layer and the interdependency of information flow between each of the layers and command information flowing down.

PART IV

REFERENCE MATERIAL

20

LANGUAGE INTERFACE

An interesting topic of discussion is the language interface supported by the data grid. The access of data is not apparent and not as simple as in Structured Query Language (SQL) since the structure of the data in the data grid is not restricted to tables and relationships that normally exist in a relational database. Structural type can vary from simpler to more complex than that of the two-dimensional table of the relational model. However, there are some standards emerging such as SQL99 (SQL3) that address data access into object–relational data structures. In this chapter we will examine three language interfaces from the distributed data management: (1) programmatic, which is a program language interface such as C++; (2) Java; and (3) C# language binding. The second language interface that we will examine will be a query based on an interface similar to that of SQL. Finally, a XML-based descriptive data language interface will also be examined.

In this chapter we will look at the three approaches for language interface into the data grid, including their scope and the pros and cons of each. In summary, all three language interfaces are required for the data grid for the same reasons that all three are needed for the relational technologies. The relational database technology does have a programmatic interface [Application Programmatic Interface (API)], a string-based query interface (SQL), and XML bindings as highlighted below:

- The advantage of the Programmatic Language Interface is speed and performance. The developers can access the database natively without having to go through the layers of SQL.

Distributed Data Management for Grid Computing, by Michael Di Stefano
Copyright © 2005 John Wiley & Sons, Inc.

- SQL is the simplest and most effective way of accessing data in a structured data store or database. Currently, it is not clear which is the best and most efficient method to perform a stringlike query interface into the data grid. Therefore, we will discuss the current available methods, and as the industry moves forward, a clearer path will be chosen through the user community. Note that precompiled SQL queries do provide levels of performance boost over straight SQL even though they are considered as part of the SQL interface.
- Web content is mostly XML-based. Web pages and applications need data access to and from a database. In addition to XML, data structural descriptions and representation typically used for Internet access that are being "bunched" into this category are

   Document type definition (DTD)

   Standard Generalized Markup Language (SGML)

   eXtensible Style Language (XSL)

PROGRAMMATIC

Programmatic interfaces are limited to the audience of developers who can program in a 3GL (third-generation language) type of language such as C++, Java, and C#. Developers as a community are accustomed to programmatic interfaces since just about every data management system has one that includes relational databases. These interfaces are supplied by the data management vendors (e.g., Sybase Open Client API) or through third-party toolkits (e.g., JDBC). A good rule of thumb is that the native language bindings supplied by the database vendor yield the best performance. Performance decreases the farther away you go from a native binding.

The language bindings for the data grid are quite different from the one that you would use with relational databases. Let us take a moment to review the typical flow of work when building an application:

- Through the programmatic interface, the business objects issues a query.
- Result sets are returned.
- The result sets are then parsed and the business objects are populated.

The results sets that are returned by the database's Application Programmatic Interface (API) are iterative, first through the table looking for appropriate rows, then through each row looking for the appropriate individual data elements or fields. In this situation, it is the responsibility of the developer to map the binding between the result set traversals and the data attributes of the business object. Note that there are some developer tools that can make this process less manual.

One objective of a data grid is to eliminate the data access bottlenecks by widening the throat of the data access funnel; this funnel can be as wide as the data grid itself. This process is achieved by bringing the data as close to the grid compute node as possible. The term that we have associated with the process of data locality is *data affinity*, which I have addressed throughout the book. However, data locality is not the complete solution. The solution for the data grid can extend beyond data affinity into providing a unified view of the business data independent of the data source. Without the data grid functionality, it would be the responsibility primarily of the business object to connect to the data source and translate the data from the external format of the data source into the data attributes of the business object. The data grid can assume the data translation responsibility from the business object through its data load and store policies. Note that data representations in business objects can range from simple single data points and lists, to more complex lists of lists forming *N*-dimensional space. Therefore, the data grid must have the flexibility to represent multidimensional data structures. With this requirement, it is important to note that the language interfaces of the data grid must support accesses, queries, and the navigation of *N*-dimensional data structures.

The requirement for the data management systems to support multidimensional data structures is not new; for example, there are object databases. However, these data management systems are not in wide use. In addition, anyone who has programmed with an object database can attest that they are not the easiest systems to use, architect, manage, maximize performance with, and maintain.

I would like to focus on examples that are currently in use and are understood by majority of the developers in the technology field. The two that come to mind are the Standard Template Library (STL) and the SourcePro product (formally known as RWTools), which is a commercially available toolkit, offered by Rogue Wave Software (www.roguewave.com). Most developers are fairly familiar with these concepts; therefore a data grid programmatic interface should be these straightforward APIs. This would reduce the barrier to entry, minimizing the learning curve, and increasing the likelihood of acceptance by the community. The example provided in this book is based on a data grid product offered by Integrasoft called the Integrasoft Grid Fabric (IGF). This product, whose API is a Standard Template Library (STL), can be considered RWTool-like. The example illustrated below shows, through the use of a factory object, the connection to the data grid, querying the data grid via the *GET*( ) command, and the simple iteration through an array to access and print the data atoms stored in the data grid. The code represented by this interface is illustrated below:

```
1  public static void main (String argv[])
2      {
3      java.util.Properties props = new java.util.Properties();
4      IGFCartridge cart = IGFBasicCartridgeFactory.instance().
          create(``Default'',
5          props);
6      IGFBasicDataCartridge dCart = (IGFBasicDataCartridge)
          cart.data();
7
8      IGFBasicList testList = (IGFBasicList) dCart.getRoot
          (``YieldCurve1'');
```

```
9     for (int i = 1; i < 10; i++)
10    {
11      IGFCustomObject o = (IGFCustomObject)testList.get(i);
12      System.out.println(''Index:''+i+''yield:''+o.m_yield.
          getValue()+''mat:''+
13                        o.m_maturity);
14    }//for ()
15
16    }
```

Most developers understand the use of factories, which are the things that can be collected and the things that can contain them. So, when reviewing this example, most developers will intuitively understand how to "data-grid-enable" systems with little or no learning curve. Complex issues such as data atom granularity are simply handled through inheritance (coarse in grain) or via attribute declaration (fine in grain). Once a data atom is defined, it lives in the data grid and not in the local memory of the process itself. It can be inserted into any data grid collection, thus automatically making it available to all on the data grid.

The data grid supporting similar programmatic constructs is commonly used by application developers, enabling the reuse of existing code in the current production applications as well as other legacy systems. Thus, the data integration that is required in the data grid can leverage the existing straight-through processing (STP) adapters, which are used today to "load" the data into the data grid and "store" the data out of the data grid. The use of middleware, whether provided through a third-party vendor or internally developed, is prevalent throughout most information technology organizations to achieve STP. Normal implementations of middleware solutions leverage the concept/technique of data loaders (typically referred to as "adapters"). These adapters possess the logic of translating data to and from systems, including legacy systems into business objects. Therefore, to transform from STP to enterprise information integration (EII) into the data grid, the use of the well-known programmatic API style discussed above can easily enable the conversion of the existing STP adapters into the data grid adapters for both data load and store.

QUERY-BASED

The most commonly used query-based interface is Structured Query Language (SQL). The relational model is steeped in mathematical principles, thus enabling complex data relationships ranging from simple two-dimensional table structures to an optimized method of querying the resulting structures. However, SQL is not inherently suited as a query interface into a data management system of the data grid since its needs to support varying types of data atoms and multidimensional structures.

There are other data management systems with similar data structural chrematistics of a data grid, specifically object databases and object–relational databases. Building on the existing work to determine how similar problems have been addressed with these systems is an excellent place to start moving forward and standardizing on what is the best query-based interface required by the data grid. The story starts in the early days of extending SQL for querying object databases. What has evolved from those efforts is the object–relational standard, SQL99. SQL99, formally known as SQL3, extends SQL to include concepts of object–relational bindings. SQL99's object–relational bindings do support object-oriented concepts such as inheritance and instances, but they do not support object-oriented standards fully. However, this is the most reasonable starting point for adopting a query-based interface as required for the data grid. Even though the object-relational mapping is not fully object-oriented, it does support many of the concepts and has industry standards bodies supporting it. The alternative of starting from scratch and creating an entirely new standards body and organizations to revisit some of the problems already addressed by SQL99 should be considered if one does determine that SQL99 cannot support the requirements of a data grid. The following references provide additional information on SQL99:

- ANSII Standards Body
- "Practical PostgreSQL" by John Worsley and Joshua Drake, O'Reilly, January 2002

Why focus on SQL99 alone, one may ask. SQL99 is something that is architected to support object relational bindings and mappings as opposed to something that's more native and optimized for the data grid. The object–relational standard, SQL99, has a well-established community behind it, including myself, since I am a firm believer of building on what is a successful versus starting from scratch. SQL has been proved to work well, and as such a majority of the user community understands and knows how to use it. Therefore, it makes sense to build on a technology that enjoys a broad knowledge base that is widely accepted, thus lowering the barrier of entry of any new technology, including grid technology. Granted this approach is not the best technical answer, but it is a practical one. Any future extensions to SQL99 to support the "data grid" can be organized through the existing standards bodies. Therefore, it is the opinion of this author that this is the most logical and practical place to start binding a query-based language suited to the data grid. The following is the syntax example for the select statement in PostgreSQL, a forerunner to SQL99, from which many features can be found:

```
1   SELECT [ALL | DISTINCT [ON (expression [, ...])]]
2       target [AS name] [, ...]
3       [FROM source [, ...]]
4         [[NATURAL] join_type source
5         [ON condition | USING (column_list)]]
6         [, ...]
7       [WHERE condition]
8       [GROUP BY expression [, ...]]
9       [HAVING condition [, ...]]
```

```
10      [{ UNION | INTERSECT | EXCEPT } [ALL] sub-query]
11      [ORDER BY expression
12      [ASC | DESC | USING operator]
13      [,...]]
14      [FOR UPDATE [OF table [,...]]]
15      [LIMIT { count | ALL } [{ OFFSET |, } start]]
```

With all of this said, individual vendors should not work in a vacuum, creating their own query-based language or adding their own extensions to SQL/SQL99 in support of their own data grid product. This may generate fractures in the community, thus hindering the adoption of grid technology. Hence, this will result in every vendor having their own flavor of a query-based interface, for example, their own personalized version of SQL99. Should individual vendors venture down this path, I would encourage them to contribute their work into the community with the possible inclusion and adoption of a uniform standard moving forward.

XML-BASED

XML is quickly becoming a common way to exchange data between applications primarily because its markup language supports metadata or information that describes the data that are contained within a message. XML also supports some of the complex relationships of data and data attributes found within most of programming languages such as object-oriented programming.

Database companies have an XML interface built into their respective products, Oracle has an XML SQL utility, and DB2 has DB2 XML, for example. These examples are of how an emergent technology has been leveraging complex data relationships (such as those supported in XML). Other databases such as object–relational databases take the object representations of data as described in XML and more readily map them into a relational database model. Some object databases are also utilizing XML to store data. Therefore, the use of XML as an interface into data grid is something that should be explored further and definitely supported.

Initially, an XML-based query language would be a cross between SQL, a language that is easy to understand and learn and the more complex programmatic interfaces, which are tightly bound to the 3GL programming languages. The XML query interface sits in between the two extremes; one needs to have some programming experience to understand XML and XML structures and formats, and even to read the XML syntax. Tools that simplify the XML process are available; however, they do not completely reduce the complexity level of a SQL query. So, while going beyond the object–relational limits of SQL99, XML does not completely reduce the barrier of entry to the mass development resources.

Today, most of the Web page contents are XML-based. As with relational, object, and object–relational databases, XML interfaces are essential to the data grid.

21

BASIC PROGRAMMING EXAMPLES

I am a partner and co-founder of Integrasoft. We have dedicated the company to highly distributed computing environments in the financial sector since its inception in 1997. In 2001, we focused our collective experience on bridging the chasm of data management in relation to the grid compute environments. Many of the principles discussed in this book are a direct result of our work and are addressed in our product known as the Integrasoft Grid Fabric (IGF), a distributed data management system for the compute grid.

IGF is a purely data management system that is designed to sit on top of any vendor's "data distribution engine." Currently, IGF's data distribution engine is a distributed cache that spans the entire grid space.

IGF supports data regions and the various data management policies discussed below. Three working code examples developed using the IGF product are described below. The first two are simple "HelloWorld" examples that show fine and coarse granularity of data atoms in a data grid. The latter is more involved, covering a random-number surface used in a Monte Carlo simulation. I hope that these examples will be found useful in further expansion of the theories or application that we have covered.

HELLOWORLD EXAMPLE

Coarse Granularity

This example shows a coarse-grained object whose entire data attributes will be stored in the IGF data grid as a single IGF data atom. Note that the business logic of "IGFCustomObject" does not need any modifications to be able to support the data grid. Through its inheritance from IGFCacheable, the IGFCustomObject becomes an entity that can be stored in any IGF data grid collection. When placed in an IGF collection, it will be assigned a "logical" name that can be used by the collection's "get( )" command for later retrieval. Since IGFCustomObject is an IGFCacheable entity, it through any IGF Collection's "put( )" command can be placed into the collection. The collection and all its entities are live data atoms in the data grid. By default, the collection and its entities are now under the data grid's management policies, which include the regionalization, synchronization, replication, and distribution policies. Any application connected to the data grid can open the collection and via the collection's "get( )" command can "query the data grid" for any individual entity in the collection by name, for example. Because of the coarse granularity of the data grid atom, IGFCustomObject is "queryable" as a single data point (data atom); applications cannot see into the IGFCustomObject and thus query the data grid for it by any of its data attributes of "m_yield," "m_maturity," and "m_pointName." The object is opaque to the outside world; this is what is meant by "coarse granularity." However, once retrieved from the data grid through the get( ) command, the application can operate on the object and its attributes as any other normal object. Any resulting changes of state of the object are reflected in the data grid once it is "put" back (updated) into the collection.

The following is an example of the code required to define ("coarse data atom"), store ("writer program"), and access ("reader program") a coarse data atom:

Coarse Data Atom

```
1    import com.integrasoftware.GridFabric.Cartridges.
     Framework.model.*;
2    import com.integrasoftware.GridFabric.Cartridges.Basic.
     DataCartridge.model.*;
3    import com.integrasoftware.GridFabric.Cartridges.Basic.
     DataCartridge.*;
4    import com.integrasoftware.GridFabric.Integration.Data.
     Framework.model.*;
5    /**
6    *Title: IGFCustomObject<
7    *Description: This custom object demonstrates the ability
     to store leaf nodes with both IGF
8    *and generic Java values. Leaf nodes can be inserted in a
     variety of IGF collections
9    *Copyright: Copyright (c) 2003
10   *Company: Integrasoft LLC
```

```
11  *@version 1.0
12  */
13
14  public class IGFCustomObject implements IGFCacheable
15          //Leaf nodes MUST implement IGFCacheable
16  {
17  public IGFBasicFloat m_yield;
18  public java.util.Date m_maturity;
19  public String m_pointName;
20
21  public IGFCustomObject()  //These are empty for now
22  {
23  }
24
25  public IGFCachePolicy cachePolicy()  //These are empty for now
26  {
27  return null;
28  }
29
30  public void cachePolicy(IGFCachePolicy policy)//These are
    empty for now
31  {
32  }
33  }
```

Writer Program

```
1   import com.integrasoftware.GridFabric.Cartridges.Basic.
    DataCartridge.model.*;
2   import com.integrasoftware.GridFabric.Cartridges.Basic.*;
3   import com.integrasoftware.GridFabric.Cartridges.Basic.
    DataCartridge.*;
4   import com.integrasoftware.GridFabric.Cartridges.Frame-
    work.control.*;
5   import java.util.*;
6
7   import java.io.*;
8
9   /**
10  *Title: IGFObjectGraph3Writer
11  *Description: This example demonstrates the creation of a
    custom leaf object, a leaf can
12  *contain any number and type of attributes as long as it
    implements IGFCacheable
13  *Copyright: Copyright (c) 2003
14  *Company: Integrasoft LLC
15  *@version 1.0
16  */
```

```
17
18  public class IGFObjectGraph3Writer {
19  public IGFObjectGraph3Writer()
20    {
21    }
22
23  public static void main (String argv[])
24  {
25  java.util.Properties props = new java.util.Properties();
26
27
28  //Create a cartridge on region called "Default", pass in
    properties in event more configuration parameters are needed
29  //
30  IGFCartridge cart = IGFBasicCartridgeFactory.instance().
    create("Default",
31    props);
32
33  //Obtain a handle to the Data Cartridge associated w/Region
    "Default"
34  IGFBasicDataCartridge dCart = (IGFBasicDataCartridge)
    cart.data();
35
36  //Construct a new List associated w/Region "Default"
37  IGFBasicList testList=(IGFBasicList) dCart.
    obtainCacheableEntityNamed(
38    "IGFBasicList");
39
40  //Iterate through list and populate a custom leaf object
41    for (int i = 1;i < 10; i++) {
42
43  //Create a leaf object
44  IGFCustomObject o = new IGFCustomObject();
45
46  //Create an IGF Float associated w/Region "Default"
47  IGFBasicFloat mYield=(IGFBasicFloat)dCart.
    obtainCacheableEntityNamed("IGFBasicFloat");
48
49  //Populate IGFFloat
50  mYield.setValue((float)Math.random()*100);
51
52  o.m_yield = mYield;
53  o.m_maturity = new Date();
54  o.m_pointName = "3YR";
55
56  //Add custom leaf object to list
57  testList.add(o);
58
59  System.out.println("Index:"+i+"yield:"+o.m_yield+"mat:"+
```

```
60        o.m_maturity);
61    }
62
63    //Insert list into region "default"
64    dCart.putRoot("YieldCurve1", testList);
65  }
66
67 }
```

Reader Program

```
1    import com.integrasoftware.GridFabric.Cartridges.Basic.
     DataCartridge.model.*;
2    import com.integrasoftware.GridFabric.Cartridges.Basic.*;
3    import com.integrasoftware.GridFabric.Cartridges.Basic.
     DataCartridge.*;
4    import com.integrasoftware.GridFabric.Cartridges.Frame-
     work.control.*;
5    import java.util.*;
6
7    import java.io.*;
8
9    /**
10   *Title: IGFObjectGraph3Writer
11   *Description: This example reads IGFCacheable objects from
     the Data Grid
12   *Copyright: Copyright (c) 2003
13   *Company: Integrasoft LLC
14   *@version 1.0
15   */
16
17    public class IGFObjectGraph3Reader {
18
19      public IGFObjectGraph3Reader() {
20      }
21
22      public static void main (String argv[])
23        {
24        java.util.Properties props = new java.util.Properties();
25        IGFCartridge cart = IGFBasicCartridgeFactory.instance().
     create("Default",
26          props);
27        IGFBasicDataCartridge dCart=(IGFBasicDataCartridge)
     cart.data();
28
29        IGFBasicList testList = (IGFBasicList) dCart.getRoot
     ("YieldCurve1");
30        for (int i = 1; i < 10; i++)
31          {
```

```
32      IGFCustomObject o = (IGFCustomObject)testList.get(i);
33      System.out.println("Index:"+i+"yield:"+o.m_yield.
   getValue()+"mat:"+
34                  o.m_maturity);
35      }//for ()
36
37  }
38  }
```

Fine Granularity

Now let us investigate an example of a fine-grained data atom. The first thing to notice is that there is no IGFCustomObject that inherits from the IGFCacheable. In this situation the object to be data-grid-enabled is IGFObjectGraph1Writer, where some of its data attributes are natively data-grid-enabled. It is important to note that not all of an object's data attributes need to be data-grid-enabled. Those attributes that are data-grid-enabled "live" in the IGF data grid and are managed by its distributed data management policies. Those that are not data-grid-enabled will reside in the local heap of the process space of the IGFObjectGraph1Writer instance.

The IGFObjectGraph1Writer instance is "put" into the IGF data grid with the logical name of ROOTOBJECT, the name that will be used for later queries and retrieval. Some of the data attributes of the IGFObjectGraph1Writer are collection classes, maps, lists, and arrays. The other data attributes are basic, such as IGFInteger and IGFFloat. Any program that accesses the IGF data grid can get the IGFObjectGraph1Writer from the data grid and directly access any of the "data-grid-enabled attributes." Those programs can change or update the values of these attributes via their respective "put( )" operations, which will immediately take effect in the IGF data grid and can be accessed by any other program viewing or accessing the IGFObjectGraph1Writer "ROOTOBJECT" instance in the IGF data grid. The fact that the internal data attributes of the IGFObjectGraph1Writer are directly IGF data-grid-enabled means that access to these data attributes is direct and transparent to all on the IGF data grid. Therefore, the IGFObjectGraph1Writer is said to be a fine-grained data atom. A sample code for loading of the data atom into the data grid ("writer program") and retrieval of data atom ("reader program") is

Writer Program

```
1  import com.integrasoftware.GridFabric.Cartridges.Basic.
   DataCartridge.model.*;
2  import com.integrasoftware.GridFabric.Cartridges.Basic.*;
3  import com.integrasoftware.GridFabric.Cartridges.Basic.
   DataCartridge.*;
4  import com.integrasoftware.GridFabric.Cartridges.
   Framework.control.*;
```

```
5   import com.integrasoftware.GridFabric.Integration.Data.
    Framework.model.*;
6   import java.util.*;
7
8   import java.io.*;
9
10  /**
11  *Title: IGFObjectGraph1Writer
12  *Description: This object demonstrates the creation and
    population of a custom Root Object.
13  *Root Objects MUST inherit from IGFBasicObject, and can
    contain both native as well as IGF types
14  *Copyright: Copyright (c) 2003
15  *Company: Integrasoft LLC
16  *@version 1.0
17  */
18
19  //Must inherit from IGFBasicObject
20  public class IGFObjectGraph1Writer extends IGFBasicObject
    {
21  public IGFBasicMap m_map1, m_map2;
22  public IGFBasicList m_list1, m_list2;
23  public IGFBasicInt m_int1;
24  public IGFBasicFloat m_float1;
25  public IGFBasicNativeDoubleArray m_dArray;
26  public int foo;
27
28  public IGFObjectGraph1Writer() {
29  super();
30  }
31
32  public static void main(String[] args) {
33   try {
34    IGFObjectGraph1Writer graph1 = new
    IGFObjectGraph1Writer();
35    java.util.Properties props = new java.util.Properties();
36
37
38    //Create a cartridge on region called "Default", pass in
    properties in event more configuration paramemeters are
    needed
39    IGFCartridge cart = IGFBasicCartridgeFactory.instance().
    create("Default",
40      props);
41
42    //Obtain a handle to the Data Cartridge associated
    w/Region "Default"
43    IGFBasicDataCartridge dCart = (IGFBasicDataCartridge)
    cart.data();
```

```
44
45   //Start populating graph1 attributes
46   graph1.foo=-90;
47
48   //Construct new objects for attributes of graph1
49   graph1.m_map1 =
50         (IGFBasicMap) dCart.obtainCacheableEntityNamed
     ("IGFBasicMap");
51
52   graph1.m_map2 =
53         (IGFBasicMap) dCart.obtainCacheableEntityNamed
     ("IGFBasicMap");
54
55   graph1.m_list1 =
56         (IGFBasicList) dCart.obtainCacheableEntityNamed
     ("IGFBasicList");
57
58   graph1.m_list2 =
59         (IGFBasicList) dCart.obtainCacheableEntityNamed
     ("IGFBasicList");
60
61   graph1.m_int1 =
62         (IGFBasicInt) dCart.obtainCacheableEntityNamed
     ("IGFBasicInt");
63
64   graph1.m_float1 =
65         (IGFBasicFloat) dCart.obtainCacheableEntityNamed
     ("IGFBasicFloat");
66
67   IGFBasicDouble dbl2 =
68         (IGFBasicDouble) dCart.obtainCacheableEntityNamed
     ("IGFBasicDouble");
69
70   graph1.m_dArray = (IGFBasicNativeDoubleArray)
71               dCart.obtainCacheableEntityNamed
     ("IGFBasicNativeDoubleArray");
72
73   //populate ints/floats/doubles
74   graph1.m_int1.setValue(94);
75   graph1.m_float1.setValue((float) 95.443);
76   dbl2.setValue(97.998);
77
78   //add int/float into list1
79   graph1.m_list1.add(graph1.m_int1);
80   graph1.m_list1.add(graph1.m_float1);
81
82   //add int/double into list2
83   graph1.m_list2.add(graph1.m_int1);
84   graph1.m_list2.add(dbl2);
```

```
85
86    //add double/int into map1
87    graph1.m_map1.put("TESTDOUBLE", graph1.m_float1);
88    graph1.m_map1.put("TESTINT", graph1.m_int1);
89
90    //add double into map2
91    graph1.m_map2.put("TESTDOUBLE", dbl2);
92
93    //populate native double array
94    for (int i = 1; i < 100; i++)
95     graph1.m_dArray.putAt(i, Math.log(10.332*i));
96
97    //insert object as root node into region "default"
98     dCart.putRoot("ROOTOBJECT", graph1);
99  } catch (Exception ex)
100 {
101 ex.printStackTrace();
102 }
103 }
104
105 public IGFCachePolicy cachePolicy()
106 {
107  return null;
108 }
109
110 public void cachePolicy(IGFCachePolicy policy)
111 {
112 }
113
114 }
```

Reader Program

```
1    import
     com.integrasoftware.GridFabric.Cartridges.Basic.DataCar-
     tridge.model.IGFBasicObject;
2
3    /**
4    *Title: IGFObjectGraph1Reader
5    *Description: This object demonstrates how to read a Custom
     Root Node and traverse it
6    *Copyright: Copyright (c) 2003
7    *Company: Integrasoft, LLC
8    *@version 1.0
9    */
10
11   import com.integrasoftware.GridFabric.Cartridges.Basic.
     DataCartridge.model.*;
12   import com.integrasoftware.GridFabric.Cartridges.Basic.*;
```

```
13  import com.integrasoftware.GridFabric.Cartridges.Basic.
    DataCartridge.*;
14  import com.integrasoftware.GridFabric.Cartridges.Frame-
    work.control.*;
15  import java.util.*;
16
17
18  import
    com.integrasoftware.GridFabric.Cartridges.Basic.DataCar-
    tridge.model.IGFBasicObject;
19
20
21  public class IGFObjectGraph1Reader extends IGFBasicObject {
22    public IGFObjectGraph1Reader() {
23    }
24     public static void main(String[] args) {
25      IGFObjectGraph1Writer graph1;
26      java.util.Properties props=new java.util.Properties();
27
28    //Create a cartridge on region called "Default", pass
    in properties in event more configuration parameters are
    needed
29    IGFCartridge cart=IGFBasicCartridgeFactory.instance().
    create("Default", props);
30
31    //Obtain a handle to the Data Cartridge associated
    w/Region "Default"
32    IGFBasicDataCartridge dCart=(IGFBasicDataCartridge)-
     cart.data();
33
34    //get root custom object from region "Default"
35     graph1=(IGFObjectGraph1Writer)dCart.getRoot
    ("ROOTOBJECT");
36
37    //get a previously inserted int from m_map1
38     IGFBasicInt mapInt=(IGFBasicInt)graph1.m_map1.get
     ("TESTINT");
39
40    //get a previously inserted double from m_map1
41     IGFBasicFloat mapDouble=(IGFBasicFloat)graph1.m_map1.
    get("TESTDOUBLE");
42
43    //get a previously inserted double from m_map2
44   IGFBasicDouble mapDouble2=(IGFBasicDouble)graph1.m_map2.
    get("TESTDOUBLE");
45
46    //get a previously inserted int from m_list1
47   IGFBasicInt listInt=(IGFBasicInt)graph1.m_list1.get(1);
48
```

```
49      //test for quality to ensure that the objects are actu-
   ally identical
50      boolean cmpAre=(mapInt.equals(graph1.m_int1) && mapDou-
   ble.equals(graph1.m_float1));
51
52      double [] dblArr = new double[100];
53      for (int i = 1; i < dblArr.length; i++)
54      {
55        dblArr[i] = graph1.m_dArray.getAt(i);
56        System.out.println("dblArr[+"+i+"]: "+dblArr[i]);
57      }
58
59
60      for (int i = 1; i < graph1.m_list1.size()+1;i++)
61      {
62        System.out.println("List1:"+graph1.m_list1.get(i).
   toString());
63      }
64
65      for (int k = 1; k < graph1.m_list2.size()+1; k++)
66      {
67        System.out.println("List2:"+graph1.m_list2.get(k).
   toString());
68      }
69
70    }
71
72 }
```

RANDOM-NUMBER SURFACE EXAMPLE

This example is a random-number surface used in a Monte Carlo simulation. Traditionally, Monte Carlo simulations are run from start to finish before any results are visible. In grid-enabled environment, the Monte Carlo simulation can be optimized by slicing the simulation across the compute grid as worklets with small input data sets generating large amounts of interim data to ultimately return a simple result(s). One of the interim data sets is a random-number surface. Providing a "schema" for such interim surfaces and data-grid-enabling them yields two optimizations: further parallelization through finer-grained compute worklets to build the interim surfaces and the reuse of previously built surfaces. The first optimization allows what was one worklet, "build random-number surface," to become many worklets, each contributing to a single entry of data point of the random-number surface.

The second optimization enables data reuse from one Monte Carlo simulation to the next. For example, a random-number surface "FooBar" built in one simulation can be reused in subsequent simulations, thus eliminating the need for additional computation cycles, which would be required to rebuild the data surfaces. In order for other applications to reuse the data surface, the IGF data grid must allow the application to "query" the data surface that it needs.

If a data surface can be queried, then not only can subsequent Monte Carlo simulations benefit from the preexisting data surfaces, which are stored in the IGF data grid, but also any "observer" program can read and monitor data surfaces as they are being built in real time. Thus, this creates a new class of applications instead of batch applications, which used to run overnight. For example, a running Monte Carlo simulation can be monitored, if diverging it can be terminated in the middle of its processing. Conversely, if convergence is satisfied prior to completion, it can be terminated early. This is yet another form of optimization offered through the smart utilization of compute resource.

All the optimizations highlighted above and the possibility of new business observer programs are possible only through data-grid-enabling a Monte Carlo simulation. The example random-number surface illustrated below is a common part of any Monte Carlo simulation:

```
1   /**
2    *Title: IGFObjectGraph1Reader
3    *Description: This object demonstrates how to read a
     Custom Root Node and traverse it
4    *Copyright: Copyright (c) 2003
5    *Company: Integrasoft, LLC
6    *@version 1.0
7    */
8   \\RandomField\\Harness\\SurfaceDemo\\IGFEuropeanCallOp-
    tionPopulator.java
9   package com.integrasoftware.GridFabric.Cartridges.Random-
    Field.Harness.SurfaceDemo;
10
11  import com.integrasoftware.GridFabric.Cartridges.Frame-
    work.control.IGFPopulator;
12  import com.integrasoftware.GridFabric.Cartridges.Frame-
    work.control.IGFDataCartridge;
13  import com.integrasoftware.GridFabric.Cartridges.Random-
    Field.DataCartridge.IGFRandomFieldDataCartridge;
14  import com.integrasoftware.GridFabric.Integration.Data.
    Framework.model.IGFCacheable;
15  import com.integrasoftware.GridFabric.Cartridges.Frame-
    work.model.IGFScenario;
16  import com.integrasoftware.GridFabric.Cartridges.Frame-
    work.model.IGFPathList;
17  import com.integrasoftware.GridFabric.Cartridges.Frame-
    work.model.IGFDataPoint;
18  import com.integrasoftware.GridFabric.Cartridges.Frame-
    work.model.IGFPath;
19  import com.integrasoftware.GridFabric.Cartridges.Random-
    Field.IGFRandomFieldFactory;
```

```
20  import com.integrasoftware.GridFabric.Cartridges.Frame-
    work.model.IGFDataPointList;
21  import com.integrasoftware.GridFabric.Cartridges.Frame-
    work.control.IGFCartridge;
22  import javax.swing.JFrame;
23  import java.awt.GridLayout;
24  import java.awt.Dimension;
25  import java.awt.Color;
26  import javax.swing.JPanel;
27  import com.klg.jclass.chart3d.*;
28  import com.klg.jclass.chart3d.j2d.*;
29  import com.klg.jclass.chart3d.data.*;
30
31  public class IGFEuropeanCallOptionPopulator implements
    IGFPopulator, Service
32  {
33    private IGFCartridge m_cartridge;
34    private String m_scenarioName;
35    private int m_dimensionality;
36    private double m_strikePrice;
37    private double m_timeInterval;
38    private double m_assetPrice;
39    private double m_sigma;
40    private double m_contIR;
41    private double m_divYield;
42    private double m_timeStep;
43    private double m_dT;
44    private double m_nudt;
45    private double m_sigsdt;
46    private double m_lnAssetPrice;
47    private JobContext m_context;
48
49    public IGFEuropeanCallOptionPopulator()
50    {
51      m_strikePrice = 100;
52      m_timeInterval = 1;
53      m_assetPrice = 100;
54      m_sigma = 0.2;
55      m_contIR = 0.06;
56      m_divYield = 0.03;
57      m_timeStep = 100;
58      m_dT=m_timeInterval/m_timeStep;
59      m_nudt = (m_contIR-m_divYield-1/2*m_sigma*m_sigma)*m_dT;
60      m_sigsdt = m_sigma*Math.sqrt(m_dT);
61      m_lnAssetPrice = Math.log(m_assetPrice);
62    }
63
64  public static final void main(String argv[])
65  {
```

```
66  IGFEuropeanCallOptionPopulator pop = new IGFEuropeanCall
    OptionPopulator();
67    pop.connectToRandomFieldWith(10,"MonteCarlo","Random-
    FieldCartridge");
68    pop.cartridge().compute().populator(pop);
69    for (int i = 0; i < 10; i++)
70      pop.populate();
71  }
72
73  public void populate()
74  {
75
76    IGFRandomFieldDataCartridge dCart = (IGFRandomFieldData-
    Cartridge)cartridge().data();
77    IGFScenario scene = dCart.scenarios().findScenario
    (scenarioName());
78    IGFPathList paths=scene.paths();
79    IGFPath path=dCart.makePath();
80    paths.add((IGFCacheable)path);
81    IGFDataPointList points = path.points();
82    for (int i=0; i < m_timeStep-1; i++)
83    {
84      IGFDataPoint aPointInPath = dCart.makeDataPoint();
85      double stdNormal = Math.random();
86      aPointInPath.point().put(0, stdNormal);
87      points.add(aPointInPath);
88      }
89
90    int lastPath = paths.size();
91    java.util.Vector vector=new java.util.Vector();
92    vector.addElement(new Integer(lastPath));
93    dCart.generateEventForNameSpace("STR", vector);
94
95  }
96
97  public IGFCartridge cartridge()
98  {
99    return m_cartridge;
100 }
101
102 public void cartridge(IGFCartridge cartridge)
103 {
104   m_cartridge = cartridge;
105 }
106
107 public void connectToRandomFieldWith(int dimensionality,
    String scenarioName, String cartridgeName)
108 {
109   java.util.Properties props = new java.util.Properties();
```

```
110     props.setProperty(IGFDataPoint.DIMENSION, String.
     valueOf(dimensionality));
111     scenarioName(scenarioName);
112     dimensionality(dimensionality);
113     cartridge(IGFRandomFieldFactory.instance().create
     (cartridgeName, props));
114   }
115
116   public String scenarioName()
117   {
118   return m_scenarioName;
119   }
120
121
122   public void scenarioName(String sceneName)
123   {
124     m_scenarioName=sceneName;
125   }
126
127   public int dimensionality()
128   {
129     return m_dimensionality;
130   }
131
132   public void dimensionality(int dim)
133   {
134     m_dimensionality = dim;
135   }
136
137
138   public void invoke(JobContext arg0, InputMessage arg1,
     OutputMessage arg2) throws Exception, SystemException
139   {
140     connectToRandomFieldWith(10,"MonteCarlo","RandomField-
     Cartridge");
141     m_context = arg0;
142     cartridge().compute().populator(this);
143     for (int i=0; i < 10; i++)
144     populate();
145     StringBuffer sb_test = new StringBuffer();
146     String a = ((TextInputMessage)arg1).get();
147     //perform a simple transformation (to upper case) and
     append its task ID
148     sb_test = sb_test.append(a.toUpperCase()+"... Task
     ID:"+arg1.getTaskID().getValue());
149     ((TextOutputMessage)arg2).set(sb_test.toString());
150   }
151
152   }
```

22

ADDITIONAL READING

In this chapter I list useful reference material on grid computing in general, including data management in the grid, and what has brought us to this point in grid computing and the direction(s) in which it is headed. The research material is broken down by category ranging from research and standards bodies that are rich in information (some of which is specifically referenced here) and technology topics. I encourage the reader to regularly track the activities of the standards bodies such as The Global Grid Forum, IEEE, and W3C and follow the publications of the "father of grid computing," Ian Foster.

One of the key objectives of a data grid is to unite the locality of where work is done and where the data naturally reside. Terms used throughout this book include the minimization of data movement and data affinity. It is imperative for anyone involved in data management for grid computing to understand data affinity, including its benefits, and how to best achieve it. The papers referenced here describe in detail the fundamentals of data affinity, and others describe advanced methods of data distribution policy and data synchronization policy that will be helpful in achieving data affinity.

Happy reading!

USEFUL INFORMATION SOURCES

- IEEE Distributed Systems Online (http://dsonline.computer.org)
- John Narghton, *A Brief History of the Future*, Overlook Press, May 2000

Distributed Data Management for Grid Computing, by Michael Di Stefano
Copyright © 2005 John Wiley & Sons, Inc.

WHITE PAPERS

Grid Computing

- Ian Foster, Carl Kesselman, and Steven Tuecke, *The Anatomy of the Grid Enabling Scalable Virtual Organizations* (available online at http://www.globus.org/research/papers/anatomy.pdf)
- Michael Di Stefano and Steve Yalovitser, "Grid Computing with a Data Grid Plane," September 27, 2002
- Ian Foster, Carl Kesselman, and Steven Tuecke, "The Anatomy of the Grid, Enabling Scalable Virtual Organizations," *Int. J. Supercomput. Appl.* (2001) (available online at http://www.globus.org/research/papers/anatomy.pdf)
- Ian Foster, Jens Vöckler, Michael Wilde, and Yong Zhao, "The Virtual Data Grid: A New Model and Architecture for Data-Intensive Collaboration," *Proceedings of the 2003 CIDR Conference* (available online at (http://www.griphyn.org/chimera/papers/CIDR.VDG.crc.submitted.pdf)
- Reagan W. Moore (San Diego Supercomputer Center), Scott Studham (Pacific Northwest National Laboratory), Arcot Rajasekar (San Diego Supercomputer Center), Chip Watson (Jefferson National Laboratory), Heinz Stockinger, and Peter Kunszt (CERN), "Data Grid Implementations," February 19, 2002 (available online at http://www.ppdg.net/docs/WhitePapers/Capabilities-grids.v12.pdf)
- Ann Chervenak, Ian Foster, Carl Kesselman, Charles Salisbury, and Steven Tuecke, "The Data Grid: Towards an Architecture for the Distributed Management and Analysis of Large Scientic Datasets" (available online at http://www.globus.org/documentation/incoming/JNCApaper.pdf)

GridFTP

- The Globus Project, "GridFTP Universal Data Transfer for the Grid," September 5, 2000 (copyright 2000, The University of Chicago and The University of Southern California) (available online at http://www.globus.org/datagrid/deliverables/C2WPdraft3.pdf)
- Bill Allcock, Lee Liming, and Steven Tuecke (ANL), and Ann Chervenak (USC/ISI), "GridFTP: A Data Transfer Protocol for the Grid, Grid Forum Data Working Group on GridFTP" (available online at http://www.sdsc.edu/GridForum/RemoteData/Papers/gridftp_intro_gf5.pdf)

Distributed File Systems

- *Distributed File System: A Logical View of Physical Storage*, Microsoft
- Peter J. Braam (School of Computer Science, Carnegie Mellon University), *The Coda Distributed File System* (available online at http://www.coda.cs.cmu.edu/)

- M. Satyanarayanan, "Coda: A Highly Available File System for a Distributed Workstation Environment" (available online at http://www-2.cs.cmu.edu/afs/cs/project/coda/Web/docdir/ieeepcs95.pdf)
- See http://www.eecs.harvard.edu/~vino/web/push.cache/node7.html

STANDARDS BODIES

Globus—Data Grid

- See http://www.globus.org/datagrid/
- GridFTP Universal Data Transfer Protocol for the Grid: The University of Chicago and The University of Southern California, September 5, 2000 (available online at http://216.239.51.104/search?q = cache:b0sOC7xSLh8J:www.globus.org/datagrid/deliverables/C2WPdraft3.pdf + GridFTP&hl = en&ie= UTF-8)

Global Grid Forum

- See http://www.ggf.org/L_About/about.htm
- *GridFTP*: http://www.gridforum.org/6_DATA/gridftp.htm

W3C

- Definition of Web Services: http://www.w3.org/TR/2003/WD-ws-arch-20030808/

PUBLIC AND UNIVERSITY GRID EFFORTS

- NASA; *Information Power Grid* (available online at http://www.ipg.nasa.gov/ipgusers/globus/6-globus.html)
- The DataGrid Project: "DataGrid is a project funded by European Union. The objective is to build the next generation computing infrastructure providing intensive computation and analysis of shared large-scale databases, from hundreds of TeraBytes to PetaBytes, across widely distributed scientific communities" (project report available online at http://eu-datagrid.web.cern.ch/eu-datagrid/)
- *In-Vigo*, University of Florida (available online at http://invigo.acis.ufl.edu/docs/aboutInVigo.html)
- *Virtuoso: Resource Management and Prediction for Distributed Computing Using Virtual Machines* (available online at http://www.cs.northwestern.edu/~plab/Virtuoso)
- *OceanStore*: http://oceanstore.cs.berkeley.edu/info/overview.html

SCIENTIFIC RESEARCH USE OF GRID COMPUTING

- *Grid Embedded Optimization and Design Search for Engineering*: http://www.geodise.org/
- *NEESgrid* (http://www.neesgrid.org/index.php): *Earthquake Engineering*
- *FusionGRID* (http://www.fusiongrid.org/index.html)
- Ayon Basumallik, Seung-Jai Min, and Rudolf Eigenmann, "Towards OpenMP Execution on Software Distributed Shared Memory Systems," School of Electrical and Computer Engineering, Purdue University, West Lafayette, IN (available online at http://www.ece.purdue.edu/ParaMount)
- Lee Liming of the George E. Brown, Jr., "Network for Earthquake Engineering Simulation (NEES). The MOST Experiment: Earthquake Engineering on the Grid," presentation at The Application Research Group of the Global Grid Forum, meeting on Case Studies on Grid Applications in Munich, Germany, March 2004 (available online at http://www.zib.de/ggf/apps/index.html)
- Kate Keahey at the Argonne National Laboratory, "The National Fusion Collaboratory Project: Applying Grid Technology for Magnetic Fusion Research," presentation at The Application Research Group of the Global Grid Forum, meeting on Case Studies on Grid Applications in Munich, Germany, March 2004 (available online at http://www.zib.de/ggf/apps/index.html)
- Professor Simon Cox of Geodise (www.geodise.org), "Geodise: Grid Enabled Design Optimisation and Design Search, Applications and Testbeds Working Group Workshop," presentation at The Application Research Group of the Global Grid Forum, meeting on Case Studies on Grid Applications in Munich, Germany, March 2004 (available online at http://www.zib.de/ggf/apps/index.html)
- Alex Rodriguez, Dinanath Sulakhe, Elizabeth Marland, Natalia Maltsev, Ian Foster, Michael Wilde, and Veronika Nefedova, "Grid Enabled Server for High-throughput Analysis of Genomes," presentation at The Application Research Group of the Global Grid Forum, meeting on Case Studies on Grid Applications in Munich, Germany, March 2004 (available online at http://www.zib.de/ggf/apps/index.html)
- Dr. F. M. Brochu at the University of Cambridge (UK), "Running MadGraph on the LHC Computing Grid (LCG)," presentation at The Application Research Group of the Global Grid Forum, meeting on Case Studies on Grid Applications in Munich, Germany, March 2004 (available online at http://www.zib.de/ggf/apps/index.html)

WEB SERVICES

- Gunjan Samtani and Dimple Sadhwani, "Web Services and Straight Through Processing, Web Services in the Financial Industry," June 26, 2002 (available online at http://www.webservicesarchitect.com/content/articles/samtani06.asp)

- Service-Oriented Architecture Explained by Sayed Hashimi 08/18/2003 (available online at http://www.ondotnet.com/pub/a/dotnet/2003/08/18/soa_explained.html)
- Hao He, What is Service-Oriented Architecture? September 30, 2003 (available online at http://webservices.xml.com/pub/a/ws/2003/09/30/soa.html)
- Greg Goth, "Web Services Easing toward the Mainstream" (available online at http://dsonline.computer.org/0310/f/d10newp.htm)
- Michael Stevens, "Service-Oriented Architecture Introduction, Parts 1 and 2" (available online at http://www.developer.com/java/ent/article.php/10933_1010451_2)
- "The Benefits of a Service-Oriented Architecture" (available online at http://www.developer.com/tech/article.php/1041191)
- Greg Goth, "Web Services Easing toward the Mainstream," IEEE Distributed Systems Online (http://dsonline.computer.org/0310/f/d10newp.htm)
- Larry Peterson, Tom Anderson, David Culler, and Timothy Roscoe, "A Blueprint for Introducing Disruptive Technology into the Internet," *Proceedings of the 1st ACM Workshop on Hot Topics in Networking* (HotNets), October 2002.

DISTRIBUTED COMPUTING

- Jim Gray, *Distributed Computing Economics*, Microsoft Research, San Francisco, CA, March 2003
- D. Gelernter and A. J. Bernstein, "Distributed Communication via Global Buffer," *Proceedings of the ACM Principles of Distributed Computing Conference*, 1982
- D. Gelernter, "Generative Communication in Linda," *TOPLAS* **7**(1), 80–112 (1985)
- N. Carriero and D. Gelernter, "Linda in Context," *Commun. ACM* **32**(4) (April 1989)

COMPUTE UTILITY

- Vadim Kotov, *On Virtual Data Centers and Their Operating Environments*, Computer Systems and Technology Laboratory, Hewlett-Packard Laboratories Palo Alto, HPL-2001-44, March 8, 2001
- Integrasoft, L.L.C. (www.integrasoftware.com), Platform Computing, Inc. (www.platform.com), Corosoft, Inc. (www.corosoft.com), "Presentation: The Virtual Data Center"
- "On demand business: The new agenda for value creation" (www.ibm.com)
- The Global Grid Forum (http://www.gridforum.org/)
- Duke University Department of Computer Science, *COD, Cluster on Demand* (available online at http://issg.cs.duke.edu/cod/)

SERVICE-ORIENTED ARCHITECTURES

- Hao He, "What is Service-Oriented Architecture?" O'Reilly webservices.xml. com, September 30, 2003 (available online at http://webservices.xml.com/ pub/a/ws/2003/09/30/soa.html)
- John Fontana, "Resurrecting the Distributed APP Model," *Network World* (September 29, 2003) (available online at http://www.nwfusion.com/buzz/ 2003/0929soa.html)

DATA AFFINITY

- Research possibilities to pursue in peer-to-peer networking (see http:// www.praxagora.com/andyo/professional/p2p_research.html#affinity)
- Large-scale distributed systems (LSDS) (see www.inria.fr/rapportsactivite/ RA2003/grand-large2003/LSDS.html)
- Artur Andrzejak, Sven Graupner,Vadim Kotov, and Holger Trinks, *Algorithms for Self-Organization and Adaptive Service Placement in Dynamic Distributed Systems*, Internet Systems and Storage Laboratory, HP Laboratories, Palo Alto, CA, HPL-2002-259, September 17, 2002* (available online at http:// www.zib.de/andrzejak/my-papers/HPL-2002-259.pdf)
- Kavitha Ranganathan and Ian Foster, "Decoupling Computation and Data Scheduling in Distributed Data-Intensive Applications"
- Jeremy Stribling, Kirsten Hildrum, and John D. Kubiatowicz, *Optimizations for Locality-Aware Structured Peer-to-Peer Overlays*, Report UCB/CSD-03-1266, Computer Science Division (EECS), University of California, Berkeley, CA, August 2003
- Open MP (available online at http://www.openmp.org/and http://www.hpc. unimelb.edu.au/vpic/omp/perf/4.html)
- Active Harmony (http://www.dyninst.org/harmony/)

23

WHITE PAPER: NATURAL ATTRACTION FORCES OF DATA BODIES WITHIN A DATA GRID TO DESCRIBE EFFICIENT DATA DISTRIBUTION PATTERNS

Proposed by
Michael Di Stefano
mdistefano@integrasoftware.com
Integrasoft, L.L.C.
September 14, 2004

INTRODUCTION

This paper puts forth the premise that a practical and optimal data distribution pattern of data bodies within a data grid can be described through forces of attraction between data bodies and the force of friction as exerted on them by the physical properties of the data grid.

As bodies in space, the planets, stars, satellites, and other celestial bodies follow natural laws of attraction and movement within the fabric of space; single data bodies will follow their own set of natural laws of attraction within the physical fabric of the data grid. Similar to the views expressed in Newtonian, Einsteinian, and quantum physics, I will apply both the micro and macro views of data distribution within a data grid. Similar to how quantum physics describes orbits of electrons around the nucleus guided by discrete quantum energy levels, the micro view for the data distribution concerns the manner in which data distribution is present within a single data body.

On the other hand, the macro view of data distribution is concerned with the physical data distribution patterns of *multiple* data bodies in relation to each other within the space of the data grid fabric. Newtonian laws accurately describe a physical body in terms of mass and force, such as apples falling to Earth in contrast to quantum physics, which describes the internal atomic structure of the apple. I will follow the same approach, being less concerned with the internal data atoms and the distribution pattern that form a single data body and more interested in the fact that the single data body exists, having definite and measurable quantities. These single data bodies exhibit forces of attraction to one another that will result in an optimal distribution pattern that best meets the requirements of the larger system, thus resulting in minimal data movement of the overall system.

Einstein's theory of relativity describes the bending or warping of the fabric of space and time by mass. Separately, Newton's laws and the theory of relativity do not describe the complete picture; a unified view that has been advanced but not yet proven states that the curvature of space and time causes mass. The forces of attraction of single data bodies cannot be fully described by the forces of attraction that they exert on each other. Similarly, the unified view in physics, the physical characteristics of the data grid fabric (DGF) will have some influence on a single data body and the distribution patterns among the single data bodies in the data grid space (DGS).

OBSERVATION

Most systems are composed of many different data types. For example, a portfolio management system requires market data, a holdings portfolio, and risk exposure data in order to determine the best course of action for when and what to buy or sell. When this system resides in a grid topology, the data types of market data, portfolio, and risk form their own respective single data bodies in the data grid.

Initially, the system running in the grid may not be optimized since the optimal data distribution patterns have not been discovered yet. One may assume some mathematical model of data distribution for initial deployment followed by continued analysis of natural data movement patterns over time. The resulting data movement patterns will suggest manual adjustments of the optimal data distribution pattern of the single data bodies in the data grid in order to minimize data movement within the DGF during normal operation. This process will ultimately result in the formation of single data bodies of definite size and shape in relation to each other to minimize systemwide data movement.

While this process will ultimately result in a steady state of single data body size, shape, and correlation to other single data bodies of the system; it is one of trial and error that can span long periods of time. During this discovery phase, the data grid will not be operating at optimal performance levels. This is an unacceptable behavior, as grid computing is starting to gain wide acceptance in both the public and private sectors, with new systems migrating in mass from client/server onto the compute grid.

Therefore, a data distribution model that accurately describes a systemwide distribution pattern is mandatory in order to start the system closer to the optimal distribution pattern, which will minimize the settlement time required to achieve a steady state. This initial optimal behavior can be achieved by defining the single data bodies in quantifiable terms: the laws of attraction between the data bodies and the effect that the "warping" of the DGF has on them.

Hypothesis

There are fundamental principles that govern the optimal distribution patterns of single data bodies in a DGS, just as there are natural laws that govern the distribution and motion of planetary bodies in space.

Laws of Attraction. Newton's laws predict the motion of objects based on basic principles of mass, force (gravity), and acceleration. All bodies have mass and shape. The shape of a body can be either symmetric or asymmetric. Symmetric bodies (see Figure 23.1) have a center of gravity that is centered within the body's shape regardless of the mass distribution. The mass distribution can be concentrated close to the surface, close to the center, or evenly throughout. Asymmetric

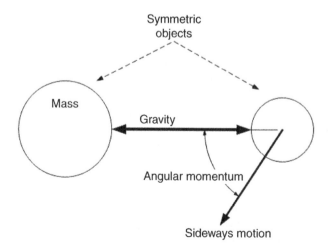

Figure 23.1. Mass, gravity, and sideways motion of symmetric objects.

bodies, on the other hand, have a center of gravity that is uniquely placed based on the irregular shape of the object and the mass distribution within.

The force of attraction between two bodies is directly related to each body's respective mass and the distance between them. The closer two bodies get, the greater the force of gravity becomes by the inverse of the square of the distance separating them. The formula is reflected as follows:

$$F = G\frac{M_1 M_2}{r^2}$$

As the force of gravity increases, the distance between the two masses decreases until the objects collide. However, when an external force is applied to give a body a sideways (lateral) motion, the object may end up on an orbit, just as the (Earth's) moon orbits Earth. Alternatively, if the sideways motion is great enough, the object will escape the gravitational pull of the other body.

Where Newton's laws fail, Einstein's theory of relativity picks up. The mass of an object affects the fabric of space. Einstein showed that space–time continuum is warped around a body, with amount of the warping related to the mass of the body. The warping of space is immediately evident by its effect of the bending of light around an object. However, Einstein's theory does not explain planetary motion as accurately as do Newton's laws. So an alternative theory has been put forth in an attempt to create a unified view in which the mass of an object does not warp space but rather the mass of an object is an expression of the curvature of space.

How Does This Fit in with Data Distribution Patterns of Single Data Bodies Within a Data Grid Fabric? Let's begin by defining some of the terms used so liberally thus far. A single data body is a homogenous data type such as market data, security master, stock inventory, portfolio, or risk, that is used in or shared with a larger system (application, business service, Web service, etc.) or systems of applications. Table 23.1 gives definitions for both objects and single data bodies.

As a body in the physical space, each single data body has its own unique boundary, shape, and internal data distribution pattern. The force of attraction (or the force of gravity) between two bodies in the physical space is described by one of the most famous formulas known, Newton's second law, where "force" is equal to "mass" times "acceleration": $F = ma$. The key component in determining the force of gravity is mass. *Mass* is defined as the force required to change the velocity of a body in space.

Applying this theory to single data bodies, the concept of mass is essential in describing the properties of the body. Mass is key to determining the force of attraction between two single data bodies, as well as other forces in the system. Is the mass of a single data body represented as a single expression or a collection of expressions? This answer requires closer analysis of what constitutes a single data body, which this chapter (white paper) will not address in detail. However, one

TABLE 23.1. Terminology

Shape	Symmetric or asymmetric	Symmetric or asymmetric
Mass	Internal/gravitational force per unit of acceleration	Property or collection of properties paramount in defining the force of attraction between two bodies
Internal atom distribution	Mineral, water, air, etc. atoms are distributed within the confines of the body	Data atoms distributed within the confines of the body
Center of gravity	Point where line of action of the force of gravity passes through	Point where line of action of the force of attraction passes through

such component is the *coefficient of attraction* between two single data bodies, which *cannot be included* in the expression of mass of a single data body.

The *coefficient of attraction* between two single data bodies is analogous to acceleration in the equation for force. The combination of this coefficient with the expression for mass will define the force of attraction between two single data bodies.

Collision of Single Data Bodies. The *center of gravity* is the point through which the line of action of the force passes. The force passing through the points of center of gravity of the two objects indicates the direction or the line of impact on the respective bodies should they actually collide.

Extending this analogy, single data bodies have size, shape, and mass, as well as a center of gravity. Therefore, the force of attraction between two single data bodies passes through the centers of gravity of the respective bodies (see Figure 23.2).

Differences in these analogies appear in the following areas: traverse motion (angular momentum), collision, and the introduction of equilibrium distance. Without traverse motion, bodies will collide. We see this often, for example, in "shooting stars," which are meteorites that collide with Earth. If the body is too big to burn up in Earth's atmosphere, a violent collision will take place on Earth. With no sideway (lateral) motion or angular momentum, our moon would collide into Earth!

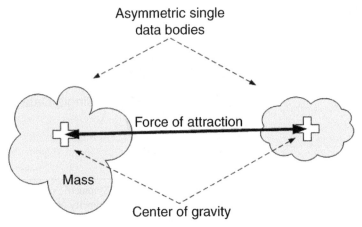

Figure 23.2. Center of gravity of single data bodies.

However, within a DGS, there is no traverse motion, so the single data bodies will collide (see Figure 23.3). Or will they? In the physical world, two particles cannot occupy the same space at the same time, without a violent collision. This is the first area where the fabric of the data grid will affect the movement behavior of single data bodies distributed within it. The physical nodes of the data grid are the computers with storage space. Provided the physical storage capacity at any one node is sufficient, that node will be capable of "holding" multiple data atoms at any one instant in time. Therefore, collisions of single data bodies will not occur; in fact, they will overlap with each other.

The degree to which data bodies overlap will vary from no overlap to complete overlap. In an attempt to achieve minimal data movement throughout the system, the forces of attraction will bring two or more single data bodies in physical proximity to each other. However, there will come a point where the force of attraction may cause single data bodies to "overshoot" their equilibrium distance (see Figure 23.4), the point at which minimal data movement is reached. Therefore, a counterbalancing force is needed to move the bodies back to equilibrium distance.

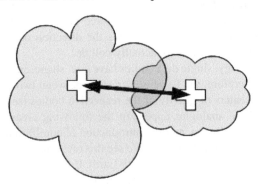

Figure 23.3. Collision of single data bodies.

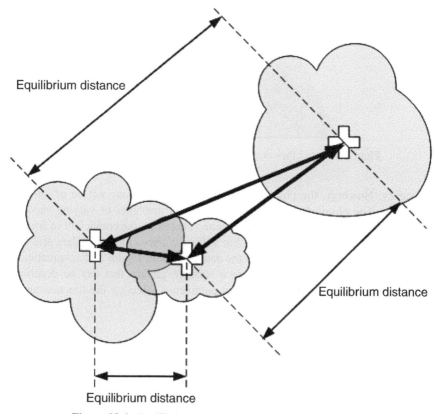

Figure 23.4. Equilibrium distance between single data bodies.

The equilibrium distance between two single data bodies is reached when the force of attraction between the bodies is counterbalanced by an equal and opposite force, thus resulting in the optimal distance with minimal data movement within a DGS. To stay within the realm of Newtonian law, this force is similar to that of the force of friction

$$F_f = \mu N$$

where the force of friction (F_f) is equal to the coefficient of friction (μ) times the "weight" (N) of the single data body on the fabric of the data grid. The expression for the weight of the single data body must include the mass of the single data body; therefore the expression for the force of friction becomes

$$F_f = \mu m$$

In the physical world the coefficient of friction is a single number mainly because it is usually applied at the point of contact between two objects of uniform

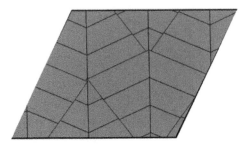

Figure 23.5. Coefficient of friction for the surface of a data grid.

consistency. However, the physical fabric of a data grid may not be of uniform consistency. The physical data grid is composed of machines of varying capacity connected by a network of varying bandwidth. Therefore, the coefficient of friction of the data grid will not be a constant but will vary across the entire data grid as a reflection of the physical properties of the data grid itself. Figure 23.5 schematically represents the coefficient of friction as a variable surface that can be described by some function $\mu(x)$; some of the input parameters affecting the function are as follows:

$$\mu \begin{pmatrix} NetworkBandwidth, \\ Network,\ Latency, \\ ComputeNodeStorageCapacity, \\ ComputeNodeServiceExecutionCapability, \\ \ldots\ldots \end{pmatrix}$$

The data grid's functions for its surface coefficient of friction, the force of friction, and the equilibrium distance have an interesting connection to the properties of the networks connecting the nodes within the DGS. One of the key parameters in determining the function for the coefficient of friction of a data grid is the cost of moving data between the source node (the node where the data physically reside) and the destination node (the node where the data are needed to perform an operation). This cost of moving data within the data grid is inversely proportional to network bandwidth. Therefore, the greater the network bandwidth, the greater the coefficient of friction, and thus the greater the equilibrium distance between the two single data bodies will be.

In summary, by defining the "mass" of a single data body, and an expression of the force of attraction [e.g., Force of Gravity] between single data bodies, and a force of friction exerted by the data grid on the single data bodies, models can be formed to determine the optimal single data body distribution pattern within a data grid for minimal data movement for a system. This minimized data movement increases system performance and efficiency.

Effects of the Data Grid on a Single Data Body. The model cannot be complete until expressions for determining the center of gravity of a single data body, the force of friction, and equilibrium distance are defined. These are not simple questions to answer; however, great insight is gained from the effects of the data grid fabric on the single data bodies.

Einstein's theory of relativity predicts that with mass warping of the fabric of space and time, the mass of a single data body will have no effect on the fabric of the data grid. In fact, it is quite the opposite. The data grid is a tangible physical entity consisting of many machines of finite compute power and data storage capacity. The maximum speed at which matter can travel in the data grid is not a constant, unlike the speed of light in our physical universe. The speed with which data move in the data grid is determined by the bandwidth, throughput, and latency parameters of the physical network connecting the nodes of the data grid.

Where the fabric of space and time is assumed to be homogeneous, the fabric of the data grid is not. The nodes of the data grid can vary in power and capacity, and the networks connecting the nodes can vary from infiniband, to 100baseT, to something less than is typically found on a WAN. Therefore the fabric of the data grid is not homogeneous, and it is not a constant. Over time the fabric of the data grid will change as old machines are cycled out by new ones, as networks are upgraded, and as hardware outages restrict the data grid itself.

The relation of the data grid fabric to the data bodies contained within it is closer to the "unified view" in physics, which states that mass does not warp space and time; rather, it is the warping of space and time that defines mass. Compute tasks are sent to the machines best capable of performing the task (grid computing), and part of that determination should be data locality. If the data are not already local on that machine, the data grid must move them there; the exact phenomenon must be minimized. Therefore, the capacity of each individual grid node and the characteristics of the network connecting the nodes will determine

- Where on the data grid the data must be and the quantity of data that can be held at a node. These conditions will determine the shape and density of the single data body, which has a direct impact on the single data body's center of gravity.
- The shape of the coefficient of friction surface of the data grid, which will influence the force of friction between two single data bodies and in turn the equilibrium distance between the two single data bodies.

Conclusions

There exists a family of expressions that represent the physical fabric of the data grid, the macro properties that describe single data bodies, and the forces that they exert on each other, resulting in a steady-state data distribution pattern so that systemwide data movement is minimized.

These expressions include, most importantly, the mass of a single data body. Mass is used in the expressions for the force of attraction between two single data bodies and the force of friction that counterbalances the force of attraction to achieve the equilibrium distance between the two single data bodies. The expression for the mass of a single data body should describe external and measurable properties of the single data body that describe the composition of the body.

Unique to any two pairs of single data bodes is the coefficient of attraction. This is the measure of the interdependencies between two single data bodies in the larger system. For example, in a risk management system, risk exposure is dependent on the holding's portfolio and market data. Thus, there will be a coefficient of attraction between the risk exposure single data body and the market data single data body and the portfolio single data body.

The expressions of the forces for data distribution are as follows:

- The *force of attraction* (F) is equal to the mass of the single data body (m) times the coefficient of attraction between two single data bodies (a):

$$F = ma$$

- The *force of friction* (F_f) is the product of the *mass of a single data body* (m) times the *coefficient of friction* (μ), which describes the physical properties of the fabric of the data grid:

$$F_f = \mu m$$

The physical properties of the data grid have a direct effect on the size, shape, density, and therefore the center of gravity of a single data body. They are collectively expressed in a coefficient, called the *coefficient of friction* of the fabric of the data grid. It is more realistic that the coefficient of friction is not a single number, but rather a mathematical function that will exhibit different results in different areas of the data grid.

$$\mu \begin{pmatrix} NetworkBandwidth, \\ Network,\ Latency, \\ ComputeNodeStorageCapacity, \\ ComputeNodeServiceExecutionCapability, \\ \ldots\ldots \end{pmatrix}$$

Thus, the force of attraction between two single data bodies, countered by the force of friction between the same two single data bodies, will result in an equilibrium distance that represents the steady state of the two single data bodies where the data movement within the data grid space is at a minimum.

24

GLOSSARY OF TERMS

For the reader, the following glossary is provided for terms used throughout this book. The vocabulary words range from business-specific, financial/accounting terms, information technology in origin, grid computing jargon, and other terms introduced in this book that may or may not make their way into the grid technology jargon mainstream.

API   See definition for *Application Programmatic Interface.*

Application Programmatic Interface   Application Programmatic Interface (API) is a standard programming language (e.g., C++, Java) that allows access to the information from the system with which it is communicating. "Standard" in this context refers only to the product or system.

C#   This is an object-oriented language used in a Microsoft.Net environment for building applications and systems.

compute grid   This is a grid that enables sharing, management, and distribution of tasks based on configurable service-level policies. It provides the core resource and task management services for grid computing.

compute utility   This provides for customer resource consolidation and location independence, extending their capability to optimize the center for their business needs and for a particular pattern of workload, thus making the data center actually platform-architecture-transparent and providing a much more simple and convenient "high-level" virtual architecture (see Ref. 35, p. 2).

Distributed Data Management for Grid Computing, by Michael Di Stefano
Copyright © 2005 John Wiley & Sons, Inc.

data affinity   This is a key data management feature or objective of any data grid that describes data locality or "physical closeness" of data in the grid to compute nodes where a running task is accessing that data.

data atom   As described in this book, the data atom is the smallest element of data for which a data set can be broken down. The data grid will apply the management policies of synchronization, distribution, and replication to the data atoms of a data region.

data grid   This provides the data management functions that are required for data access, synchronization, and distribution of a grid.

data marshaling   A process of packaging the data in formats that other applications understand. Often, the format of the marshaled data is common and machine-independent.

data region   See the definition of *regionalization*.

distributed file system   In a client/server environment, this is a collection of files, physically distributed across any number of machines on a network that are logically structured into a hierarchical organization by one or more coordinating servers. Clients of the logical file system access it via the distributed file system servers.

distribution policy   The data distribution policy describes the distribution pattern of data within a data grid. The scope of the data distribution policy can range from a subset of data atoms within a data region to the distribution of data regions within the entire data grid space. The finest data granularity point on which a data distribution policy can operate is a data atom.

document type definition   Document type definition (DTD) is a schema specification method for SGML and XML documents where the definition for the data is represented.

DTD   See definition for *document type definition*.

EAI   See definition for *enterprise application integration*.

EII   See definition for *enterprise information integration*.

enterprise application integration   Enterprise application integration (EAI) is a best-practices method of architecture and implementation using technology tools (typically termed *middleware*) enabling the integration of applications across an enterprise (data integration). It integrates information at the application level.

enterprise information integration   Enterprise information integration (EII) is a best-practices method of architecture and implementation using technology tools enabling the integration of information at the business level across an enterprise.

event notification policy   The event notification policy describes events and how they are to be managed with the data grid. Subscribers of events can range from other data grid management policies (e.g., synchronization policies) to external user programs. The event itself indicates that a data atom has changed state and an action must be taken.

eXtensible Markup Language eXtensible Markup Language (XML) consists of self-describing data with customized user tags for data definition, data processing, and data parsing among applications, systems, and any organizations. The programs written to process XML data structures normally obtain the data structure from the document type definition (DTD).

eXtensible Style Language eXtensible Style Language (XSL) is a language used to create a style sheet for specifying the style of an XML document.

Globus Project This is an organization that conducts research to create fundamental technologies for grid computing and offers a toolkit called the *Globus Toolkit* (more information can be found on the Web site www.globus.org).

grid computing Grid computing is any distributed cluster of compute resources that provide an environment for the sharing and managing of the resource for the distribution of tasks based on configurable service-level policies.

GridFTP This is an attempt by the Globus Project to establish a universal data transfer protocol for grid computing through the use of a common File Transfer Protocol (FTP).

high availability High availability (HA) is the ability of a resource or service to withstand failure, typically through resource duplication in a hot-standby, monitoring, failure detection, and finally automated failover to the hot-standby resource in such a fashion that the user of the resource detects only a reduction in resource response time during the failover process.

Java Database Connection Java Database Connection (JDBC) is a set of Java APIs that allow access to any database that supports SQL. The API executes the appropriate SQL command to perform the respective operation.

JDBC See the definition for *Java Database Connection*.

LAN See the definition for *local-area network*.

level 0 data grid These data grids are optimal for data sets that are static in nature.

level 1 data grid These data grids are optimal for data sets that are dynamic in nature.

local-area network A local-area network (LAN) consists of local computers networked together and confined to a limited geographic space such as a floor or a building.

Monte Carlo simulation This is a mathematical method that uses statistical techniques (e.g., randomness) to model complex systems in a variety of disciplines such as physics, biopharmaceuticals, and finance.

object–relational database management system Object–relational database management (ORDBMS) is a data management system that enhances the relational data model by supporting arrays, inheritance, and functions that represent some of the basic concepts of object-oriented programming.

OLAP Online analytical processing (OLAP) is the collection, management, process, and reporting of multidimensional data.

ORDBMS See definition of *object–relational database management system*.

Parallelize   This is a unit of work that can be subdivided into smaller atomic sub-units of work called "worklets" in such a way that each subunit of work can be run in parallel across physically dispersed computers (compute grid).

PostgreSQL   PostgreSQL is an object–relational database management system (ORDBMS).

QoS   See definition of *quality of service.*

quality of service   Quality of service (QoS) is the level of service as defined by the business unit that the grid architecture needs to meet.

regionalization   Also referred to as a *data region*, this is the logical grouping of data atoms within the data grid space. A simple analogy would be a data region in a distributed data management system or a database in a relational data management system.

replication policy   Data replication policy describes exactly how the data atoms are to be replicated within a data grid.

SGML   See definition for *Standard Generalized Markup Language.*

SQL   See definition for *Structured Query Language.*

SQL3   See the definition for *SQL99.*

SQL99   Also referred to as SQL3, this is an ANSI/ISO standard that replaces SQL92 addressing advanced topics such as object–relational database concepts, call level interfaces, and integrity management not found in SQL92.

Standard Generalized Markup Language   Standard Generalized Markup Language (SGML) is a standard metalanguage, a description of how to specify a document markup language or tag set; for example, XML is a SGML-based language.

Standard Template Library   The Standard Template Library (STL) is a C++ library of container classes, algorithms, and iterates.

STL   See definition for *Standard Template Library.*

STP   See definition for *straight-through processing.*

straight-through processing   Straight-through processing (STP) is a best-practices method of architecture and implementation using technology tools (typically termed *middleware*) that automates end-to-end processing of transactions from a business perspective.

Structured Query Language   Structured Query Language (SQL) is a data management and query language for databases. There is no standard SQL today, but there are many extensions to the ANSI-SQL.

synchronization policy   The data synchronization policy describes how the data atoms within a data region are to synchronize with each other. Types of synchronization are optimistic (showing complete trust in the data grid to synchronize the data atoms in a best-faith method), pessimistic (complete end-to-end transactional behavior), or somewhere in between these two extremes.

WAN   See description for *wide-area network.*

wide-area network   A wide-area network (WAN) is a collection of LANs typically spanning vast geographic distances.

worklet   This is a unit of work that has counterparts, all of which are atomic with respect to each other and contribute to a larger work unit.

XML   See the definition for *eXtensible Markup Language*.

XSL   See definition for *eXtensible Style Language*.

REFERENCES

1. Source of Data: David Moschella and from the following presentation: Dave Cohen and Steve Yalovitser, "Paradigm Shift: Middleware Convergence to Web Services," presentation at the 2004 Web Services on Wall Street Conference and Show, February 2004 (available online at http://lighthouse-partners.com/wsonws/presentations/yalovitser_cohen.ppt, slide 6).

2. John Fontana, "Resurrecting the Distributed APP Model," *Network World* (September 29, 2003) (available online at http://www.nwfusion.com/buzz/2003/0929soa.html).

3. Hao He, "What Is Service-Oriented Architecture?" (available online at http://webservices.xml.com/pub/a/ws/2003/09/30/soa.html), O'Reilly Web Services, September 30, 2003.

4. Greg Goth, *Web Services Easing toward the Mainstream*, IEEE Distributed Systems (available online at http://dsonline.computer.org/0310/f/d10newp.htm).

5. Global Grid Forum, *Open Grid Service Infrastructure Primer*, February 11, 2004.

6. John Narghton, *A Brief History of the Future*, Overlook Press, May 2000.

7. Ian Foster, Carl Kesselman, and Steven Tuecke, "The Anatomy of the Grid, Enabling Scalable Virtual Organizations," *Int. J. Supercomput. Appl.* (2002) (available online at http://www.globus.org/research/papers/anatomy.pdf).

8. Ann Chervenak, Ian Foster, Carl Kesselman, Charles Salisbury, and Steven Tuecke, "The Data Grid: Towards an Architecture for the Distributed Management and Analysis of Large Scientific Datasets," p. 1 (available online at http://www.globus.org/documentation/incoming/JNCApaper.pdf).

9. Reagan W. Moore (San Diego Supercomputer Center), Scott Studham (Pacific Northwest National Laboratory), Arcot Rajasekar (San Diego Supercomputer Center), Chip Watson (Jefferson National Laboratory), Heinz Stockinger, and Peter Kunszt (CERN), "Data Grid

Implementations," p. 1, February 19, 2002 (available online at http://www.ppdg.net/docs/WhitePapers/Capabilities-grids.v12.pdf).

10. Bill Allcock, Lee Liming, Steven Tuecke (ANL), and Ann Chervenak (USC/ISI), "GridFTP: A Data Transfer Protocol for the Grid, Grid Forum Data Working Group on GridFTP" (available online at http://www.sdsc.edu/GridForum/RemoteData/Papers/gridftp_intro_gf5.pdf).

11. The Globus Project, "GridFTP Universal Data Transfer for the Grid," September 5, 2000 (copyright 2000, The University of Chicago and The University of Southern California) (available online at http://www.globus.org/datagrid/deliverables/C2WPdraft3.pdf).

12. M. Satyanarayanan, "Coda: A Highly Available File System for a Distributed Workstation Environment," p. 1 (available online at http://www-2.cs.cmu.edu/afs/cs/project/coda/Web/docdir/ieeepcs95.pdf).

13. Ian Foster, Jens Vöckler, Michael Wilde, and Yong Zhao, "The Virtual Data Grid: A New Model and Architecture for Data-Intensive Collaboration," *Proceedings of the 2003 CIDR Conference*, p. 1 (available online at http://www.griphyn.org/chimera/papers/CIDR.VDG.crc.submitted.pdf).

14. "Data Sheet Avaki 5.0 Software," www.avaki.com (available online at http://www.avaki.com/file/pdf/public/adg50_data_sheet.pdf).

15. Tuplespace is a concept created by the Linda project at Yale University; see D. Gelernter and A. J. Bernstein, "Distributed Communication via Global Buffer," *Proceedings of the ACM Principles of Distributed Computing Conference* (1982), pp. 10–18; D. Gelernter, "Generative Communication in Linda," *TOPLAS* 7(1), 80–112 (1985); N. Carriero and D. Gelernter, "Linda in Context," *Commun. ACM* 32(4) (April 1989).

16. See http://oceanstore.cs.berkeley.edu/info/overview.html.

17. See http://www.openmp.org/.

18. Ayon Basumallik, Seung-Jai Min, and Rudolf Eigenmann, "Towards OpenMP Execution on Software Distributed Shared Memory Systems," School of Electrical and Computer Engineering, Purdue University, West Lafayette, IN (available online at http://www.ece.purdue.edu/ParaMount).

19. Michael Di Stefano and Steve Yalovitser, "Grid Computing with a Data Grid Plane," p. 11, September 27, 2002.

20. E. F. Codd, "A Relational Model of Data for Large Shared Data Banks," *Commun. ACM* 13(6), 377–387 (1970).

21. James Fallows, "Free Flight, From Airline Hell to a New Age of Travel," *Public Affairs* (2001).

22. Jeremy Stribling, Kirsten Hildrum, and John D. Kubiatowicz, *Optimizations for Locality-Aware Structured Peer-to-Peer Overlays*, Report UCB/CSD-03-1266, Computer Science Division (EECS), University of California, Berkeley, August 2003.

23. Jim Gray, *Distributed Computing Economics*, Microsoft Research, San Francisco, CA, March 2003.

24. Artur Andrzejak, Sven Graupner, Vadim Kotov, and Holger Trinks, *Algorithms for Self-Organization and Adaptive Service Placement in Dynamic Distributed Systems*, HPL-2002-259, Internet, Systems and Storage Laboratory, Hewlett-Packard Laboratories, Palo Alto, CA, September 17, 2002.

25. Kavitha Ranganathan and Ian Foster, "Decoupling Computation and Data Scheduling in Distributed Data-Intensive Applications."

26. Professor Simon Cox of Geodise (www.geodise.org), "Geodise: Grid Enabled Design Optimisation and Design Search," presentation at The Application Research Group of the Global Grid Forum, Applications and Testbeds Working Group Workshop, meeting on Case Studies on Grid Applications in Munich, Germany, March 2004 (available online at http://www.zib.de/ggf/apps/index.html).

27. Alex Rodriguez, Dinanath Sulakhe, Elizabeth Marland, Natalia Maltsev, Ian Foster, Michael Wilde, and Veronika Nefedova, "Grid Enabled Server for High-throughput Analysis of Genomes," presentation at The Application Research Group of the Global Grid Forum, meeting on Case Studies on Grid Applications in Munich, Germany, March 2004 (available online at http://www.zib.de/ggf/apps/index.html).

28. Dr. F. M. Brochu at the University of Cambridge (UK), "Running MadGraph on the LHC Computing Grid (LCG)," presentation at The Application Research Group of the Global Grid Forum, meeting on Case Studies on Grid Applications in Munich, Germany, March 2004 (available online at http://www.zib.de/ggf/apps/index.html).

29. Kate Keahey at the Argonne National Laboratory, "The National Fusion Collaboratory Project: Applying Grid Technology for Magnetic Fusion Research," presentation at The Application Research Group of the Global Grid Forum, meeting on Case Studies on Grid Applications in Munich, Germany, March 2004 (available online at http://www.zib.de/ggf/apps/index.html).

30. Lee Liming and George E. Brown, Jr., "Network for Earthquake Engineering Simulation (NEES). The MOST Experiment: Earthquake Engineering on the Grid," presentation at The Application Research Group of the Global Grid Forum, meeting on Case Studies on Grid Applications in Munich, Germany, March 2004 (available online at http://www.zib.de/ggf/apps/index.html).

31. Larry Peterson, Tom Anderson, David Culler, and Timothy Roscoe, "A Blueprint for Introducing Disruptive Technology into the Internet," *Proceedings of the First ACM Workshop on Hot Topics in Networking (HotNets)*, October 2002.

32. IBM, *On Demand Business: The New Agenda for Value Creation* (www.ibm.com).

33. The Global Grid Forum (http://www.gridforum.org/).

34. Duke University Department of Computer Science, *COD, Cluster on Demand* (available online at http://issg.cs.duke.edu/cod/).

35. Vadim Kotov, *On Virtual Data Centers and Their Operating Environments*, HPL-2001-44, Computer Systems and Technology Laboratory, Hewlett-Packard Laboratories, Palo Alto, CA, March 8, 2001.

36. Integrasoft, L.L.C. (www.integrasoftware.com), Platform Computing, Inc. (www.platform.com), Corosoft, Inc. (www.corosoft.com), "Presentation: The Virtual Data Center."

INDEX

Access:
  data grid comparisons, 75–76
  data management (traditional), 62–63
Adapter, data regionalization,
    load-and-store policy, 93–94
Affinity. *See* Data affinity
Amdahl's law:
  grid computing, 15
  Web Services, 208, 214
APL, grid topology, data management
    evolution, 43
Application, defined, grid topology
    application, 54
Application policies, grid topology, 53–58.
    See also Policies
Application server, client/server
    technology, 7–10
Atomic task applications, 145–146
Availability, data management
    (traditional), 64

Backup, data management
    (traditional), 64
Bandwidth:
  data synchronization patterns, 104
  geographic boundary problems, 184–185
  grid topology application, 55

Batch schedulers, grid computing, 3
Best-faith delivery, enterprise
    information integration (EII),
    synchronization, 128
Bottlenecks, grid computing, 10–12
Business applications, Integrity, data
    management (traditional), 63
Business forces, service-oriented
    architecture (SOA), 25–26
Business models, grid computing
    rationale, 14, 19
Business use cases, geographic boundary
    problems, 178–183
  financial services, 178–180
  following the sun shift, 183
  operations, 180–183

Calculation-intensive applications,
    147–148, 153–164
  data grid analysis, 160–164
  described, 153–154
  general architecture, 156–160
  use cases, 154–156
Centralized synchronization, peer-to-peer
    synchronization versus,
    core engine, 75

Centralized synchronization manager,
     102–103
Client/server technology:
   data management evolution,
      grid topology, 44
   grid computing, 4–5, 7–10
   relational data management, 68
Coarse granularity. *See also*
      Fine granularity
   Integrasoft Grid Fabric (IGF)
      programming example, 236–240
   OpenMP, level 1 data grids, 51
CODA, distributed file systems, level 0
      data grids, 47
Command and control, 191–202
   architecture, 192–196
      comparisons, 195–196
      with data grid, 194–195
      without data grid, 193–194
   data grid analysis, 196–201
   described, 191–192
   spinoffs, 202
Command-and-control systems, compute
      utility, 221–223
Commercial industry, grid computing
      rationale, 14
Common Object Request Broker
      Architecture (CORBA):
   enterprise information integration (EII)
      and, 114, 115–116
   grid computing, 7
   service-oriented architecture (SOA), 22
   Web Services, 206, 211
Complex data set applications, 146
Compute clusters, defined, 3
Compute farms, compute grids, 33
Compute grids. *See also* Data grid(s)
   data grids and:
      data affinity, 139–141
      parallel planes, 35–36
   grid planes, 33–34
Compute utility, 217–225
   architecture, 220–225
      command-and-control systems,
         221–223
      geographic boundary, 221
      macro/microscheduling, 223–225
   overview, 218–220
   resource listing, 255
   service-oriented architecture, 217–218
Computing power, service-oriented
      architecture (SOA), 29
Coordination, data management function,
      parallel grid planes, 36–37

Core engine (data grid comparisons), 73–75
   centralized versus peer-to-peer
      synchronization, 75
   generally, 73–74
   replicated versus distributed architectures,
      74
Costs:
   data affinity, measurable quantity,
      134–135
   grid computing, 11, 12
   grid computing rationale, 13–14, 17
   service-oriented architecture (SOA), 24
   supply-demand economics, 27–29

Data, defined, grid topology application,
      54–55
Data affinity, 133–142
   achievement of, 135–139
      regionalization, synchronization, and
         distribution, 135–139
      task routing, 139
   calculation-intensive applications, 160
   examples, 141–142
   expectations, 135
   grid integration, 139–141
   level 1 data grids, grid topology, 51
   measurable quantity, 134–135
   overview, 133
   resource listing, 256
Data center applications, 148–149
Data center automation, service-oriented
      architecture (SOA), 25
Data collection applications, 146
Data distribution:
   data affinity, 135–139
   forces of, Integrasoft Grid Fabric (IGF)
      White Paper, 257–266
Data distribution policy, data
      regionalization, data management,
      85–88. *See also* Policies
Data granularity. *See* Granularity
Data grid(s). *See also* Compute grids
   administration, data grid comparisons,
      traditional data management, 76
   calculation-intensive applications,
      160–164
   command and control, 194–201
   compute grids and:
      data affinity, 139–141
      parallel planes, 35–36
   data mining and data warehouses, 172–175
   evolution of, parallel grid planes, 38–39
   geographic boundary problems, 185–190
   grid computing, 5–6

grid planes, 34–35
relational data management, engine, 70
Data grid comparisons, 73–78
  access, 75–76
  core engine, 73–75
    centralized versus peer-to-peer
      synchronization, 75
    generally, 73–74
    replicated versus distributed
      architectures, 74
  grid computing data management, 76–78
  traditional data management, 76
Data grid plane (DGP), data
  regionalization, 79–80
Data grid resources, data regionalization,
  data management, 84
Data integration. *See* Enterprise information
  integration (EII)
Data load/save policy. *See also* Policies
  data regionalization, data
    management, 90–95
  enterprise information integration (EII),
    grid computing, 120–124,
    124–129, 126–129
  grid computing data management, 78
Data locality (distribution), grid computing
  data management, 77–78
Data management. *See also* Relational data
  management
  data regionalization, 84–96
    data distribution policy, 85–88
    data replication policy, 88–90
    event notification policy, 95–96
    generally, 84–85
    load-and-store policy, 90–95
    synchronization policy, 90
  evolution of, 43–45
    client/server technology, 44
    grid computing, 44–45
    historical perspective, 43–44
  grid computing, 5–7, 10, 12
  parallel grid planes, 36–39
  Web Services, 206–207
Data management engine, relational
  data management,
  grid computing, 69
Data management (traditional), 59–66
  features of, 60–65
    access, 62–63
    backup/recovery/availability, 64
    data structure, 61–62
    events, 64
    integrity, 63
    mechanics, 60–61

security, 64–65
transactions, 63
historical perspective, 59–60
usability, 65–66
Data mining and data warehouses, 165–175
  benefits of, 174–175
  data grids, 172–174
  described, 165
  general architecture, 168–172
  use cases, 166–168
Data passing, data grids, parallel grid
  planes, 38
Data pulling, data grids, parallel grid
  planes, 38
Data regionalization, 79–97
  data affinity, 135–137
  data management, 84–96
    data distribution policy, 85–88
    data replication policy, 88–90
    event notification policy, 95–96
    generally, 84–85
    load-and-store policy, 90–95
    synchronization policy, 90
  defined, 80
  overview, 79–80
  quality-of-service (QoS) levels, 96–97
  traditional terms, 80–84
Data region transactional, enterprise
  information integration (EII),
  synchronization, 128–129
Data reorganization, grid computing data
  management, 76–77
Data store policy. *See* Data load/save
  policy
Data structure, data management
  (traditional), 61–62
Data surfaces, data management function,
  parallel grid planes, 37
Data synchronization, 99–109
  architectures, 102–104
  of data, grid computing data
    management, 77
  data affinity, 135–137
  enterprise information integration (EII),
    grid computing, 126–129
  grid computing data management, 77
  interregion, 101–102
  intraregion, 100–101
  overview, 99–100
  patterns, 104–109
    generally, 104
    granularity, 105–106
    policy expression, 106–108
    simulations, 108–109

Data synchronization (*Continued*)
  policies, data regionalization, data
    management, 90
  as standard interface, 109
  transactional, grid computing data
    management, 77
Data warehouses. *See* Data mining and data
    warehouses
DB2:
  data management evolution,
    grid topology, 44
  history of, 60
  usability, 66
Defense spending:
  grid computing, 11, 12
  Web Services, 214
Demand, supply-demand economics, 28
Dependability, service-oriented architecture
    (SOA), 29
Desire, supply-demand economics, 28
Destination addressing, Web Services, 209
Development costs, grid computing
    rationale, 17–18
Disconnected operation, distributed file
    systems, level 0 data grids, 47
Distributed architectures, replicated
    architectures versus, core engine, 74
Distributed Component Object Model
    (DCOM), service-oriented
    architecture (SOA), 22
Distributed computing:
  client/server technology, 8
  resource listing, 255
  service-oriented architecture (SOA), 25
  supply-demand economics, 29
Distributed Computing Environment (DCE),
    grid computing, 7
Distributed data integration, level 0 data
    grids, grid topography, 48
Distributed data policy, data
    regionalization, data management,
    85–88. *See also* Policies
Distributed file systems:
  grid computing, data management
    evolution, 45
  information sources, 252–253
  level 0 data grids, grid topology, 47
Distributed memory, level 1 data grids,
    grid topology, 50–51
Distributed middleware products,
    client/server technology, 8
Distributed resource managers, relational
    data management, grid
    computing, 69–70

Distributed shared memory (DSM)
    architecture, data synchronization
    patterns, simulations, 108
Distribution (locality), of data, grid
    computing data management, 77–78
DNA sequencing, grid computing, data
    management evolution, 45
Dynamic-data movement pattern analysis,
    data regionalization, data
    management, 86
Dynamic data sets, level 1 data grids, grid
    topology, 48–52
Dynamic discovery, service-oriented
    architecture (SOA), 22–23

Elasticity:
  grid computing, 11
  service-oriented architecture (SOA), 29
Energy exploration, grid computing, data
    management evolution, 45
Engine element. *See also* Core engine
    (data grid comparisons)
  data management (traditional), 60–61
  relational data management, 68
  grid computing, 69–70
Engineers, grid computing
    rationale, 14–17
Enterprise application integration (EAI),
    enterprise information integration
    (EII) and, 111–116. *See also*
    Enterprise information
    integration (EII)
Enterprise data grid integration
    (EDGI), 130
Enterprise information integration
    (EII), 111–131
  data mining and data warehouses, 169
  grid computing, 116–131
    data load policy, 120–124, 126–129
    data store policy, 124–129
    integration, 129–131
    load, store, and
      synchronization, 126–129
    natural separation, 118–120
    straight-through processing (STP),
      enterprise application integration
      (EAI) and, 111–116
Ethernet, service-oriented architecture
    (SOA), 24–25
Event notification, grid computing data
    management, 78
Event notification policy, data
    regionalization, data management,
    95–96. *See also* Policies

Events:
  data management (traditional), 64
  data regionalization, 82
Excess supply, supply-demand
    economics, 28
eXtensible Markup Language (XML):
  language interface, 230, 234
  Web Services, 203

Fault-tolerant transactional:
  enterprise information integration (EII),
    synchronization, 129
  geographic boundary
    problems, 181–183
Feedback control loop, command and
    control, 191. *See also* Command
    and control
File Transfer Protocol (FTP):
  enterprise information integration (EII)
    and, 113
  grid computing, data management
    evolution, 45
  level 0 data grids, grid topology, 46
Financial factors, grid computing
    rationale, 17–18
Financial services, geographic boundary
    problems, 178–180
Fine granularity. *See also* Coarse granularity
  Integrasoft Grid Fabric (IGF)
    programming example, 240–245
  OpenMP, level 1 data grids, 51
First-generation compute grids,
    grid planes, 34
Following the sun shift, geographic boundary
    problems, 183
FooBar, enterprise information integration
    (EII), grid computing, 120–123, 124
Foreign key, data structure, data
    management (traditional), 61–62
Fungibility, service-oriented architecture
    (SOA), 29

Gaussian distributed data policy, data
    regionalization, data management, 85
Geographic boundary, 177–190
  benefits, 188–190
  business use cases, 178–183
    financial services, 178–180
    following the sun shift, 183
    operations, 180–183
  compute utility, 221
  data grids, 185–188
  described, 177
  general architecture, 184–185

Geography, defined, grid topology
    application, 55
Global Grid Forum, information
    sources, 253
Global replication, level 1 data grids, grid
    topology, 50
Globus:
  compute grids, 34
  GridFTP, 46
  information sources, 253
Granularity. *See also* Coarse granularity;
    Fine granularity
  data regionalization, load-and-store
    policy, 91, 93
  data synchronization patterns,
    105–106
  geographic boundary problems, 185
  Integrasoft Grid Fabric (IGF)
    programming example, 236–245
  OpenMP, level 1 data grids, 51
  service-oriented architecture (SOA), 29
Grid computing, 3–12. *See also*
    Compute grids; Data grid(s)
  basics of, 3–7
  data management evolution, grid
    topology, 44–45
  defined, 4
  enterprise information integration
    (EII), 116–131
    data load policy, 120–124, 126–129
    data store policy, 124–129
    load, store, and
      synchronization, 126–129
    natural separation, 118–120
  new topology of, 10–12
  overview, 3
  paradigm shift in, 7–10, 15
  parallel grid planes, 31–39 (*See also*
    Parallel grid planes)
  rationale for, 13–20
    business drivers, 19
    financial factors, 17–18
    historical perspective, 13–17
    technology, 19–20
  relational data management, 68–71
    data management features, 70–71
    engine, 70
    functional tier analysis, 69–70
  service-oriented architecture (SOA), 25
GridFTP:
  data grids, 34–35
  information sources, 252
  intraregion data synchronization, 100
  level 0 data grids, grid topology, 46

Grid planes, 32–35
  compute grids, 33–34
  data grids, 34–35
Grid topology, 43–58
  application characteristics, 53–58
  data management evolution, 43–45
    client/server technology, 44
    grid technology, 44–45
    historical perspective, 43–44
    implementations, 45–52
      level 0 data grids, 45–48
      level 1 data grids, 48–52
        case study, 51–52
        foundations, 48–51
Grouping/frequency, data regionalization,
    load-and-store policy, 91–92

Hierarchy. *See* Grid topology
High availability techniques:
  data management (traditional), 64
  geographic boundary problems, 181–183

Index feature:
  data grid comparisons, traditional data
    management, 76
  data regionalization, 82–83
Information sources, 251
Information technology (IT):
  grid computing rationale, 19–20
  service-oriented architecture (SOA), 24–25
Integrasoft Grid Fabric (IGF):
  data distribution forces (White Paper),
    257–266
  level 1 data grids, grid topology, 48, 51–52
  programming examples, 235–245
Integrity, data management (traditional), 63
Interface. *See also* Language interface
  data synchronization as standard, 109
  service-oriented architecture (SOA), 23
  usability, data management
    (traditional), 65–66
Interface Definition Language (IDL),
    service-oriented architecture
    (SOA), 22
Internet. *See* Web Services
Internet bubble:
  grid computing rationale, 14, 17, 19
  service-oriented architecture
    (SOA), 25–26
Interregion data synchronization, 101–102
Intraregion data synchronization, 100–101
Invocation, data regionalization,
    load-and-store policy, 92
Isomorphism, Web Services, 215

JavaSpaces, level 1 data grids, grid
    topology, 48, 49–50, 52

Language interface, 229–234.
  See also Interface
  data grid comparisons, access, 75–76
  eXtensible Markup Language (XML), 234
  overview, 229–230
  programmatic, 230–232
  query-based, 232–234
  relational data management, grid
    computing, 68–69
Layered architecture, Web Services, 209
Level 0 data grids, grid topology,
    implementations, 45–48
Level 1 data grids, grid topology, 48–52
  case study, 51–52
  foundations, 48–51
Linda project, 49
Load-and-store policy. *See* Data load/save
    policy
Local-area networks (LAN). *See* Bandwidth
Locality:
  of data, grid computing data
    management, 77–78
  data regionalization, data
    management, 86, 87
Localized catching, data grids, parallel
    grid planes, 38
Location manipulation, data regionalization,
    data management, 87
Locking, data regionalization, 83
Logical data groupings, data
    regionalization, 81
Loose couplings, service-oriented
    architecture (SOA), 22

Macro/microscheduling, compute utility,
    223–225
Maintenance costs, grid computing
    rationale, 17–18
Management policies, data
    regionalization, data
    management, 85. *See also* Policies
Market forces:
  grid computing rationale, 14, 15
  supply-demand economics, 27–29
  Web Services, 214
Mathematics, grid topology, data
    management evolution, 43
Mechanics, data management
    (traditional), 60–61
Message, service-oriented architecture
    (SOA), 23

Messaging, client/server technology, 8
Messaging-oriented
    middleware (MOM):
  enterprise information integration (EII)
    and, 114–115, 116
  Web Services, 211
Metadata hubs, level 0 data grids, grid
    topography, 48
Metcalfe's law:
  grid computing, 15
  Web Services, 209, 214, 215
Metered data, operational
    applications, 146–147
Middleware architecture, service-oriented
    architecture (SOA), 22
Monte Carlo simulation:
  calculation-intensive applications,
    159, 160–161
  grid topology, 55–56
  programming example, 245–249
Moore's law:
  grid computing, 11, 12, 15
  Web Services, 208, 214, 215

Natural separation, enterprise
    information integration (EII), grid
    computing, 118–120
Network proliferation, grid computing
    rationale, 15–16
Networking, service-oriented architecture
    (SOA), 24–25

OceanStore, level 1 data grids, grid
    topology, 50, 52
Online analytical processing (OLAP):
  command and control, 197
  data analysis applications, 148
  data mining and data warehouses, 169,
    170, 172, 175
  grid topology, 56–58
Open Grid Services Architecture (OGSA),
    compute grids, 34
OpenMP, level 1 data grids, grid topology,
    48–49, 50–51
OpenStore, level 1 data grids, grid
    topology, 48
Operational applications, 146–147
Operational costs, grid computing
    rationale, 13, 18
Optimistic transactional data
    synchronization, grid computing data
    management, 77, 99
Optimizations, data regionalization, 82

Oracle:
  history of, 60
  usability, 66

Parallel grid planes, 31–39
  compute/data grids, 35–36
  data management function, 36–39
    data grid evolution, 38–39
    requirements, 36–37
  grid planes, 32–35
    compute grids, 33–34
    data grids, 34–35
  overview, 31–32
Parallel processing, calculation-intensive
    applications, 154–156
Partial objective function (POF), data
    affinity, measurable quantity,
    134–135
Peak loads, client/server technology, 8
Peer-to-peer (P2P) platforms:
  data grid comparisons, 74
  grid computing, 3
  synchronization, 103–104
  synchronization, centralized
    synchronization versus, core
    engine, 75
Persistence, JavaSpaces, level 1
    data grids, 49
Pervasiveness, grid computing, 11, 12
Pessimistic transactional data
    synchronization, grid computing
    data management, 77
Poisson distributed data policy, data
    regionalization, data
    management, 85
Policies:
  data grid comparisons, 73–74
  data load policy, enterprise information
    integration (EII), grid computing,
    120–124, 126–129
  data store policy, enterprise information
    integration (EII), grid computing,
    124–129
  data synchronization as standard
    interface, 109
  data synchronization patterns, 106–108
  event notification, data regionalization,
    data management, 95–96
  grid topology applications, 53–58
  management, data regionalization, data
    management, 85
Prices, supply-demand economics, 27–29
Processing capacity, client/server
    technology, 10

Programmatic API:
  data grid comparisons, access, 75–76
  language interface, 229
Programmatic language
  interface, 230–232
Protein folding, grid computing, data
  management evolution, 45
Public resources, listing of, 253

Quality assurance (QA):
  data center applications, 149
  enterprise information integration (EII)
    and, 114
  grid computing rationale, 17–18
Quality-of-service (QoS) levels:
  data regionalization, 96–97
  enterprise information integration (EII),
    synchronization, 126
  geographic boundary problems, 180
  grid computing, 7
  grid topology:
    applications, 56–58
    data management evolution, 44
  intraregion data synchronization, 101
  level 0 data grids, grid
    topography, 47–48
Query:
  data grid comparisons, traditional data
    management, 76
  data regionalization, 83–84
  defined, grid topology application, 55
  JavaSpaces, level 1 data grids, 49
Query-based language interface, 232–234

Random-number surface, programming
  example, 245–249
Random (white-noise) distributed data
  policy, data regionalization, data
  management, 85
Real-time event processing. See
  Straight-through processing (STP)
Recovery, data management (traditional), 64
Regionalization, data affinity, 135–137.
  See also Data regionalization
Relation, data regionalization, 83
Relational database:
  grid computing, 5–6
  technology, data management
    evolution, 44
Relational data management, 67–71.
  See also Data management
  grid computing, 68–71
    data management features, 70–71
    engine, 70

functional tier analysis, 69–70
  historical perspective, 67–68
Reorganization, of data, grid computing
  data management, 76–77
Replicated architectures, distributed
  architectures versus, core engine, 74
Replicated resource managers, relational data
  management, grid computing, 70
Replication:
  data grid comparisons, traditional data
    management, 76
  data regionalization, data management,
    86–87, 88–90
Resource management engine, relational
  data management, grid
  computing, 69–70
Resource provisioning, service-oriented
  architecture (SOA), 25
Return on investment (RoI), grid
  computing rationale, 13, 17
Round-robin distributed data policy, data
  regionalization, data management, 85

Scaling. See Grid topology
Schema, data regionalization, 81–82
Scientific research, resource listing, 254
Secondary key, data structure, data
  management (traditional), 61–62
Second-generation compute grids, grid
  planes, 34
Securities and Exchange Commission
  (SEC), 178
Security, data management
  (traditional), 64–65
Seismic data analysis, grid computing, data
  management evolution, 45
Semiconductor manufacturing, grid
  computing, data management
  evolution, 45
Server replication, distributed file systems,
  level 0 data grids, 47
Service-oriented architecture (SOA),
  21–29. See also Web Services
  compute utility, 217–218
  defined, 21–23
  forces driving, 23–27
    business, 25–26
    technology, 24–25
    world events, 26–27
  overview, 21
  paradigm shift, 29
  resource listing, 256
  supply-demand economics, 27–29
  Web Services, 203–215

Service-oriented network architecture
(SONA). *See also* Web Services
grid computing rationale, 15
shift toward, 29
Web Services, 203–215
Simulations, data synchronization
patterns, 108–109
Speed, level 0 data grids, grid
topography, 47–48
Standard Query Language (SQL), 5
data regionalization, 83–84
language interface, 229–230
relational data management, 68
Storage area network (SAN),
service-oriented architecture
(SOA), 24–25
Straight-through processing (STP). *See also*
Enterprise information
integration (EII)
enterprise information integration (EII)
and, 111–116
event notification policy, data
regionalization, 95
String-based interfaces, data grid
comparisons, access, 76
Structured English Query Language (SEQL):
data management access (traditional), 62–63
history of, 59
Structured Query Language (SQL):
data management evolution, grid
topology, 44
history of, 59
language interface, 232–234
Supply, supply-demand economics, 28
Supply-demand economics,
service-oriented architecture
(SOA), 27–29
Switching, Web Services, 209
Sybase:
history of, 60
usability, 66
Synchronization policy. *See* Data
synchronization
System/R project, 59

Tables, data structure, data management
(traditional), 61–62
Task routing, data affinity, 139
Technology bubble:
grid computing rationale, 14, 17, 19
service-oriented architecture
(SOA), 25–26
Terrorism, service-oriented architecture
(SOA), 26–27

Third-generation compute grids,
grid planes, 34
Time, defined, grid topology application, 55
Transactional data synchronization, grid
computing data management, 77
Transactions:
data management (traditional), 63
JavaSpaces, level 1 data grids, 49

Universities:
grid computing rationale, 14
resource listing, 253
Unix workstations, distributed file systems,
level 0 data grids, 47
Usability, data management
(traditional), 65–66
Use cases:
applications, 149–151
calculation-intensive
applications, 154–156
data mining and data
warehouses, 166–170
geographic boundary problems, 178–183
financial services, 178–180
following the sun shift, 183
operations, 180–183
User-level programmatic API, data grid
comparisons, access, 75
Utility, supply-demand economics, 28

Venture capital, grid computing rationale, 14

Warehouses. *See* Data mining and data
warehouses
War on terror, service-oriented architecture
(SOA), 26–27
Web Services, 203–215
compute grids, 34
computing power, 214–215
data management, 206–207
defined, 203–205
described, 205–206
historical perspective, 208–210
resource listing, 254–255
service-oriented architecture
(SOA), 22–25
SONA, 210–212, 212–214
White papers, 252–253
Wide-area networks (WAN).
See Bandwidth
Work, defined, grid topology application, 54
Worklets, client/server technology, 9

XML, Web Services, 203

Printed and bound by CPI Group (UK) Ltd, Croydon, CR0 4YY

27/10/2024

14580261-0002